Key Concepts in
Sport and Exercise
Research Methods

Recent volumes include:

Key Concepts in Sport Psychology
John M D Kremer, Aidan Moran,
Cathy Craig and Graham Walker

Key Concepts in Sports Studies
Stephen Wagg, Belinda Wheaton,
Carlton Brick and Jayne Caudwell

**Key Concepts in Sport and Exercise
Sciences**
David Kirk, Carlton Cooke, Anne
Flintoff and Jim McKenna

Key Concepts in Tourist Studies
Melanie Smith, Nicola MacLeod and
Margaret Hart Robertson

Key Concepts in Leisure Studies
David Harris

Key Concepts in Public Health
Frances Wilson and Andi Mabhala

Key Concepts in Health Psychology
Ian Albery and Marcus Munafo

Key Concepts in Health Studies
Chris Yuill, Iain Crinson and Eilidh
Duncan

The SAGE Key Concepts series provides students with accessible and authoritative knowledge of the essential topics in a variety of disciplines. Cross-referenced throughout, the format encourages critical evaluation through understanding. Written by experienced and respected academics, the books are indispensable study aids and guides to comprehension.

MICHAEL ATKINSON

Key Concepts in
Sport and Exercise
Research Methods

Los Angeles | London | New Delhi
Singapore | Washington DC

First published 2012

Apart from any fair dealing for the purposes of research or private study, or criticism or review, as permitted under the Copyright, Designs and Patents Act, 1988, this publication may be reproduced, stored or transmitted in any form, or by any means, only with the prior permission in writing of the publishers, or in the case of reprographic reproduction, in accordance with the terms of licences issued by the Copyright Licensing Agency. Enquiries concerning reproduction outside those terms should be sent to the publishers.

SAGE Publications Ltd
1 Oliver's Yard
55 City Road
London EC1Y 1SP

SAGE Publications Inc.
2455 Teller Road
Thousand Oaks, California 91320

SAGE Publications India Pvt Ltd
B 1/I 1 Mohan Cooperative Industrial Area
Mathura Road
New Delhi 110 044

SAGE Publications Asia-Pacific Pte Ltd
33 Pekin Street #02-01
Far East Square
Singapore 048763

Library of Congress Control Number: 2011922511

British Library Cataloguing in Publication data

A catalogue record for this book is available from the British Library

ISBN 978-1-84860-728-6
ISBN 978-1-84860-729-3 (pbk)

Typeset by C&M Digitals (P) Ltd, Chennai, India
Printed in Great Britain by CPI Antony Rowe, Chippenham, Wiltshire
Printed on paper from sustainable resources

contents

contents

v

key concepts in sport and
exercise research methods

List of Figures and Tables

FIGURES

TABLES

About the Author

Michael Atkinson is Associate Professor, Faculty of Physical Education and Health, University of Toronto. He was previously Senior Lecturer in the School of Sport and Exercise Sciences at Loughborough University, leading the instruction of research methods and skills at the undergraduate and postgraduate levels therein. Michael received a PhD in Sociology from the University of Calgary in 2001 (BA, University of Waterloo, 1995; MA, McMaster University, 1997). Since then, he has researched and taught courses on the sociology of sport, bodies, deviance and research methods (qualitative, quantitative and historical) at Memorial University of Newfoundland (Canada), McMaster University (Canada), and University of Western Ontario (Canada). For his contributions to the Canadian social sciences, Michael was the recipient of the Social Sciences and Humanities Research Council of Canada's prestigious Aurora Award in 2004.

Introduction: Using this Book

With the mushrooming of undergraduate programmes in sport and exercise science, kinesiology, and physical activity and health, on both sides of the Atlantic, modules in research skills and methods have expanded and diversified considerably. In many universities, methodology courses at the undergraduate level cater to students with wide ranging sub-disciplinary interests such as psychology, physiology, sociology, biomechanics, pedagogy, health, economics, management and others. Within this context of diversity, one of the primary pedagogical hurdles to negotiate in an undergraduate methods module is finding a comprehensive and panoramic introductory reader within a literature that contains a relative dearth of accessible and down-to-earth options. What students and instructors are forced to do is read from several commonly used sport and exercise sciences methods textbooks (written from either a predominantly quantitative or qualitative slant), or employ methods books from other disciplines (biology or sociology, for example) that are simply not written for sport, exercise and health students. These books do not often articulate the significance and practice of core methodological concepts in straightforward and plain language.

I feel that to engage students more directly with research skills, a book is needed that outlines many of the main concepts in research methods that all students in an undergraduate programme in sport, exercise, kinesiology or health should understand clearly. Each of the concepts presented in the book is, I hope, delivered to students in a way that diverges from standard 'textbook definition' modes of presentation. The concepts under examination in this book are presented using a form of narrative analysis which relays what the concepts mean in plain language, their significance in research, their bearing on how research is conducted, and how they are engaged in sport and exercise research. Entries revolve around a core methodological concept, practice or debate that students need to know before conducting research on their own subjects of interest, or for truly grasping research studies presented to them in other undergraduate modules.

Given all of the above, I selected 40 core concepts in research methodology for inclusion. Not all aspects of the concept are tackled in each section (such would be impossible!). Though the tone and content of

ix

the entries varies in certain degrees depending on the concept under review, each of the entries is structurally formatted in a similar manner. Following a brief introduction to the concept at hand, we unpack the significance of the concept by discussing:

(i) *What is this concept?* A definitional introduction to the concept is presented, but only in a quasi-standardised format. Included briefly in this section is a statement of when and why in the research process the concept is important.

(ii) *Why is this relevant to me?* In this section, the significance of the concept or practice will be reviewed.

(iii) *Show me how it's used!* In this section, some of the more technical aspects of the concept will be discussed, using sport and exercise to further illustrate the significance of the concept or practice. Particular emphasis is given to how the concept relates to the ways by which knowledge is framed and accumulated in research.

(iv) *Problems, pitfalls and controversies.* In the final section, a concluding set of remarks regarding the methodological problems or debates about the concept or practice is included in order to highlight how the practice of knowledge production in sport and exercise research is contested terrain.

In the end, students are encouraged neither to memorise the contents of this book nor to receive it in an uncritical manner. This book is one that presents a series of arguments about many core concepts in methodology, but does not attempt to provide the definitive gospel about each concept. With this in mind, *Key Concepts in Sport and Exercise Research Methods* is offered as a tool to help students think like researchers, and, ultimately, to be knowledge-producers in their own right.

Michael Atkinson
Faculty of Physical Education and Health
University of Toronto

Academic Journals

By the end of your first week of university or college, you have been exposed to and affected by research that has been published in academic journals. I am often surprised and usually more than a bit deflated to learn that many of my research methods students neither know what an academic journal is, nor have pored over the contents of one first hand. More's the pity, because we often treat the contents of academic journals as canonised information in our respective sub-disciplines. The contents of your professor's lectures and the very tests and papers you will be required to write are all, in some way, linked to research that has appeared in academic journals. In this entry, let's analyse some of the critical features, components and uses of academic journals.

WHAT IS THIS CONCEPT?

Students sometimes have difficulty understanding what original empirical research refers to when we talk about the papers that appear in academic journals. Your garden variety 'research article/paper' appearing in a journal, is a sole- or multi-authored summary and analysis of first-hand research which has been conducted by the author(s). A research article's contents generally follow a similar structure: it introduces you to the question or idea underpinning the author's research project (e.g. 'Is there a culture of violence in professional ice hockey?'); what we know about the subject (in this case, a literature review of other people's research on ice hockey violence or sport violence in general, taken from books and journal articles); how the data or 'evidence' were collected within the project (e.g. interviews, experiments, surveys, media analysis, and so on); a theoretical and conceptual analysis of what the researchers think the data they gathered mean, or what the data show related to our research question (e.g. 'Yes, there is a culture of violence in the sport of ice hockey, and here is how it seems to form'); and a conclusions/discussion section where the researchers usually summarise what they found and suggest future directions for other researchers.

An academic journal is like an ongoing diary where research efforts within a specific field of study that have been identified as important, innovative, compelling and informative are published and debated. In more specific terms, an academic journal is a periodical in which research relating to a particular academic discipline or sub-discipline is regularly published. Normally, an academic journal is published any-where from three to six times yearly and contains a number (anywhere from 2 to 12, or more) of published research articles. Journals often contain theoretical and philosophical essays as well (e.g. let's say I pro-pose a new theory which explains why ice hockey players fist fight), reviews of books that have been published by academics (e.g. imagine I read and provided my own assessment of a new book on ice hockey violence), meta-reviews of selected published research on a specific topic (i.e. where someone has actually read everything published on a subject like ice hockey violence and then summarised this collectively for us), or statements about 'research in progress' authored by a researcher (we often refer to these as 'Research Notes'). Academic jour-nals serve as forums for the introduction and presentation of research conducted by academics all over the world. They are, in many ways, the lifeblood of academic research and the critical medium in the circula-tion of academic knowledge.

WHY IS THIS RELEVANT TO ME?

Very early on in your career as a student, you should become familiar with articles published in academic journals. They are invaluable tools for the successful completion of your own coursework and research projects. A proper and reflexive use of sport and exercise science literatures in a term paper or report is always impressive. But a review of published research and theory in academic journals is also essential for understand-ing how to think like a psychologist, economist or historian of sport. Reading and knowing the academic literature relevant to your sub-discipline of interest in sport and exercise sciences are components of the 'apprenticeship' role a student adopts. Journal articles provide you with a more rounded and deeper overview of the material in your courses, they add flesh to the skeletal structure of ideas presented to you in textbooks, and they unpack and explain the significance (and real-world practical-ity!) of the complex issues you will be exposed to in your studies.

To all intents and purposes, reading academic journal articles about a subject of your interest is probably the first step you will ever take in conducting research. Reviewing what has been published in academic journals in your substantive field of interest is indeed truly vital in the research process. But an important hurdle to overcome at first (at least something my students complain about all the time) is that many journal articles are dense, inaccessible and filled with technological or theoretical lingo. Because academic journal articles are generally written by and for full-time academics, the style of writing can be distracting and discouraging for undergraduate students. I think this might be one of the reasons why so many of my students 'read' an article by only skimming the article's 'Abstract' (a summary of the article placed on its first page) and/or the 'Conclusion' section. Do not be discouraged if there are many parts of the article that seem daunting at first; with time, patience and experience, you will become very familiar with all of the terms and lingo. Reading and understanding journal articles is a learned skill; and thankfully, as my physiology and coaching colleagues remind me, it does not take the same time and physical effort as learning a physical skill in sport that may require 15,000 repetitions to master!

SHOW ME HOW IT'S USED!

In every one of our sub-disciplines in sport and exercise science, there may be a handful or even dozens of academic journals in which your professors and instructors strive to publish their original research findings. Psychologists of sport, for example, regularly seek to publish in journals such as *Psychology of Sport and Exercise*, *Journal of Applied Sport Psychology*, and the *International Journal of Sports Psychology*. While there are quite a few journals in every sport or exercise sub-discipline, there are literally hundreds, and in some academic fields thousands, of researchers seeking to publish their findings in the journals. An average journal may be published say four times yearly, and accept four to eight articles for publication in each of its editions – a total of only 16–32 research articles for the entire year. Hundreds of research papers may have been submitted to the journal for consideration. So, when an article appears in print it has won quite a competitive struggle. Why is this important?

One of the main differences between academic journals and trade publications where research is published (like magazines, newspapers, or even academic books) is that a research paper appearing in an academic journal has been *peer reviewed*. To have a significant understanding of why academic journal articles are treated in such high regard, and why researchers use them so frequently, we need to briefly discuss the process of peer review.

A journal of high esteem for sport and exercise sciences researchers (especially for some of our 'hard science' colleagues) is the *Journal of*

academic journals

Sport Sciences (JSS). The *JSS* is physically published and distributed by the book company Routledge, but is organised, administered and managed by members of the British Association of Sport and Exercise Sciences (BASES), the World Commission of Science and Sports, and the International Society for the Advancement of Kinanthropometry. These organisations may sound rather fancy and exclusive, but they are not, really. Academic societies and associations like BASES are comprised of groups of professors from a particular country, or from around the world, who work in the same field, for instance, sports nutrition or biomechanics. They pay a yearly membership (normally) to be in the society, and may frequently meet with other members to discuss their research (often, in three- or four-day academic conferences sponsored by the societies). One of their self-appointed tasks is to create and manage an academic journal that publishes important, innovative, critical or path-breaking research in their disciplinary area. Any journal, like the *JSS*, is overseen by an editor and an editorial board comprised of members from BASES who review research papers submitted to the journal by authors. Now here's where we get to the consequential bit.

I recently finished a three-year study of pain tolerance techniques among ultra marathon runners, wrote a paper summarising the project and its findings, and now want to publish it in a journal such as the *JSS*. So, my next step would be to send them my paper, and cross my fingers! Upon receipt of my submitted manuscript (our language for a written, but not published paper), the journal editor at the *JSS* would first determine whether to reject the submission outright (i.e. if the article does not meet their standard of research quality, or focuses on a subject not usually published in the journal), or begin the process of peer review. If they thought the article decent enough to be fully reviewed, my submission would become subject to anonymous peer review by other academics (who are experts in the area of, say, ultra-endurance sport or pain processes in sport).

The number of peer reviewers (or 'referees') varies according to each journal's policies – typically, no fewer than two, and usually at least three outside peers review the article. The editor sends them my paper (without my name or university affiliation anywhere on it), and they are given several weeks to conduct the review. I do not know who is reviewing my paper, nor do the reviewers know I have written it. This 'double blind' process is standard at journals and is critical for ensuring that our own biases and beliefs about a colleague or their past work do not get factored into the review process. The editor(s) uses the reviewers' opinions (submitted in the form of standardised reports) in determining whether to publish my article, Typically, because the process is lengthy, an accepted article will not be published until months after its initial submission, while publication after a period of several years is not unknown. What all of this means in practice is that by the time a published article appears in print, it has typically gone through a very rigorous process of review, scrutiny, revision and defending. Furthermore, researchers collectively use journals to validate the legitimacy of our research abilities, efforts and findings. Because they have been so extensively peer reviewed and critiqued through the submission process, articles become considered among academics as signs of a person's own competence as a researcher.

PROBLEMS, PITFALLS AND CONTROVERSIES

A professor of mine told me once that there are students who read articles in academic journals and those who use them. The statement perplexed me at the time, but after several years of reading journal articles and assigning course tasks requiring their employment, I came to fully understand his message. Using journals is a process that involves critically evaluating their contents. I cannot impress upon my students this lesson with enough enthusiasm. There is a natural tendency for students to read and then simply describe or repeat what lies on the pages of a journal article; perhaps out of deference to academic authority, due to their hurrying through a research assignment, or for many other reasons. But research knowledge needs to be scrutinised by both the most seasoned and neophytic of academic eyes. When I assign a research assignment requiring the use of academic literature, students tend to magically agree with the theories, methods and findings in the literature. Students of mine who have studied representations of femininity in sports advertisements or codes of masculinity in the pain and injury process, all tend to find themselves in total agreement with the dominant theories explaining either phenomenon. Students and faculty members alike must remember that arguments contained in our literatures are living, breathing (of course metaphorically) things, which need constant critical evaluation. Although the charge might be a cliché or rather passé in certain respects, never completely accept an argument just because it appears in a journal article.

Also, researchers can often find considerable creative benefit in exploring academic articles beyond their disciplinary boundaries. In my own research on eating cultures in sport, I have come to learn quite a bit from psychologists, nutritionists and physiologists about athlete eating behaviours. My own sociological questioning of the rise of eating problems in sport cultures has been markedly influenced by other theoretical ways of seeing eating disorders brought forward through non-sociological journals. In short, our tendency to be uni- rather than multi-disciplinary when starting a project can sometimes severely limit how much we learn about a subject of our interest.

A relatively new trend among academic journals is their mass migration to online spaces. When I first started undergraduate school, online access to journal articles was universally unknown. Today, most journals are published as online texts that may be accessed for a fee, and share archives of their journal editions dating back a decade or more (see the entry on Literature Reviews for a description of how to search online journals). Among the more controversial trends in contemporary publishing is what we call the online open accessing of journals. An open access journal is one which is published online and requires no subscription (normally your university pays a subscription fee to access an academic journal for the entire school). The aim of open accessing is to literally 'open up' academic research to communities of students, researchers and members of the general public, while reducing the environmental impact of paper-based forms of publishing. To the advocates of open access, paying academic societies and publishing companies huge sums for important knowledge is a bit unsavoury and exclusionary. Some researchers express concern, perhaps in a knee-jerk fashion, about the quality of open access journals and have been reluctant to accept them as legitimate. Others are simply unaware of the mass existence of online journals in fields such as sport and exercise science. Yet others express concern that if the journal eventually disappears into virtual space, our research efforts will be lost forever.

See also: Archival Research; Literature Reviews; Meta-Analysis; Research Proposals; Research Questions.

KEY READINGS

The best way to learn about the wide-ranging scope and content of sport-related academic journals is by delving deeply into them. Here is a partial list of the most common academic journals used by sport and exercise researchers.

American Journal of Physiology
American Journal of Sports Medicine
Applied Bionics and Biomechanics
Athletic Insight: The Online Journal of Sport Psychology
Biomechanics
British Journal of Sports Medicine
Canadian Journal for Women Coaching
Coaching: An International Journal of Theory, Research and Practice
Coaching Psychologist
European Journal of Applied Physiology
European Journal of Nutrition
European Journal of Sport Science
European Sport Management Quarterly
Human Movement Science
International Journal of Behavioral Nutrition & Physical Activity
International Journal of Food Sciences & Nutrition
International Journal of Sport & Exercise Psychology
International Journal of Sport Nutrition & Exercise Metabolism
International Journal of Sport Psychology
International Journal of Sports Marketing & Sponsorship
International Journal of the History of Sport
International Review for the Sociology of Sport
International Sports Law Review
Journal of Applied Biomechanics
Journal of Applied Physiology
Journal of Applied Sport Psychology
Journal of Athletic Training
Journal of Biomechanics
Journal of Electromyography and Kinesiology
Journal of Exercise Physiology
Journal of Hospitality, Leisure, Sports and Tourism Education
Journal of Human Nutrition & Dietetics
Journal of Leisure Research
Journal of Sport Behavior
Journal of Sport & Exercise Psychology
Journal of Sport & Tourism
Journal of Sport Tourism
Journal of Sports Sciences
Journal of the International Society of Sports Nutrition
Legal Aspects of Sport
Leisure Management
Leisure Sciences
Leisure Studies
Nutrition Research
Operative Techniques in Sports Medicine

academic journals

PE & Sport Today
Pediatric Exercise Science
Physical Education & Sport Pedagogy
Physical Therapy in Sport
Professionalization of Exercise Physiology Online
Psychology of Sport and Exercise
Recreation
Research Quarterly for Exercise & Sport
Science & Sports
Sociology of Sport Journal
Sport, Education & Society
Sport, Ethics & Philosophy
Sport in History
Sport in Society
Sport Journal
Sport Management Review
Sport Marketing Quarterly
Sport Psychologist
Sport Sciences for Health
Sports Biomechanics
Strength and Conditioning Journal
Training & Coaching Today
Women in Sport & Physical Activity Journal

Analytic Epidemiology

My brother contracted a very rare form of epilepsy when he was 46 years old. The disease changed his life immeasurably, and every day seems like an uphill battle for him. Knowing that he played quite a bit of contact sport in his youth, his doctors were quite eager to explore whether or not his brain suffered permanent trauma as a teenager; and whether or not such trauma might be aetiologically linked to his epilepsy. The manifestation of epilepsy in adults is poorly understood by neurologists and other specialists. Some common causes of epilepsy in children are cerebral palsy (most often due to complications related to childbirth), infections of the brain, metabolic and certain systemic diseases, any structural disease of the brain, head trauma and a range of hereditary conditions. In adults, structural brain disease, trauma, infections and the presence of toxins are more often the cause. In about 50–75% of cases of adult epilepsy, no cause can be determined even with the best of technology and science, and thus epilepsy is believed to be 'idiopathic' in these cases. I now see the field of play in quite different terms in my roles as an ice hockey and soccer coach. I wonder whether or not every hit, knock, bump or bash one of my players experiences might produce catastrophic results later in their lives. As a researcher, I am interested in studying whether or not involvement in contact sport as a youth may be, in addition to other factors, a known risk related to the development of adult epilepsy. When I venture into this research territory, I am in the area of population health research; or, in other terms, *epidemiology*.

WHAT IS THIS CONCEPT?

Epidemiology is the study of the distribution and determinants of disease, injury, and other health outcomes in human populations. Unlike clinical medicine, which focuses on improving the health of one individual at a time, the goal of epidemiological analysis is to improve the health of the population (or in some cases, a sub-group of the population) as a whole. Of course, if the health of the population is improved, so is that of many individuals. But epidemiologists argue that only with population data can the relationships between risk or protective factors and health outcomes for individuals be fully described and quantified. A population health focus shifts attention towards the role of public health programmes and policies in identifying and combating illness. An epidemiologist might study, for example, whether involvement in sport is a robust predictor of adult epilepsy; and if so, what types of new health/sport policies might be developed to protect children.

Typically, epidemiological research is divided into two strands, or methodological approaches: *descriptive epidemiology* and *analytic epidemiology*. *Descriptive epidemiology* focuses on identifying and reporting both the pattern and frequency of health events in a population (e.g. how many children who play contact sports end up with adult epilepsy); *analytic epidemiology* focuses on the search for the determinants of health outcomes (e.g. whether or not involvement in sport is a good predictor – that is, cause – of adult epilepsy). These two components work together to increase our understanding of the health of a population.

analytic epidemiology

9

Let's discuss descriptive epidemiology in a bit more detail. Descriptive epidemiology focuses both on the pattern of health events in a population and on their frequency in a population. Within the field of epidemiology, there are three types of data that are necessary for describing the patterns of health and disease in human populations. These three pillars of descriptive epidemiological analysis are: person, place and time. *Person characteristics* include socio-demographic characteristics such as age, race/ethnicity, education, income, occupation, parity and marital status, as well as behaviours such as substance abuse, diet, sexual activity or use of health care services. If we were studying adult epilepsy, researchers would be interested in whether certain person characteristics are shared by people who contract the disease later in life. *Place characteristics* include geographic location (e.g. urban vs. rural), features of the geography (e.g. mountainous region, area with wells as the major water source), population density, as well as geo-political boundaries (e.g. census tracts, cities, counties or states), and location of worksites, schools and health facilities. *Time characteristics* include cyclical changes, long-term secular trends, and even daily or hourly occurrences during a developing 'epidemic'. While person characteristics are attributes of individuals, place and time characteristics are attributes of the physical and social environment. By jointly considering person, place and time, epidemiology advances the idea that health and diseases like epilepsy result from the interaction between individuals and their environment. While we can all list various person, place and time characteristics without much effort, it is important to understand what these characteristics actually represent so that we use them appropriately.

Analytic epidemiology is far more complex than simple descriptive approaches to the study of health and illness patterns in a population. There are two main types of analytic epidemiological techniques: *cohort studies* (often referred to as prospective studies) and *case-control investigations*. While descriptive studies of population health are heavily correlation-oriented (examining the common correlates of disease outcomes within a population), analytic epidemiology is, by contrast, far more aetiological (cause) preoccupied. Cohort studies are longitudinal research efforts, where an academic, or normally a team of them, will follow a group of people over time and examine their health outcomes given their exposure to a variety of health-related variables. Here's an example. Imagine I examine the existing literature and find that a descriptive epidemiological connection has been made between involvement in minor American football or ice hockey and the onset of adult epilepsy. So, I assemble a sample of 2,000 young people aged 15–18 and track them over 30 years to examine whether or not the kids in the sample who played football or hockey contract adult epilepsy at a higher rate than kids who did not. The aim of the study would be to track the rate of incidence of adult epilepsy in the youth, and to determine whether or not the various person, place and time characteristics in the group account for more of the adult epilepsy outcomes than sport involvement.

Case-control investigations are retrospective studies investigating people who already have an illness/disease under our academic interest. In our example, they would be adults who have already been diagnosed with epilepsy. In these designs, the person, place and time characteristics of people who already have adult epilepsy are compared with those who do not (often, from a similar generational cohort). What is the logic of this method? It's simple, really. The people who develop adult epilepsy in our study would be called 'cases' and those who do not are referred to as 'controls'. Based on our background research before the sample of people was gathered, we would have developed a series of theoretical hypotheses to be tested against the data; for instance, that people who played contact sport would be greatly over-represented in the case group by comparison to the control group. We are simply testing whether or not our theoretically predicted causes of epilepsy are evidenced within the empirical data. If we are correct, a huge preponderance of the people with epilepsy would have played contact sport, while those without epilepsy would have no history of minor sport involvement.

WHY IS THIS RELEVANT TO ME?

Epidemiological research and the associated techniques of population health analysis is a rapidly growing, multi-disciplinary field. Epidemiological research not only challenges traditional boundaries of health and illness research within universities and colleges, it pushes academic researchers beyond the level of theory and towards the use of clinical or field research in the way of praxis. The methods discussed above are indeed powerful techniques for identifying the correlates of illness in a population, and epidemiological research findings are quickly becoming sought after as important knowledge to be used for shaping public health policies. Why? There has recently been an invigorated push within academic departments to engage more in 'evidence-based' research that speaks directly to the health and wellness management problems encountered across social institutions, including the family, the school system, the workplace and, of course, the sport and exercise domain. Because epidemiology focuses on the correlates and predictors of health/illness outcomes in a population, it is key for identifying what is going 'wrong' in social institutions that produce illness, and what can be changed within them to encourage wellness. By definition, epidemiological research techniques are designed to be practical and interventionist.

SHOW ME HOW IT'S USED!

For students averse to statistical analysis in even its simplest form, epidemiological research can be both frustrating and scary. Descriptive epidemiological studies need not be scary to even the most unseasoned student. The general goal of descriptive research on population health is to gather a working sense of the distribution of an illness in a population (i.e. the common person characteristics among those with it), rates of contraction in the population and a general sense of the *risk markers* of the illness. Risk markers can be thought of as the person, place and time characteristics people are 'exposed to' that may be correlated with one's contraction of the illness. Risk markers for developing adult epilepsy are childhood head trauma, exposure to certain neurotoxins, sex (more males than females contract it), residence in an urban environment, and so forth. Now, we cannot be sure that any one of these causes adult epilepsy; people not fitting this profile do contract it, and people with all of these risk markers may never contract the illness. We normally refer to variables as risk markers in descriptive research when we know, clinically, very little about the aetiology of a disease or when new correlates with disease outcomes are being investigated and researchers are theoretically/substantively unsure as to how/if the variable operates causally at all.

Descriptive epidemiological studies analyse population health outcomes (like the contraction of adult epilepsy) via the use of descriptive rather than inferential statistics; hence the name of the approach! If I gathered an appropriate sample of 10,000 people aged 35–50 in London, England, and measured them on a whole series of health, physical activity and exercise variables (including whether or not they had been diagnosed with adult epilepsy) I could use descriptive statistics to paint a preliminary portrait of who is at risk of the illness, its relative presence in the city, and the main person, place and time correlates (at least, among those I have measured) in the study associated with the outcome. Simple statistics like frequencies and sample proportions can be utilised to calculate the *prevalence* of epilepsy. The prevalence is the number of people with the illness divided by the number of people in the study. This statistic provides a working estimate of the proportion of people in a society with the illness (indicating, potentially, something about its seriousness). The *incidence* is yet another statistic commonly used by epidemiological researchers. Incidence rates are calculated by dividing the number of new cases in a population over a specific time period by the number of people in the population at risk. This rudimentary statistic offers researchers a working sense of the average (at risk) person's probability of contracting the illness. In future, pay close attention to news media accounts of new illnesses and how publics are informed about the relative risks of contracting … these are almost always based on incidence rates calculated via epidemiological research.

Analytic epidemiological research builds on knowledge of risk markers in a population, but ventures further towards the study of *risk factors*. Something becomes a risk factor when researchers are testing the factor's potential causal role in the contraction or transmission of a disease. Descriptive statistical procedures are no longer appropriate, and so inferential statistics are employed. There is a full arsenal of inferential statistical techniques available to the field of population health research. Which one(s) a researcher will employ depends on how variables have been measured (their level of measurement), over what time period (cross-sectional, longitudinal, time-series, etc.) and the nature of the sample being used in the research. Common inferential techniques of data analysis used include linear regression, logistic regression, structural equation modelling, cluster analysis, path analysis, multi-level modelling, time-series analysis, hazard rate/event history analysis, and ANOVA models.

PROBLEMS, PITFALLS AND CONTROVERSIES

Although epidemiological research is not mired with serious pitfalls and controversies, there are several pertinent issues worth noting. As with all quantitative research involving the analysis of variables, the measurement of concepts with invalid indicators is a significant stumbling block in poorly designed projects. Measuring a variable like 'involvement in contact sport' might seem easy and straightforward; we could simply ask respondents if they have played any contact sport and for how long. But this is not a great measure at all. What we are really interested in is whether or not a person has received head trauma while playing one of the sports we have identified. The more imprecise, distal and approximate our measures are, the more epidemiological research remains focused on risk markers rather than risk factors. Involvement in contact sport is likely the generic risk marker, while multiple concussions are most likely a significant risk factor in the development of adult epilepsy. One must always be careful to sample appropriately in epidemiological research (biased samples always lead to biased results, let's remember) and to adequately ensure the separation of cases from controls in one's design. Finally, the standard critique of quantitative analysis dependent on cross-sectional data applies to many epidemiological research ventures. Cross-sectional data – notoriously difficult to use in the testing of potentially causal relationships between variables – will allow epidemiologists to study many risk markers and correlates with illness, but rarely allow for incontrovertible claims regarding the aetiology of disease.

See also: Causality; Descriptive Statistics; Inferential Statistics: Populations and Samples.

KEY READINGS

Brownson, R. and Petitti, D. (1998) *Applied Epidemiology: Theory to Practice*. New York: Oxford University Press.

Clayton, D. and Hills, M. (1993) *Statistical Models in Epidemiology*. Oxford: Oxford University Press.

Dishman, E., Heath, G. and Washburn, R. (2004) *Physical Activity Epidemiology*. Champaign: Human Kinetics.

Friis, R. (2009) *Epidemiology 101*. Sudbury: Jones and Bartlett Publishing.

Applied vs. Pure Research

A long, long time ago, I remember listening to an introductory lecture on research methods in which my instructor ventured into a lengthy diatribe on the differences between research for 'research's sake' and research conducted as problem-solving. Most methods textbooks I pick up and review or use in a course of mine tend to contain a chapter or a portion of one devoted to the differences between so-called pure (basic) research and applied research. In what follows, we review the apparent differences between the two research acts (pure/applied) and attempt to dispel the myth that research generically falls exclusively into either one of them.

WHAT IS THIS CONCEPT?

Making differentiations between applied and pure research is mainly an academic task. Yet students are regularly exposed to the terms 'applied' or 'pure' research, and, as such, their conceptual similarities and differences require explanation. It's fair to state that while not all pure research is applied, applied research almost always contains an implicit 'pure' element. *Pure research* refers to systematic study of life aimed at fuller knowledge or a deeper understanding of the theoretical aspects of a phenomenon. This would be done, in essence, with no precise applications of the findings of research towards any real world problem-solving. Here is an example. I conduct quite a bit of research on alternative sport subcultures like Parkour. There are many, many theories about how and why subcultures in sport form, what they mean to participants, and what they signify about broader social life. Pure or basic research on Parkour kids (who often call themselves *traceurs*) might strive to examine if and how an existing theory (or set of theories) about subcultures explains the form and content of the group's genesis and daily practices. Now, for socio-cultural theorists of sport like me, these are fascinating theoretical excursions into the world. For people outside of academia, one might struggle to see the merit of comparing what Parkour kids do against subcultural theory.

On the other hand, *applied research* is a systematic, empirical study undertaken to generate knowledge for problem-solving in a very broad sense. Applied research is defined differently by academics, but consensus exists regarding the need to apply, test or extend theoretical ideas in research for the sake of making the world a better, more efficient, enhanced place in one manner or another. In my example of Parkour, one might choose to study whether or not youth involvement in the subculture is an effective inoculant against participation in crime and delinquency. I might question whether or not involvement in alternative sports subcultures reduces youth crime rates in an area. Not only would the study probe the potential relationship between subcultural involvement and participation in contra-normative behaviours, but odds are

I would be testing or striving to develop an innovative theoretical explanation of how sports subcultures operate. Like many of my colleagues, I envision my research as a set of empirical exercises connecting both pure and applied aspects. Ingham and Donnelly (1990) describe openly hybrid kinds of research as *practical*; containing both theoretical and social/personal interventionist aims and goals.

More recently, scores of sport, exercise and physical activity researchers have turned to action research. *Action research* is a reflective process of progressive problem-solving led by academics working with others in teams or as part of a 'community of practice' to improve the way they address issues and solve problems. For example, I am working with colleagues in the UK, France and the United States on a global Parkour project to examine (among other things) whether or not Parkour is viable as a strategy to combat social exclusion and inactivity among youth. We might, as an action research project, consider involving community youth outreach workers, members of the police, health educators or others who might be able to help examine the problem – and for whom our findings might alter their tactics for managing youth 'at risk'. Action research is a collaborative knowledge exchange, a think-tank scenario of research in which academics work together and with others who need problems solved. Action research can also be undertaken by larger organisations or institutions, assisted or guided by academics or those with research skills expertise, with the aim of improving their strategies, practices and knowledge of the environments within which they practise. As designers and stakeholders, researchers work with others to propose a new course of action to help their community improve its work practices. Action research challenges traditional modes of doing science or academic research in general, by including a greater range of people (stakeholders) in the research process and working with them in the middle of problem-solving contexts.

WHY IS THIS RELEVANT TO ME?

An image of the academic as a pure or basic researcher is routinely presented to undergraduate students as the ideal type, but most of our undergraduate students will never become fully fledged 'pure' researchers. There is a tendency amongst some academics and practitioners to idealise the role of pure/basic research, but in reality, basic research is rapidly becoming a thing of the past in sport and exercise circles. With the demand for faster translations of theoretical ideas into public practice, research undertaken for theoretical purposes alone is difficult to justify. Further, there are far more job opportunities for students in applied research settings than in traditional academic research zones. As the contemporary university or college morphs into a social institution mandated the task of solving personal, collective and indeed global problems, research application is the mantra of the new millennium.

SHOW ME HOW IT'S USED!

The mean weight of a person in North America is increasing. The mean amount and intensity of daily physical activity of the typical North American is declining. These trends pose rather stark personal and social problems. Hundreds of researchers in North America devote their professional lives to the study of the physical, psychological and social consequences of sedentary lifestyles on ageing populations. What a problem to tackle, and the need for both pure and applied research is obvious!

Pure or basic research on health concerns amongst an inactive, ageing population could take shape in any number of ways. A physiologist might conduct research on the theoretical relationship between hormone therapy and the ability for women aged 55 and older to engage in heavy weight training activity – all theoretical, that is, focusing on the benefits or detriments based on what biological theories teach us as scientists. Or, a sociologist of sport could use post-colonial feminist theory to explain why older, minority women in a country like Canada are at a particular risk for being inactive. Basic research *seeks to uncover and account for* observable patterns in the world; explaining them through disciplinary theory and proposing why and how 'things' may be connected in the world. A sizeable number of undergraduate and graduate research activities are most likely pure research efforts, with little emphasis at all placed upon 'practical' application.

Applied research efforts on the health outcomes of inactivity within an ageing population take, as one might guess, a more proactive and interventionist stance. An epidemiologist might study why coronary disease clusters within identified segments of the urban environment, then use population health theory to point to the environmental risk factors in that zone, and then offer a set of recommendations for risk management. Motor behaviour researchers conduct studies of the relationship between inactivity, stair walking and injuries from falls within older populations, and provide suggestions for the elderly and their physicians for managing risks. Further still, an action research

applied vs. pure research

17

project could be launched following a call placed to a sport and physical activity psychologist from the manager of a senior citizens' group residence who is looking for innovative suggestions for motivating members to be more active. Residents routinely avoid the planned health and physical activity programmes on offer there, because they find them dull and unchallenging. The sports psychologist might go to the residence, survey and study the people regarding their perceptions of and motivations for physical activity, and work with the resident managers to help organise and implement an innovative health programme.

PROBLEMS, PITFALLS AND CONTROVERSIES

The movement towards research cultures peppered with an ethos of application and action signals the erosion of academic freedom and theoretical creativity for basic researchers. I understand this concern and criticism. In my personal research practice, breakthroughs in my own way of seeing the world of sport and exercise have come from studies leaning heavily towards the task of pure/basic research. Freedom to think creatively, to propose seemingly bizarre new ideas, to rigorously challenge dominant ways of thinking in theory, and to move into the conceptual unknown rarely occur in highly applied research ventures. Therefore, it is vital that a space must remain for research driven by the development of new ideas and perspectives alone. 'For hire' research undertaken within organisations or institutionally granted/funded research, may allow for creative thinking to help solve a problem of interest (the much valued need to think 'outside of the box' for solutions to obdurate problems), but radically innovative ideas tend to flow slowly in these scenarios.

Critics of pure research respond by claiming that traditional academics tucked away in their institutional silos are out of touch with the real world. If universities and colleges are pantheons of problem-solving, then the pressing problems of individuals and publics living beyond the tight circumference of the academic community should be privileged. Now, I'm not going to drag out an awfully clichéd line from the movie Spiderman ('with great power comes great responsibility') but there is merit in the argument against devoting one's career to theoretical problem exploration with no concern for its implementation in any social context.

Finally, despite widely accepted beliefs in the need for interdisciplinary and trans-disciplinary solutions to sport, health and exercise problems, rarely are interdisciplinary research teams assembled in practice. In the case study of Parkour, for example, there are socio-cultural, psychological and bio-physical theories explaining youth crime and how involvement in sports activities as forms of social intervention may 're-train' the body in ways that make people more compliant with social norms. But the lack of interdisciplinary co-operation and the enduring preference for (or possibly comfort in) disciplinary specialisation, leads researchers to avoid working in teams to examine many sides of a problem. As long as researchers remain committed to working within their own academic tribes and from narrow theoretical perspectives, the true potential of applied or action research may never be realised.

See also: Critical Theory; Evaluation Research; Evidence-Based Research and Practice; Theory; Translation

KEY READINGS

Bishop, D. (2008) 'An applied research model for sport sciences'. *Sports Medicine* 38: 253–263.

Blankenship, D. (2009) *Applied Research and Evaluation in Recreation*. Champaign: Human Kinetics.

Hackfort, D., Duda, J. and Lidor, R. (2005) *Handbook of Research in Applied Sport and Exercise Psychology: International Perspectives*. Los Angeles: Fitness Information Technology.

Ingham, A. and Donnelly, P. (1990) 'Whose knowledge counts? The production of knowledge and issues of application in the sociology of sport'. *Sociology of Sport Journal* 7:58–65.

Whyte, W., Greenwood, D. and Lazes, P. (1989) 'Participatory action research: Through practice to science in social research'. *American Behavioral Scientist* 32: 513–551.

Archival Research

History has been called the world's greatest social laboratory. The analysis of historical events, processes and characters can provide considerable insight into the ways in which sport and exercise has been structurally determined, culturally defined and contoured as societies take shape over time. Historical researchers do not abound in the study of sport and exercise, and more's the pity. Why? Because detailed examinations of the genesis of sport cultures, the evolution of sporting pastimes, the emergence and disappearance of folk games, the professionalisation of sport, and the study of who participates in sport and exercise historically, just to name but a few subjects, are important for grasping the form and content of what socially and culturally counts as sport and exercise today. Contemporary physical cultural problems like the resistance to activity and exercise, waning involvement in minor league sports, obesity rates and other issues in population health, as well as sedentary lifestyles, are best understood as long-term historical processes rather than *sui generis* problems of the current generation.

WHAT IS THIS CONCEPT?

Archival analysis is part of the historical research method, and refers to a form of the content analytic method whereby the researcher examines the accumulated documents or other 'physical' artefacts of a culture (e.g. diaries, novels, magazines and newspapers) in order to answer a socio-cultural research question. Historical research is, then, the process of systematically examining past events to give an account of what has happened in the past, but also a means of understanding the development of contemporary situations, conditions and events occurring today. For example, English football phenomenon Wayne Rooney signed a £60 million contract in October 2010 with Manchester United. The contract made Rooney the highest paid footballer in the country. While one might study the current bonanza of spending in the English Premier League and elsewhere as a manifestation of player greed or high ticket prices, an historical researcher sees another set of possibilities and questions. An historical researcher might conceptualise the problem as part of the long-term trend towards the capitalist commercialisation of the game or as an offshoot of ongoing globalisation in sport. Either of the two processes has complicated roots dating back at least a hundred years and involves social events, happenings, trends and organisation patterns both close to and far away from the playing field. Historical researchers would tie high player salaries in the current era to such processes and events through theory, and would need historical archives to trace out and examine the 'documented' links between the two. Thus, historical research and the use of archives as an overall method is:

- Not a mere accumulation of facts and dates or even a description of past events; it is a study of how historical events and occurrences are related to one another as part of the unfolding of a 'bigger' social process;
- Intended as a flowing, dynamic account of past events which involves an interpretation of these events in an attempt to recapture the nuances, personalities and ideas that influenced these events;
- Undertaken to communicate an understanding of past events as indicators of diffuse social processes that are ongoing today.

There is a vast array of topics in sport, exercise and health studies that may be considered for conducting historical research. For example, a researcher may choose to answer questions about the development of school sports, exercise science as a field of inquiry, the use of public space for sports spectacles, the rise of sport-media technology, the patterns of social inclusion and exclusion in sport, famous personalities, statistics detailing participation rates, or how geographical demographics affect sports cultures in a particular country. My students are generally surprised to learn that there are many places to acquire historical information about sport and exercise histories. However, as clichéd as it might sound, the library is a wonderful starting point for discovering and exploring accumulated archives. In a library/archive setting, *primary sources* are the most sought after documents. Primary sources are first-hand accounts of information. Examples of primary documents include personal diaries, letters, pictures, film, meeting notes and memos, eyewitness accounts of events and oral histories. *Secondary sources* of information are records or accounts prepared by someone other than the person, or persons, who participated in or observed an event. These may take the form of news or other media accounts, biographies, official statistics, institutional summaries of events, and even other researchers' historical accounts of past events. Secondary resources can be very useful in giving a researcher a general grasp of a subject and may provide extensive bibliographic information for delving further into a research topic.

Two important figures in historical research methods are worth noting, due to their respective influence on how academics 'see' history and method. In 1987, sociologist Charles Ragin described in his book, *The Comparative Method*, a technique known as qualitative comparative analysis (QCA). QCA is a hybrid qualitative-quantitative technique (using Boolean summaries of truth tables that compare and unpack similar historical processes across different cases). The technique is based on Ragin's argument that the historical study of something like, in our example, the commercialisation of sport, reveals processes as cross-nationally relevant phenomena, but similarly illustrates that they do not manifest causally in precisely the same linear manner in all cases. Thus, using qualitative examinations of, for instance, the historical commercialisation of sport in Canada, the UK, the US, France, Germany, Australia, South Africa, Japan and Argentina, we could tease out both the necessary and sufficient causes of sport commercialisation. Ragin (1987) refers to this process as the study of *conjunctural causation*.

Michel Foucault's impact on the socio-cultural study of history and sport is nothing less than paradigm shifting. In particular, Foucault's discussions of the need to study language (discourse) and its relationship to power and knowledge in a given phase of history has changed the manner by which socio-cultural researchers of sport and exercise understand what history can reveal about contemporary issues such as gender discrimination, homophobia and sexual inequality, racism, classism, and other forms of ideological and structural inequality in the sport and exercise worlds. In 1969, Foucault published *The Archaeology of Knowledge*, a methodological treatise that explicitly formulates what he took to be his implicit historical approach (*archaeology*) for studying how discourses emerge historically and shape social relationships between people. The premise of the archaeological method is that systems of thought and knowledge (*epistemes* or *discursive formations*), that can be observed in historical documents, are governed by ideological rules, beyond those of grammar and logic, that operate beneath the consciousness of individual subjects. These logics define a system of conceptual possibilities that determines the boundaries of thought in a given domain and period.

WHY IS THIS RELEVANT TO ME?

There are institutional archives everywhere, with innumerable documents containing historical, statistical and other information about sport, exercise and health. An *archive* is a way of sorting and organising older documents, whether it is digitally (photographs online, e-mails, etc.) or manually (putting it in folders, photo albums, etc.). Among the most sought after types of archives are *fonds*. A fond is an aggregation of documents that originate from the same source. More specifically, a fond distinguishes itself from an 'archive collection' through its organic nature, as archival documents that have been naturally accumulated (made or received) by an individual, company, institution, etc., as a by-product of business or day-to-day activities. These collections of materials are then donated to a library or other institution so that they may be preserved and/or accessed by the public. In modern archival practice, the fond is generally the highest level of arrangement, and is usually used to describe the whole of the archive of an organisation or the papers of an individual. It may be divided into sub-fonds, generally the records of different branches of an organisation or major themes within the papers of an individual. These are in turn further subdivided into series (which may in a smaller archive come directly below a fond without the presence of a sub-fond), usually used for groupings of individual types of documents' sub-series, files and items. An item is the smallest archival unit, and is usually indivisible (a single volume or letter, for instance). It is technically possible to add an infinite number of *subs* to the fonds, series or files, but in practice it is actually rare for more than one to be used.

Other than the discovery of important archives and fonds, historical research is generally advocated because it helps to:

1. Uncover the unknown (some historical events are not recorded);
2. Answer questions (there are many questions about our past that we not only want to know but can profit from knowing);
3. Identify the relationship that the past has to the present (knowing about the past can frequently give a better perspective of current events);
4. Record and evaluate the accomplishments of individuals, agencies, or institutions;
5. Assist in understanding the culture in which we live (sport and exercise are part of societies and cultures).

SHOW ME HOW IT'S USED!

There is no single approach for conducting historical research. For example, historical research, unlike the lion's share of approaches presented in this book, can adopt either quantitative or/and qualitative techniques. Nevertheless, we can draw out a general set of steps that are typically followed in an historical/archival analysis project. There are six general steps for conducting historical research:

1. The recognition of a historical problem or the identification of a need for certain historical knowledge;
2. The gathering of as much relevant information about the problem or topic as possible;

3. If appropriate, the forming of hypotheses that tentatively explain relationships between historical factors;
4. The rigorous collection and organisation of evidence, and the verification of the authenticity and veracity of information and its sources (perhaps the most critical stage in historical analysis);
5. The selection, organisation, and analysis of the most pertinent collected evidence, and the drawing of conclusions;
6. The recording of conclusions in a meaningful narrative.

After developing an appropriate research question suitable for historical analysis, the real challenge in conducting historical research involves identifying, locating and collecting information from archives/fonds pertaining to the research topic. Here are some tips for thinking about where to find information:

- The *information sources* are often contained in documents such as diaries or newspapers, records, photographs, relics and interviews with individuals who have had experience with or have knowledge of the research topic. In the case of sport and exercise, sports agencies and organisations (governmental, amateur and professional) often maintain wonderful archives
- Interviews with individuals who have knowledge of the research topic are called *oral histories*; these are often held in private collections in universities and colleges in subject-specific fonds.
- The documents, records, oral histories, and other information sources can be primary or secondary sources.
- Of late, institutions have moved towards 'digitising' historical documents and placing them online for public review. Thorough Internet searches for these special collections can uncover a treasure-trove of historical information.

Every information source used as data in an historical study must be evaluated for its authenticity and accuracy. When a document has been produced a long time ago, questions about its ability to report the 'truth' need to be asked. There are two types of evaluation tests every source of historical data must pass. First, the source must pass the test of *external criticism*: the process of determining the validity, trustworthiness, or authenticity of the source. Sometimes this is difficult to do with primary sources, but at other times it can easily be done by handwriting analysis, determining the age of the paper on which something was written, or by reviewing any other source of external validation of the document's authenticity. Second, the document must pass the test of *internal criticism*: the process of determining the reliability or accuracy of the information contained in the sources collected. If the source can be verified as authentic, its contents must also be verified as truthful. The document's reliability is evaluated by *positive and negative criticism*. *Positive criticism* refers to ensuring that the statements made or the meaning conveyed in the sources is understood. This is frequently difficult because of the problems of vagueness and presentism (*vagueness* refers to uncertainty in the meaning of the words and phrases used in the source, and *presentism* refers to the assumption that the present-day connotations of terms also existed in the past). *Negative criticism* refers to establishing the reliability or authenticity and accuracy of the content of the sources used. This is the more difficult part because it requires a judgement about the accuracy and authenticity of what is contained in the source.

Historians often use three benchmarks in making decisions about what documents can be included as evidence in a study. These are *corroboration, sourcing*, and, ultimately, *contextualisation*.

- *Corroboration*, refers to comparing different documents to each other to determine if they provide the same information;
- *Sourcing*, or identifying the author, the date of creation of a document, and the place it was created, is another technique that is used to establish the authenticity or accuracy of information;
- *Contextualisation*, or identifying when and where an event took place.

After data are collected, screened and included in a study, the process of data usage unfolds in different manners in a study. For qualitatively oriented sport and exercise researchers, interpreting/reading historical events might take on any manner of protocols, from grounded theoretical development to intensive case analysis, genealogy/archaeology, or critical discourse analysis. Quantitative studies use a series of interconnected events from the past (for example, in the commercialisation of sport) in order to test a causal theory of social behaviour or to inductively develop a better understanding of the causal sequences of events. Mixed methods designs are a blend of both interpretive readings of history and the examination of potential casual chains of events within historical processes.

PROBLEMS, PITFALLS AND CONTROVERSIES

Even though a researcher may have a brilliant and inspired idea for an historical project, the method lives and dies by the availability of credible resources. At least once a semester, a student in an undergraduate or post-graduate module I teach approaches me with an idea for historical research that is practically untenable due to the scarcity of credible evidence on the subject. Students quickly become uninterested in historical questions and related methods on these grounds alone. But historical research, even when viable, is a painstaking process involving the search for and review of dozens or even hundreds of documents. Historical researchers are self-proclaimed text lovers – and it is a rare student in sport and exercise science today who is inclined to devote most of their research energies to reading in the library!

See also: Critical Theory; Experiments; Interdisciplinary Research; Unobtrusive Methods; Variables.

KEY READINGS

Carr, E. (1961) *What is History?* Cambridge: Cambridge University Press.
Foucault, M. (1969) *L'Archéologie du Savoir*. Paris: Éditions Gallimard. [English title: *The Archaeology of Knowledge.*]
Morrow, D. and Wamsley, K. (2005) *Sport in Canada: A History*. Toronto: Oxford University Press.
Ragin, C. (1987) *The Comparative Method*. Berkeley: University of California Press.
Stolarov, V. (1976) 'Historical method in the sociology of sport'. *International Review for the Sociology of Sport* 11: 103–112.

.... Causality ....

WHAT IS THIS CONCEPT?

While there are clear differences between the concepts of causality and correlation and their implications, students struggle with their relation-ship on a yearly basis. The difference between the two is rather straight-forward in principle, but difficult to envision at times in practice. In what

Figure 1   Understanding the tentative nature of causality

(Source: http://xkcd.com)

follows, I'll attempt to strip away much of the methodological and statistical jargon typically involved in articulating their relationship. From the onset, let's remember that correlation and causation are part of the methodological lexicon of the positivist researcher. They are central in the analysis of data, and in the testing/assessment of hypotheses derived from theories. To help explain the difference, let's focus on a research example. Imagine I have developed a study to examine the relationship between television viewing ('screen time') and obesity. Logically, we would assume (based on so much past research and theorising) that the two are related: the more time spent in front of screens, the higher the obesity score for the person. I sample 5,000 people and survey them regarding their average daily screen time and weight, among other things. All of my 5,000 respondents return their surveys, fully completed (yeah, right!) and I proceed to analyse the data. Remember the concept of a distribution? Each person will have a score for average daily screen time (in hours) and present weight (say, in kilograms). Because not all scores for each variable will be the same, we will have a distribution of scores. This is a really important idea for grasping the concepts of correlation and causation (review the entry in this book on Distributions).

Correlation is a mathematic idea we can examine via descriptive statistical analysis. The Pearson's product moment (correlation) coefficient (r), for example, is part of the statistical cluster of tests called 'tests of association'. As a test of association, the correlation coefficient examines the distributions of two sets of variable scores (in this case, the distributions for average screen time and body weight in the sample of 5,000), and summarises whether or not they seem to be dependent on one another. A test of association like r examines if scores in the distribution of one variable match up with the scores from a second variable (go up together, go down together, or move oppositely from one another). From our literature review on obesity, we would bet that as people's scores for screen time in the sample went up, people's weights would go up. Additionally, as screen time went down, we would expect to see people's weight scores go down. A statistic like the correlation coefficient (r), which ranges in value from -1 to 1, tells us how numerically strongly the distributions of two variables 'match up' (i.e. the closer to -1 or 1, the stronger the statistical relationship) in our sample AND the direction of the relationship (a negative value implies an inverse relationship between the scores, and a positive value indicates a direct relationship). If there is no relationship between the two variables (or more appropriately, the distributions of two variables in a sample), then the correlation coefficient will equal 0, and we can say the two variables are independent of one another.

Two important points about correlation are worth noting. First, tests of association like the correlation coefficient (r) only tell us about the strength of linear dependence between the distributions of two variables, and nothing more. Correlation statistics are not based on any of our ideas about one variable being the predictor and the other an outcome variable in the real word. Second, correlation statistics are typically calculated with cross-sectional data (data measured on/from a group of people at one point in time only). Correlation values between two variables are therefore snapshots of distributional relationships bound at a particular time and place.

Causation is another matter entirely, and is (mostly) more a theoretical argument than a mathematical matter. Establishing causality between two variables means establishing, without a shadow of a doubt, that one's score on a particular variable (say obesity) is determined by one's score on another (say, screen time). Causality is the examination of whether one's score on an independent variable can be used to completely predict one's score on a dependent/outcome variable. Wow, that's a pretty lofty task, right? Our interest in causality has its roots in the very ontological assumptions of positivism itself; that is, a belief that standard, universal, law-like patterns govern the nature of all life. One could argue that most, if not all, positivist research is undertaken with the goal of establishing causality between two or more variables. Lazarsfeld (1955) outlines the criteria for making an argument that we have discovered a causal relationship between something like screen time and obesity:

1. Temporality (the supposed cause must precede the effect);
2. Empirical association (there must be statistical correlation between the variables);
3. Non-spurious relationships (the observed relationship cannot be caused by a third, an unexamined, variable).

Now, points (1) and (2) above are relatively, and I must emphasise relatively, easy to establish in many cases. Let's start with (2) first. In our study of screen time and obesity, lo and behold, our statistics tell us that the two are indeed correlated ($r = 0.85$; indicating a strong, direct, positive relationship between the two variables). The more you watch, the more you weigh. But let's re-examine the first criterion. I think screen time probably occurs before obesity, but do I know for sure? Maybe it is not television watching that is causing obesity but that being obese causes a person to watch more TV! Think about it. Maybe obese people are less mobile, energetic or motivated to be physically active so rely on TV more for entertainment. If my data are cross-sectional, then I might have a very difficult time convincing people of temporality between the two variables. What I would have to do is utilise evidence from past research illustrating the temporal arrangement of the sequence.

Non-spuriousness is another matter entirely. Of all the concepts I teach in methods classes, it poses the most initial problems for students. Spurious relationships between variables are ones appearing to be causally valid, but the two variables are perhaps only coincidentally related. Does watching more TV make you heavier? Well, if we accept that people watch more TV first and then become heavier, and we have a demonstrated a correlational relationship between them, is that enough? No, and here is why. What if we examine the socio-economic status of all the participants in our study? We find that the less money they have, the heavier they are, and the more time they spend watching television. I could easily postulate from this observation that one's personal resources are the root cause of both time spent watching TV (fewer entertainment opportunities) and weight gain (less money to spend on higher priced 'health' foods). One's social class determines much in one's life, with screen time and weight both directly affected by this 'root' variable. Of course TV watching and weight would be strongly correlated, then, because they are both outcome variables affected by one's social class – but the original two variables in our study are not necessarily causally related!

WHY IS THIS RELEVANT TO ME?

If you provide me with a big enough sample, I could find correlations between practically every variable imaginable in said sample. Correlations can be found between so many variables, but their substantive or potentially causal relevance can often be tangential at best. Every once in a while, for example, I hear reports that scientists have established that black cars get into more accidents than any other colour, or that the police are most likely to stop red cars for traffic violations. Well, just don't buy a black or red car and you'll be safe, right? Think about how this might be a spurious argument about car colour and safety. If you need a creative push, consider some other examples (all of these findings have been reported at one time or another in the international media):

* People who sleep 6 hours a night live longer than those who sleep eight or more.

So the research says that if you decrease the number of hours you sleep then you will live longer. Number of hours slept (X) is positively correlated with a person's age when they die (Y). But maybe people who are more active sleep less and live longer? It could be the person's lifestyle (C) which causes both X and Y!

* Second-hand smoke lowers a child's IQ.

The research says that the more second-hand smoke a child inhales, the lower their IQ. That second-hand smoke (A) is negatively correlated with IQ (B). But it could be that parents with lower IQs are more likely to be smokers and are more likely to have children with lower IQs!

* Breastfed babies may grow up to be smarter adults.

A study says: the longer babies are breastfed (P), the smarter they will become (Q). But maybe it is that women who can afford to stay at home to breastfeed their children, also have time to read to them and better prepare them for the critical first couple of years of school.

* Children who diet may actually gain weight in the long run.

Maybe a child's body gets 'fixed' at a certain fat level at a young age. Children who have to go on diets early may still have a problem re-setting their fat level when they are older. It is not the diet that caused the weight gain.

* Parental restrictions on movies influence adolescent use of tobacco and alcohol.

The more X-rated movies you let your kids watch, the more smoking and drinking they will do? Well, maybe parents who do not take the time to limit their children's access to X-rated movies,also tend to be more liberal about limiting access to cigarettes and alcohol.

In all of the cases above, correlation-based analysis has been used, and perhaps misused, to make potentially spurious causal arguments. Therefore, we must always be mindful that demonstrating statistical correlation is only one small step in making valid claims about relationships between processes, entities, events and systems in the world. Responsible science begins with this fundamental assumption. This is why we often pause to emphasise that rarely will any individual study (or small collection of studies on a specific subject) demonstrate causality or prove anything; rather they have the power potentially to discount rival or alternative hypotheses about a phenomenon.

SHOW ME HOW IT'S USED!

The first thing to remember in an attempt to demonstrate causality, especially in the non-physical sciences, is that it is impossible to establish complete causality. That seems a bit strange to some students who listen to me speak about the goals and aims of positivism! The magical figure of 100% proof of causality is what every researcher must strive for, to ensure that a group of their peers will accept the results. The only way to do this is through a strong and well-considered and controlled experimental design, often containing pilot studies, to establish potential cause and effect relationships before venturing ahead with a complex and expensive study. In controlled, experimental designs, researchers are able to directly observe the cause and effect process unfold, and potentially hold constant or 'control for' competing and potentially confounding variables. The temporal factor is usually the easiest aspect to examine in a controlled experiment, simply because most experiments involve administering a treatment and then observing the effects, giving a linear temporal relationship. In experiments that use historical data this can be a little more complex. Most researchers performing such a programme will supplement it with a series of individual case studies, and interviewing a selection of the participants, in depth, will allow the researchers to find the order of events.

PROBLEMS, PITFALLS AND CONTROVERSIES

Good science is good science, and bad science is bad science. What can distinguish the former from the latter (apart from the technical aspects of conducting research) is responsibility in analysis and claims making. New, innovative, challenging and potentially policy-shifting claims can be offered through research based solely on correlations between variables evidenced in a study. Don't buy a red car, watch too much television, or feed your baby bottled formula because each has causal implications to bad events in the real world. Bad science results when researchers use the statistical language of evidenced correlations to speak in tongues of causality to audiences. In the rush to publish research, secure grants, achieve tenure or receive other accolades, claims making through correlations can be a dangerous and misleading academic practice. Only when researchers have discounted all rival hypotheses, replicated results dozens of times using dozens of different samples over years of research, and provided explanations of observed phenomena through accepted theoretical ideas do we even begin to whisper about potentially causal relationships.

In a totally different vein, critics of positivism and the statistical analysis of theoretical relationships between things in the world often fail to recognise or accept how cautious and conservative quantitative researchers are about the conclusions in any given study. Correlations may be found as statistically significant and theories generally supported in a given study, but most published research openly and reflexively warns against overinterpreting from the data. Qualitatively oriented researchers occasionally overlook the cautious claims-making nature of quantitative science and prefer to castigate the approach outright. Further still, the news media care little about caveats and warnings stitched into published research about the causal implications of observed relationships, and hardly distinguish between correlation and causation. This is a dangerous practice and detrimental to science as publics are led to believe that researchers are arguing for causality in published work. Over time, the general public becomes sceptical of scientists who apparently find causality in everything!

See also: Distributions; Experiments; Hypotheses; Inferential Statistics; Positivism; Variables.

KEY READINGS

Lazarsfeld, P. (1955) *The Language of Social Research: A Reader in the Methodology of Social Research*. Glencoe: Free Press.

Lewis, D. (1973) 'Causation'. *The Journal of Philosophy* 70: 556–567.

key concepts in sport and exercise research methods

Pearl, J. (2000) *Causality: Models, Reasoning, and Inference*. Cambridge: Cambridge University Press.

Rodgers, J. and Nicewander, A. (1988) 'Thirteen ways to look at the correlation coefficient'. *The American Statistician* 42: 59–66.

Salmon, W. (1984) *Scientific Explanation and the Causal Structure of the World*. Princeton, NJ: Princeton University Press.

Critical Theory

I chose to devote my professional life to the study of sport, exercise and human movement because I firmly believe that research on these subjects can make a difference in people's lives. Not just my life or the lives of my students and colleagues, but difference on a wide social scale. Only time will tell whether any of my research makes a difference. I learned to think about the use of research to make a difference from my readings in critical theory as an undergraduate student in sociology. Critical theory is unique as a methodological subject in many respects, but ties into concepts and ideas throughout this book such as interpretivism, action and applied research, knowledge translation and qualitative methodology. Critical theory is arguably the concept in this book furthest from traditional modes of scientific inquiry, but I believe it has a rightful place in the discussion of research as an effort in knowledge production and dissemination.

WHAT IS THIS CONCEPT?

The subject of critical theory is not common in most methodology textbooks in sport, exercise and health studies, perhaps other than as a footnote. Critical theory neither is one theory *per se*, nor does it provide a set of principles or steps for conducting socio-cultural research on sport and exercise. Critical theory is at once a set of assumptions about the world, a perspective guiding investigation into the socio-cultural analysis of lived experience, and a *practice*.

With respect to the guiding assumptions of critical theory, we must turn to its genesis in the university. *Critical theory* was first defined by

critical theory

33

Max Horkheimer of the Frankfurt School of sociology in 1937. Horkheimer believed that a useful social theory is one oriented toward critiquing and changing society as a whole – in contrast to traditional theory oriented only to objectively understanding or explaining it. Horkheimer wanted to distinguish critical theory as a radical, emancipatory form of social analysis. Horkheimer joined forces with Theodor Adorno, and later defined critical theory as a perspective on society and culture, drawing from knowledge across the social sciences and humanities. Critical theory, in the sociological context, refers to a style of Marxist theory with a tendency to engage with non-Marxist influences (for instance the work of Friedrich Nietzsche and Sigmund Freud). Critical theory in the Frankfurt School arose from a desire to critique the 'status quo' thinking of positivist theory and method, the emerging interpretivist sociologies of Max Weber and Georg Simmel, and the neo-Marxist theory of Georg Lukács and Antonio Gramsci. Other notable members of the Frankfurt School included Herbert Marcuse, Walter Benjamin and Jürgen Habermas. 'Critical' scholars in the social sciences would later adopt the Frankfurt School's principles of critiquing cultures, social structures and power imbalances in society, in the development of feminist theory, postmodernist and post-structuralist theory, critical race theory, queer theory and post-colonial studies.

Specifically, critical theorists share a common set of perspectives regarding the focus of observation, analysis and critique. The following features, to varying degrees, inform all varieties of critical socio-cultural theory:

- Critical theorists believe that it is necessary to understand the lived experience of real people in the cultural contexts of their lives. Critical theory thereby shares the ideas and the methodologies of some interpretive theories.
- Critical theorists study the contexts and mechanisms of oppression in a society.
- Critical approaches examine social conditions in order to uncover hidden structures of power and cultural dominance. This means that understanding the ways one is oppressed in seemingly 'hidden' or 'silent' manners enables one to take action to change oppressive forces.
- Critical socio-cultural investigations blend both theory and action. Critical theories thus strive serve to bring about change in the conditions that affect our lives.

- Critical theory is directed at the totality of society in its historical specificity (i.e. how it came to be configured at a specific point in time).
- Critical theory seeks to improve understanding of society by integrating all the major social sciences, including geography, economics, sociology, history, political science, anthropology and psychology.

To sum up, then, researchers working in this tradition align themselves with the interests of those opposed to the dominant order of society. They ask questions about the ways in which competing interests clash and the manner in which conflicts are resolved in favour of particular groups. As such, critical theory is described as a practice: a form of public intellectual work or praxis.

WHY IS THIS RELEVANT TO ME?

Critical theory has been around and has thrived in the socio-cultural analysis of sport for well over four decades. In 1983, Gruneau's *Class, Sports and Social Development*, Whannel's *Blowing the Whistle: The Politics of Sport*, and Morgan's article in the *Journal of Sport and Social Issues* titled, 'Toward a critical theory of sport', simultaneously called for more critical sport studies. Nearly three decades on, scores of critical theory efforts pepper published research on sport and physical culture, and contour situated analyses of the geo-political relevance of sport, exercise and leisure. Though neither mutually exclusive nor exhaustive, critical race theories, queer theories, feminist theories, (new) media theories, post-colonial theories, post-structuralist theories, (neo)Marxist and other political economic theories, existentialist theories, actor-network theories, critical pedagogy theories, identity crisis theories, theories of intersectionality, globalisation and cultural fragmentation theories, risk theories, new social movement theories, environmentalist theories, victimologies, postmodern theories, figurational theory, theories of consumption, and a swathe of theories loosely collated as 'cultural studies', are woven into research on structures of cultural power in sports, leisure and health cultures.

SHOW ME HOW IT'S USED!

Singularly and collectively, scholars working with and through strands of 'critical theory' expose the emancipating, constraining, humanistic, frustrating, oppressive, progressive and connecting aspects of sport, exercise and physical culture around the world. Here, there is immense potential to articulate the impacts of inequality and injustice in sport and leisure contexts, and for scholars to help direct inter-institutional policy-making. Consider some of the dominant and emerging topic areas scrutinised within critical sport/physical activity research: gender, race and class inequality in sport; cultural intolerance in sport; exploitation and violence in sport; the hyper-capitalist consumption of sport spectacles; new social movements in sport; sporting neo-liberalisms; critical sports pedagogy; the techno-scientising of contemporary sport and physical education; bioethics in sport; the economic and cultural impacts of sport mega-events; sport and globalisation; sport and trans-national migration; sport for/as international development; human rights in sport; and, environmental issues in sport, to name only a few. But of what social good is this research? How does it potentially affect social change? What are the specific mandates of critical, praxis-oriented socio-cultural research on sport and exercise?

In the first instance, critical theoretical studies of sport must account for and intervene in the barriers within sport and leisure fields that deny access to and freedom of participation/expression for all. Such (normally qualitative) research recognises that these social problems in sport are materially based and culturally mediated; critical researchers must produce theoretically informed and empirically verified proposals for policy change; and critical theorists of sport must generate models of sport as a site of social integration that celebrates diversity. A public sociology of sport utilises research to assess if and how sport is, internally, a site where health promotion (in the widest sense) is evident, and to explore human physical, intellectual, artistic and moral potentials without fear or prejudice. Critical sociology of sport research, then, frequently involves challenging the naturalness or taken-for-grantedness of 'average' or typical identities, practices, logics, institutions, and images of power in sports worlds. A critical socio-cultural study of sport must venture beyond philosophy and critique; it must engage in the process of resolution. For example, research on the denial or usurpation of minority rights, identity-based discrimination, physical exploitation and control, and economic misdemeanours by sports organisations needs to be further represented in studies of sport. Heteronormative masculinity, essentialised constructions of gender, and taken-for-granted associations of biology, ability, and race all need to be further interrogated as cultural logics that stratify actors into established and outsider sport groups.

In the second instance, critical sport studies should devote increased attention to the potential role(s) of sport, physical activity and exercise in combating larger social problems at local, national and international levels. Proponents of a sport-for-public safety model, for example, believe that sport programmes work as preventive or reactive methods for confronting a wide range of social problems (David, 2005). When sport is structured effectively, it may offer education for children who are alienated from mainstream school opportunities; shelter at-risk children within safely supervised spaces; provide children who have few or no family role models with positive socialising forces; teach non-violence, cultural diversity and interpersonal tolerance; offer a healthy leisure-time option; and, reduce child experimentation with drugs and firearms. However, such claims are often based on anecdotal, speculative or naïve empirical grounds. For example, inner-city sport programmes designed to reduce youth crime in demographically problematic urban areas achieve uncertain results.

Still, while the socio-cultural study of sport is far more critical, investigative, probing, diverse, global and politically aware than ever before, very few socio-cultural colleagues have pursued an active, deliberate or concerted interest in praxis. That is to say, it is easy to conduct research on how women continue to be marginalised in sport or denied the same chances to participate as boys and men, how racial stereotypes and barriers exist in organised sport, how sport cultures remain relatively homophobic spaces, or how the working classes are disadvantaged with respect to participation in a range of sports practices, but critical theory involves applying theory to engage practice; the researcher does more than critique, he or she becomes involved in the process of 'doing' change. Scholars devoted to the exploration of critical theory in sport including Rick Gruneau, Bob Sparkes, Susan Birell, John Loy, Wendy Frisby, Ann Hall and others provide wonderful examples of the importance of doing praxis-oriented research. It is perhaps the late Alan Ingham who comes to mind as the scholar most sensitive to the need for a wholly critical socio-cultural research practice. Ingham's (1985) call for the re-examination of the power of sport as a community-building practice revealed an interest in intervening in issues of the fragmentation of place and culture. Ingham's Gramscian-influenced call for a common goal in sport studies research reads as an incredibly sensitive and nuanced understanding of how the movement towards critical praxis work might secure the sub-discipline's future.

In clear dialogue with Ingham's call for critical theory in the socio-cultural study of sport and physical cultural studies, David Andrews's

(2008: 54–55) definitional statement of 'Physical Cultural Studies' is a contemporary rallying call for people to become more engaged with critical theory and to use socio-cultural studies of sport to try and effect social change:

> Physical Cultural Studies (PCS) advances the critically and theoretically-driven analysis of physical culture, in all its myriad forms. These include sport, exercise, health, dance, and movement related practices. PCS research seeks to locate and understand the expressions and experiences of physical culture in the broader contexts (social, political, economic, and technological) within which they are situated, and which they simultaneously help to (re)produce. More specifically, PCS is dedicated to the contextually based understanding of the corporeal practices, discourses, and subjectivities through which active bodies become organised, represented, and experienced in relation to the operations of social power. PCS thus identifies the role played by physical culture in reproducing, and sometimes challenging, particular class, ethnic, gender, ability, generational, national, and/or sexual norms and differences. Through the development and strategic dissemination of potentially empowering forms of knowledge and understanding, PCS seeks to illuminate, and intervene into, sites of physical cultural injustice and inequity.

While not every socio-cultural scholar or critical theorist of sport and physical culture might accept or follow Andrews's (2008) definitional lead, his attempt to call sociologists of sport to 'interventionist arms' is laudable. Andrews's (2008) notion of a (public) physical cultural studies is underpinned by the neo-Marxist influence of Lawrence Grossberg, Stuart Hall, Henry Giroux and a host of other cultural studies theorists. It is an endeavour seeking, despite potentially self-deprecating or humble claims to the contrary, to develop a richly layered and activist neo-Marxist cultural studies *with* guarantees.

PROBLEMS, PITFALLS AND CONTROVERSIES

Any discussion of critical theory and praxis must recognise that the barriers to its ongoing genesis in sport and health research are not only conceptual but also structural and cultural within our universities and colleges. Turner (2006: 170) claims that, 'we do not have public intellectuals because we do not have a social role for them; in sociological terms, we need to [first] look at the availability of social space for [critical] intellectuals rather than asking questions about possible inhabitants'. Bairner (2009) mentions, further, how the late modern university, as a prison of measured time, allows for little in the way of public intellectual work when it comes to faculty members' annual report cards and review processes. Those interested in critical praxis work face internal pressures 'from above' to publish in top-tier academic journals, encounter yearly metrics designed to assess traditional academic roles and responsibilities, socialise with colleagues expressing little respect for public sociology, and find their subversive and interventionist orientations jibe tangentially at best with the expansionist mood of our late modern, corporate universities. Even more micrologically, within sub-disciplinary space (the socio-cultural study of sport, sport policy studies, or the sociology of sport more broadly), questions concerning the academically and personally self-serving fetishising of critical theoretical readings of social life, non-empirically driven accounts of sport and leisure, and mass media research, have done little to engender 'warm and fuzzy' feelings among colleagues. A beleaguered focus on identity politics research without praxis and an underwritten preoccupation with representational practices over policy/change driven research is potentially crippling critical theory in the socio-cultural study of sport. Couple these trends with a general disregard for translational or knowledge-exchange research efforts, a general lack of unique or accessible theory within the sub-discipline, too few connections or dialogues with other disciplines (e.g. political science, economics, history, anthropology, philosophy, classics, media studies and communication, human geography, criminology and others), and a general treatment of critical theory as a highly specialist and esoteric enterprise, and a gloomy forecast for the future of praxis/interventionism is easily predicted.

See also: *Discourse Analysis; Ethnography; Representation; Translation; Visual Methods.*

KEY READINGS

Andrews, D. (2008) 'Kinesiology's "inconvenient truth" and the physical cultural studies imperative'. *Quest* 60: 45–62.

Bairner, A. (2009) 'Sport, intellectuals and public sociology: Obstacles and opportunities'. *International Review for the Sociology of Sport* 44: 115–130.

David, P. (2005) *Human Rights in Youth Sport*. London: Routledge.

Gruneau, R. (1983) *Class, Sports, and Social Development*. Amherst: Massachusetts University Press.

Ingham, A. (1985) 'From pubic issue to personal trouble: Well-being and the fiscal crisis of the state'. *Sociology of Sport Journal* 2: 43–55.

critical theory

Morgan, W.J. (1983) 'Toward a critical theory of sport'. *Journal of Sport and Social Issues* 7: 24–34.

Turner, B. (2006) 'British sociology and public intellectuals: Consumer society and imperial decline'. *British Journal of Sociology*, 57: 170–188.

Whannel, G. (1983) *Blowing the Whistle: The Politics of Sport*. London: Pluto.

Descriptive Statistics

Descriptive statistics often get a bad rap in research circles. In research methods classes, they are discussed quite quickly in an introductory undergraduate course and then scarcely mentioned in subsequent courses. They are like the nerdy little brother of their more socially popular big brother, inferential statistics. Descriptive statistics are used to describe the basic features of the data in a study. They provide simple summaries about the sample and the measures. Together with simple graphics analysis, they form the basis of virtually every quantitative analysis of data. Learning the place of descriptive statistics in quantitative research is foundational, and several of the descriptives are entry points into advanced and inferential statistics.

WHAT IS THIS CONCEPT?

I consider myself to be a serious (serious, to me, that is!) recreational athlete, and I am a vegan. For several years friends and nutritionists have warned me about the risks associated with being a vegan and engaging in endurance athletics. Nutritionists have instructed me to be very mindful of striking a complete mineral balance in my daily food intake, or else I run the risk of losing bone mineral density. This is dangerous because of the punishment inflicted on the bones through long bouts of running on roads, weight training and some of the other activities accompanying my tastes for sport. For the last seven years I have been very cautious and conscientious about my eating habits, and have been able to maintain a healthy bone structure. What about other vegan (and non-vegan) endurance athletes? What do their bones look like? How could a researcher acquire a straightforward portrait of bone mineral density among a group of endurance athletes?

Here come descriptive statistics to the rescue! Because I am naturally curious, I managed to gather a group of 10 well-trained endurance athletes (5 vegan and 5 non-vegan) between the ages of 30 and 60. Each one of them agrees to visit my research lab at the university and undertake a DEXA (Dual Energy X-ray Absorptiometry) scan. A DEXA scan uses low-dose x-rays (about one tenth of the radiation dose of a chest x-ray), to assess body composition. A DEXA scan is very, very cool. While you are lying on a cushioned table, the DEXA scanner arm passes over your body taking x-rays to compile a physiological portrait of your body. The test works by measuring the density of a specific bone or bones, usually the spine, hip and wrist. The density of these bones is then compared with an average index based on age, sex and size (normally, a 30-year-old male or female). The resulting comparison is used to determine risk for fractures and the stage of osteoporosis in an individual. Bone mineral density is computed as BMC/W [g/cm^2]: where BMC = bone mineral content = g/cm; and W = width of bone at the scanned line. Average density scores for a healthy 30-year-old are approximately 1,500 kg m^{-3}. Now, raw scores are typically transformed into T or S scores for patient comparisons with the expected norm, but let's not get too complicated right now.

I conducted a DEXA scan on each of my 10 athletes and compiled the results in Table 1. In this table, I have presented scores on two variables I measured among the athletes: their diet and their average bone mineral density scores. Let's focus on the second. In most research scenarios, we run a preliminary analysis of the variables, one at a time, we are centrally concerned with as a means of examining how they are 'behaving' in our sample. Remember the purpose of my data gathering exercise is to compare the bone mineral density of vegan athletes to their non-vegan peers. But let's not rush too quickly into a comparison between the two groups.

Descriptive statistical analysis is predominantly univariate, focusing on one variable at a time; and we have a portfolio of descriptive statistics to examine the characteristics of each variable in our sample. Each is used to reduce a set of total scores on each variable, like bone mineral density scores, in a sensible and meaningful way. The arithmetic average or *mean* for a variable is one such statistic. What if we wanted to know how well a major league baseball player is performing offensively during a year? Would it make sense to examine all of his at bats for 162 games during the season? No chance! Or, would I simply look at the number of hits he made in the year to assess his offensive prowess? Probably not,

Table 1 Diet and bone mineral density

Patient	Diet	BMD score
1	Vegan	1400
2	Vegan	1475
3	Vegan	1350
4	Vegan	1550
5	Vegan	1400
6	Non-vegan	1600
7	Non-vegan	1550
8	Non-vegan	1675
9	Non-vegan	1600
10	Non-vegan	1700

because hits do not tell me anything about how many chances to hit the player received over the season. One hundred hits in 100 at bats means something entirely different than 100 hits in 673 at bats! The preferred descriptive statistic in baseball is the batting average. This single number is the player's total hits divided by the number of times at bat. A batter who is hitting .333 is getting a hit one time in every three at bats; one batting .250 is hitting one time in four. The batting average captures and summarises performance over a large number of discrete events (at bats). Batting averages provide us with a first estimate of batter performance and variability in performance over the year.

Descriptive statistics reveal more than mere numeric averages for a variable of interest. Descriptives provide references points to highs, lows, middle-points, and the dispersion of scores around central anchors in our data. They quantify how much difference there is between people's scores on a particular variable, and therefore provide researchers with an indicator of the distribution of scores in a sample. So just by running a set of descriptive statistics on my gathered bone mineral density scores, I could summarise average density in the group, the range of scores (highest and lowest), and the amount of difference, and even average amount of difference, between people in the group. All of these statistics are critical for understanding how bone mineral density scores are distributed among the athletes.

WHY IS THIS RELEVANT TO ME?

The relevance of descriptive statistics is manifold, but three reasons stand out. First, they are our preliminary measures of a variable's 'behaviour' in our sample. Do people all score around the same on the variable? How do people score on average? How do scores cluster around the average? What is the highest and lowest people score? Just imagine if I measured bone mineral density among 9,894 athletes with a range of different diets, and they had an average of 1,576 kg m^{-3}. In fact, almost all of the athletes scored exactly that BMD value. Very interesting! These preliminary data tell me that diet does not seem to affect bone mineral density scores.

Second, and related to the above, most of the advanced statistics you will encounter as a student are predicated on two simple descriptive statistics, *the mean* (noted in statistical terms as $\bar{x}$) and the *standard deviation* (noted in statistical terms as s). The mean is the arithmetic average of scores in a particular variable and the standard deviation is a measure of how far away a typical person is in the sample from the mean score (we will discuss these in a bit more detail below). The mean tells us about the average in the distribution of gathered scores, and the standard deviation how much average difference there is between people's scores on the variable. The more people's scores vary in a sample, the greater the standard deviation. In our sample data of bone mineral density for the 10 athletes, the mean is 1,530 kg m^{-3} and the standard deviation is ± 120.07 kg m^{-3}. What does this tell us? Well, the average person in our sample scores slightly above the expected BMD score for a healthy person; and, on average, a person scores 120.07 away from the mean (that is, either above or below it). Means and standard deviations are usually reported together, such as, 'Bone mineral density among the athletes had a mean of 1,530 kg m^{-3} [± 120.07].' Or, we could simply write, 'Bone mineral density in the sample of athletes was $\bar{x}$ = 1,530 kg m^{-3} [± 120.07].'

Third, we can extend the univariate basis of descriptive statistics to multivariate analysis. Through the use of crosstabs, simple bar or line graphs and frequency distribution charts, we can compare how sets of scores on two variables match up. For example, what do we learn from Table 2?

What do the data shown in Table 2 teach us about the potential relationship between diet and bone mineral density? First, it reveals that on average, vegans do seem to have lower bone mineral density scores than non-vegans. Vegans seem to score, on average, below what is expected for a typical healthy adult. This is an important finding because the mean of the sample before we separated them analytically into two sub-groups was 1,530 kg m^{-3}. So it seems the non-vegans are pulling the mean up!

Table 2 Bone mineral density means and standard deviations

Diet	Mean BMD score
Vegan	1435 [± 78.25]
Non-vegan	1625 [± 61.24]

What becomes even more interesting is that the standard deviation for the vegans is higher than for non-vegans, meaning there is more variability within their group. Higher variability may indicate that diet does not affect all vegans in the same manner. All of these preliminary insights illustrate important lessons about bone mineral density in the sample.

SHOW ME HOW IT'S USED!

Everything in statistics depends on the measurement process. Everything … really, it's true. How I have chosen to measure a variable determines what statistical analyses I may run on said variable in every case, and the process commences with descriptive statistics. Depending on whether you are confronted with a continuous variable (one measured or scored as a 'naturally occurring' number, like age or weight) or a discrete/categorical variable (one in which the response categories are measured by words or phrases that are turned into numbers through the coding process … like your religion, place of birth, or favourite physical activity), your descriptive statistics options then follow.

Let's begin with discrete variables. For variables with distribution parameters set by words or phrases, there are not a million and one options for descriptive statistical analysis. When we analyse the behaviour of a discrete/categorical variable we have measured, a *frequency distribution analysis* is normally the point of departure. A frequency distribution lists in tabular form, or presents in graphic form (e.g. a bar chart such as a histogram, pie diagram, or other), how people have scored on the variable. Frequency analysis is rather straightforward in that it provides a visual summary and breakdown of a discrete variable's distribution as either the number of people scoring for each category of the variable or the percentage of people in the sample scoring on that category.

Now, continuous variables are another story entirely. We could commence the statistical analysis of the distribution of a continuous variable with a frequency analysis as in the case above (i.e. through a histogram, scatterplot or line graph) but there are three other sub-sets of descriptive statistical analysis at our disposal as well. First, we might examine the 'holy trinity' of all descriptive statistics: *the mean, median and mode*. The mean we have covered already – it is the arithmetic average of scores on a particular variable. The mode is the most frequently occurring score in our sample, and the median is the score in the sample at which 50% of the sample falls below and 50% above. Together, all of these statistics are referred to as measures of *central tendency*. Individually and collectively they provide a snapshot of where an average or typical person in the sample scores.

The Mean, Median and Mode: An Example

We measure VO_2 max scores among a group of 11 well-trained athletes. The scores are as follows:

50, 58, **59, 59, 59**, *67*, 69, 70, 70, 72, 76

Mean: 64.45, because [50, 58, 59, 59, 59, 67, 69, 70, 70, 72, 76 / 11 = 64.45]

Median: 67, because five scores fall below and five above.

Mode: 59, because three people scored 59 in the sample, more than for any other score.

The second sub-set of descriptive statistics at our disposal is called *measures of dispersion or spread*. These statistics provide an additional layer of information about the range of the scores in the distribution, the degree of variability in scores, and the relative shape of the distribution of scores. Three commonly used measures of dispersion are worth noting. The *range* is the difference between the highest and lowest scores in a sample. The range for VO_2 max in the box above would be 76–50 = 26. The range tells us how 'wide' the distribution is in the sample. The other two measures of dispersion we report are the *variance* and the *standard deviation*. The *variance* is computed as the average squared deviation of each score from the mean (complex, I know), and the *standard deviation*, remember, is the average distance of any person in the sample from the mean. We rarely report the latter and instead focus on the former. The standard deviation is an incredibly widely used statistic for reporting the degree of variability in the sample, and it is read in conjunction with the mean. If the standard deviation gets closer to zero, we know scores hover closely around the mean. As the standard deviation inflates, we know scores are spread out more widely away from the mean. So, if the mean gives an estimate of the average VO_2 max, the standard deviation would tell us whether people all score around 64.45 or if the mean is only a central point in a sea of very, very different VO_2 max scores.

Statistics – I call them our *distributional forensics* – provide us with a general sense of whether or not we have a nice, well-behaved, normally distributed sample or not (see the entry on Distributions for a summary of normal distributions). If variables that we expected to be normally distributed are not, two statistical measures in particular, called *kurtosis* and *skewness*, will tell us right away! The kurtosis statistic is another measure of how the scores in a distribution are spread around the mean, and tell us how peaked (scores very clustered around the mean) or flat (scores spread out widely away from the mean) our distribution of scores is in the sample when graphed via a histogram. When the scores are tightly peaked around the mean, we say the distribution is *leptokurtic*, and when the distribution is spread out widely from the mean and flat,

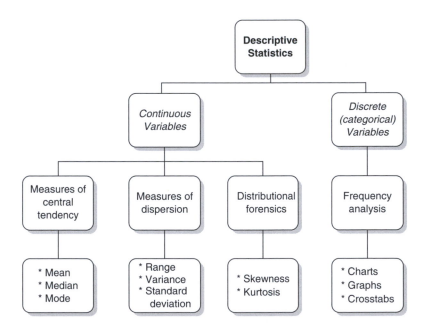

Figure 2 Descriptive statistics tree

we say the distribution is *platykurtic*. Skewness is a statistic telling us if the heart of the distribution has been shifted to the left or right of the mean, indicating a deviation from what is normally expected among many variables. Studied together and separately, skewness and kurtosis provide more detailed information regarding whether or not there might be something 'weird' going on with our distribution. If we would expect the distribution to be normally distributed and it is not, for example, we might have a problem with our measurement process or sampling procedure. Significant kurtosis or skewness issues make it very difficult to accept observed patterns in our data.

In sum, then, the basic descriptive statistics at our disposal provide a sense of empirical similarity and difference within a set of scores for a particular variable. They also provide a working understanding of whether or not the scores fall in line with expectations of variability informed by our theories of statistics.

PROBLEMS, PITFALLS AND CONTROVERSIES

There are reasons why descriptive statistics have a reputation as the nerdy little brother of the family. Descriptive statistics are first rate in the provision of sets of indicators illustrating common tendencies and patterns with univariate analysis, but that is it, really. True, they are still the mortar of inferential statistics, but in their raw form they contribute very little to the hypothesis testing process. Recall how hypothesis testing is the very engine of the scientific method. Without statistical means to robustly assess numeric relationships between variables in our hypotheses, the data collection process means very little. Descriptive statistics are limited in their fundamentally univariate focus and their inability to be generalised beyond a sample at hand. Both limitations grind the hypothesis testing process to a veritable standstill.

Sample size is another potential source of problems with descriptive statistics. In very small samples, most of our cornerstone descriptive statistics like the mean, standard deviation, and others, can be heavily influenced by one or two atypical scores in the same sample – those that are very far away from the others. Descriptive statistics are also hugely biased towards continuous variables. The vast majority of powerful tests or informative procedures at this level are geared toward continuous variables. Students are often greatly intrigued when learning about the intricacies of distributions, deviations and sample descriptives, only to be told that none of it applies to any of the categorical variables. Sure, we can run frequency tables, or dredge out the mode for categorical variables, but it's not the same. How would you feel if your parents brought home a brand new, top-of-the-range bike for your sister as a present and one roller skate for you. It is nice to receive a gift, but I would rather have the bike.

See also: Distributions; Inferential Statistics; Variables.

KEY READINGS

Fallowfield, J. (2005) *Statistics in Sport and Exercise Science*. Chichester: Lotus Publishing.
Field, A. (2009) *Discovering Statistics Using SPSS*. London: Sage.
Newell, J., Aitchison, T. and Grant, S. (2010) *Statistics for Sports & Exercise Science: A Practical Approach*. Toronto: Pearson Education.
Thomas, J. and Nelson, J. (2001) *Research Methods in Physical Activity*. Champaign: Human Kinetics.
Williams, C. and Wagg, C. (2003) *Data Analysis and Research for Sport and Exercise Science: A Student Guide*. London: Routledge.

Discourse Analysis

A very wise instructor once told me that all life is a story, and that there is no life outside of storytelling. To be honest, I thought he was full of it at first. What did he mean? How can all of life be reduced to a story, or a bunch of stories? I reflected on his idea for some time and came to the conclusion that he had shared with me a bit of brilliance. Because people speak in complex languages, assign strange and local meanings to events that happen in our lives, have diverse cultures, and narrate their innermost thoughts, feelings and desires through words and gestures, we are all storytellers in one way or another. The moment we begin to account for, recount or assign meaning to the events in our lives, we engage in the process of story creation. As individual and collective storytellers, our words both reflect bigger story systems we have learned and internalised (that we call culture, ideologies, and so on), and may serve to effect larger ways of telling stories. The analysis of, let's call them 'patterns', contained in a culture's words and language systems (and the impacts of storytelling on our social lives) is often referred to in academic circles as *discourse analysis*.

WHAT IS THIS CONCEPT?

Discourse analysis is not one technique but a house of interrelated techniques, methods, ways of writing/representing, and ways of knowing. Let's begin with the term discourse. A discourse is generally referred to as a set of representational statements made about a particular subject or object. Discourse analysis, then, is a general term for a number of approaches to analysing written, spoken, signed language use or significant semiotic (structured communicative) representations of a subject or object. The objects of discourse analysis – writing, talk, conversation, communicative events – are variously defined in terms of coherent sequences of sentences, propositions, speech acts or turns-at-talk. Discourse analysis has been taken up in a variety of social science disciplines, including linguistics, sociology, anthropology, social work, cognitive psychology, social psychology, international relations, human geography, communication and media studies, cultural studies, feminist studies and translation studies, each of which is subject to its own assumptions, dimensions of analysis and methodologies.

Discourse analytic studies are almost universally qualitative, interpreting 'readings' of texts (books, newspapers, magazines, films, online spaces, articles, television programmes, or public speech acts) and how the language of the texts illustrates something about established power relationships between people in a society. Discourse analysis is therefore a mode of performing inquiry into how stories about the world are told, disseminated, interpreted and reproduced in a society, and the effects of such storytelling on people. Discourse analysis is well suited for research questions and overall projects pertaining to how the meaning of sport, physical activity and health is shaped by the manners and modes by which people discuss them within a culture.

WHY IS THIS RELEVANT TO ME?

Discourse analysis is frequently an interpretivist/qualitative method alternative to small-scale research on how people assign meaning to identities, interaction, culture and events in the world. Discourse analysis tends to focus on diffuse patterns of language, ways of speaking and verbal means of representation in a society. Or, discourse analysts strive

discourse analysis

to uncover how enduring structural relationships between people are evidenced and reproduced through discourse. Discourse analysts illustrate how the nature of language is at once liberating for people in our pursuit of intersubjectivity (i.e. as a means of articulating and sharing complex identities, emotions and experiences with others), but equally constraining for people (i.e. what one can express is bound by the language codes one has been exposed to in life). Further, dominant discourses in a society like scientific, legal, capitalist, government, patriarchal and others tend to define conditions of 'the real' in everyday life. What does this mean? Ways of knowing in a society are transmitted through the discourses we learn in the family, school, economy and other social institutions. The dominant discourses in a setting become, more or less, incorporated into how people see the world and articulate their experiences. Have you ever wondered why so many people in Western societies believe in 'natural' differences in the role capabilities of men and women, or tend to believe that scientific knowledge is the most socially beneficial or accurate? By interrogating how people come to learn discourses, how discourses shape our lives, and how people express personal or collective meaning to others through discourse, researchers gain insight into how language plays a massive role in shaping human action.

SHOW ME HOW IT'S USED!

There are any number of variants of discourse analysis. Discourse analysis within the sport and physical activity sciences is today almost exclusively associated with a kind of *critical discourse analysis* informed by the work of Michel Foucault, Jacques Derrida, Louis Althusser, Antonio Gramsci, Jürgen Habermas, Stuart Hall, Judith Butler and Norman Fairclough. Critical discourse analysts approach language as a social and cultural practice through which identities are forged and relationships of power between people are consolidated, enforced, reproduced and even resisted. A critical discourse theorist might, for instance, examine how news media coverage of terrorism and security concerns at an Olympic event might be laden with taken-for-granted cultural (nationalistic, religious) assumptions about who terrorists and their victims are in practice. Other critical discourse analysts might look to what Foucault calls the 'genealogy' (i.e. origins and historical development) of particular discourses in sport, exercise and health fields. Foucault (1969) describes the archaeological method for doing genealogical research, whereby an analyst searches for the historical genesis and development of a term or an entire discourse, and theorises about how it emerged as such. One might study the term 'kinesiology' or 'kinesiological' discourse to examine how, when and why the field developed as a discipline in the 1960s and 1970s. Another group of critical discourse analysts engage in what Jacques Derrida (1978) described as the technique of deconstruction. The practice of deconstruction is a difficult one to describe in a sentence or two, but can be somewhat captured by the notion that deconstructionists study the texts of which a discourse is comprised in order to understand the embedded, silent or contradictory cultural meanings therein. Akin to critical discourse analysts and deconstructionists, critical feminist discourse analysts including Judith Butler illustrate how power relationships can be (re)produced between groups through performing speech acts. For example, the enduring cultural practice of 'gendering' the names of North American college and university sports teams (by placing terms like 'lady' or 'ettes' in the name of the women's teams) illustrates how men's teams are established as the norm while women's teams are secondary and thus subservient.

Narrative analysis is close conceptually to critical discourse analysis. With narrative analysis, researchers explore how people actively construct accounts of life and examine what 'narrative resources' (words, terms, language codes, perspectives, frames of reference) people choose to assemble their stories. For example, Sparkes and Smith (2002) use the study of narratives to examine how men who suffer from spinal cord injury later in life define the process as meaningful and how the event changed their sense of self. The aim in narrative analysis is to rigorously detail the maps of discursive meaning that provide people with ways of understanding the nature of their experiences. Of recent popularity among psychologists of sport is an offshoot of narrative analysis called interpretative phenomenological analysis, or simply IPA (Smith, 2007). IPA attends, like the other approaches outlined above, to how people make sense of their experiences through the process of telling stories about them. IPA researchers ask questions such as, 'What is the impact of HIV on one's interpersonal relationships?', 'How do athletes manage the retirement process?', and 'What forms of social support are useful for people diagnosed as obese?'

Of course, all of the approaches discussed above follow along a path of discourse analysis established in the American social science research in the 1960s and 1970s. Harold Garfinkel (1984), influenced heavily by the

discourse analysis

work of Alfred Schutz, emphasised the need to study how people use common stocks of (verbally transmitted) knowledge in order to navigate everyday life. To Garfinkel, cultural frames of reference could be learned by studying how people speak in regular patterns of sense-making. Garfinkel (1984) argued that if one analysed people's speech patterns, general rules of sense-making and expression could be uncovered; he called the approach *ethnomethodology*. Harvey Sacks (1995) and others adopted Garfinkel's emphasis on the speech act as a source of cultural data, and pioneered what is now called *conversation analysis*: the study of how people talk in social groups, and how meaning about life emerges in situated contexts of interaction. Others refer to conversational analysis as a form of 'interactional sociolinguistics'. One might learn a great deal, for instance, about how young male athletes construct sexuality by listening to how women and relationships are discussed in the locker-room setting.

PROBLEMS, PITFALLS AND CONTROVERSIES

Discourse analysis can seem extremely subjective and non-generalisable to those not versed in the technique(s). Discourse analysts use one or another theory to read people's stories or mass mediated 'speech acts' and, ultimately, offer highly subjective understandings of discourse. Often, and unfortunately, the subjective readings provided to audiences by discourse analysts read in almost a prefabricated manner. Stated another way, discourse analysts rarely strive to test theory in a given study, but rather apply preconceived theoretical ideas to particular discourses or discursive strategies shared among people. The result is research less informed by grounded theoretical investigations of the (many) ways in which people make sense of the world through storytelling, and research more informed by theoretical positions already held as true by research. Why is this a problem? Because the theoretical discourses of the researcher become privileged over the discourses shared among people in the world!

Discourse analysis of historical and mass mediated speech acts is criticised for yet another layer of subjectivity. Historical and mass media discourses are typically read by a researcher or group of researchers through the lens of theory, and the meaning of the discourse (and its effect on people) is inferred in a directed manner from the data. Rarely are audiences (the producers or receivers of such discourse) consulted or studied about the data and its meaning. So, the majority of discourse studies provide no opportunity for member-checking or other means of ensuring the researchers' readings actively capture the meaning or impact of discourse on people. For this reason, critics of discourse analysis have called for researchers to buttress interpretive readings of discourse with forms of 'reception' research, including audience ethnography, surveys and interviews.

See also: *Media Analysis; Representation; Visual Methods.*

KEY READINGS

Blommaert, J. (2005) *Discourse*. Cambridge: Cambridge University Press.
Derrida, J. (1978) *Of Grammatology*. London: Johns Hopkins University Press.
Fairclough, N. (2001) *Language and Power*. London: Longman.
Foucault, M. (1969) *The Archaeology of Knowledge*. London: Routledge.
Garfinkel, H. (1984) *Studies in Ethnomethodology*. Englewood Cliffs, NJ: Blackwell.
Johnstone, B. (2002) *Discourse Analysis*. Oxford: Blackwell.
Lasar, M. (2005) *Feminist Critical Discourse Analysis: Gender, Power and Ideology in Discourse*. Basingstoke: Palgrave.
Renkema, J. (2004) *Introduction to Discourse Studies*. Amsterdam: Benjamins.
Sacks, H. (1995) *Lectures on Conversation*. Oxford: Blackwell.
Smith, J. (2007) 'Hermeneutics, human sciences and health: Linking theory and practice'. *International Journal of Qualitative Studies on Health and Well-Being* 2: 3–11.
Sparkes, A. and Smith, B. (2002) 'Men, sport, spinal cord injury, embodied masculinities, and the dilemmas of narrative identity'. *Men and Masculinities* 4: 258–285.

Distributions

Understanding the concept of a *distribution* is worth its weight in gold for the neophyte research methods student. I remember struggling with my introduction to statistics lectures as an undergraduate, predominantly because I could not come to terms with the root of statistical analysis, and why distributions were so important. Now, I firmly believe that the concept of a distribution is the lynchpin for understanding (and I mean *really* understanding) the point of all statistics. I begin this brief introduction to distributions by suggesting most things in life are distributed: or simply, handed out, taken, acquired, or held differently among people. As a researcher, I want to know why. What is the likelihood of someone contracting cancer before the age of 10? Is the distribution of wealth around the world related to Olympic medal success? We need to appreciate how and why quantitative research is a practice of studying patterns among distributions of the variables we measure. This is the essence of statistics, and the claims statisticians make about the world.

WHAT IS THIS CONCEPT?

Quantitative researchers measure many, many variables. Oh so many, in fact. If you feel confident about your understanding of what a variable is, then you are well on the way to grasping the concept of a distribution and then advanced statistics. Remember that a variable is one, by definition, because people among whom it is measured score differently on it. Imagine I am conducting a study of 100m sprint times among my students in a research methods class. After dragging my 55 students out to the track, I proceed to measure each and everyone's respective 100m sprint times (not a bad way to spend class time!). Needless to say, there is going to be variability in the scores. A few people will be very, very fast, a lot more will be average for people in their age range, and a few will be very, very slow. I know this, in fact, without ever having to test their times (I'll provide the foundations of my boasting here in just a bit). The point is that we can say sprint time varies because there are different scores; not everyone runs 100 metres in exactly 12.5 seconds. Another way of summarising what we learn through the measurement process is that there will be a *distribution* of scores in the group.

We could call a distribution many things: a set, an array, a series, an arrangement, or even score frequencies. Whatever the conceptual moniker employed, a distribution is a simple idea at its core. Distribution is the term used to describe *the full set of subjects' scores* we have gathered on a particular variable. A distribution shows us the variability of scores in the group. Why are we so interested in the variability? That's simple to answer. When scores vary, for example 100m sprint times, I want to know why they vary. What makes someone run faster than someone else? I can also get a sense of how fast this group runs, on average, by studying their distribution of scores. These are essential mindsets for positivist researchers.

One of the very best methods for seeing a distribution is to produce a frequencies chart or graph for a variable you have measured through a computer program like SPSS. Because distributions are much easier to understand in reference to scale/continuous variables, let's stick with the

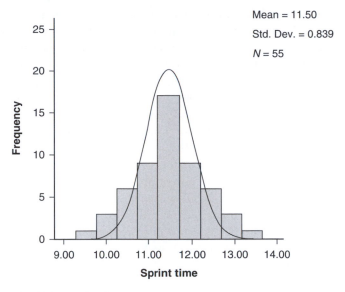

Figure 3   100m sprint times

example of 100m sprint times. After I enter all 55 scores for sprint times into SPSS, I ask it to show me the distribution in a chart called a histogram (Figure 3).

The histogram illustrates that, indeed, a few students run very quickly or very slowly, but most run around 100m in 11.5 seconds. What you are viewing in the chart is a summary of the total variability in the sample. This is how people differ in 100m sprint times, and the grand picture of the distribution/variability. Try to see this histogram as more than a series of lines on a weird looking graph – see them as actual scores for actual people in a group.

The next step in grasping the concept of a distribution is to understand its purpose and placement in the research process. This is where the ride becomes a touch bumpier, so just hang on and enjoy.

WHY IS THIS RELEVANT TO ME?

The analysis of distributions serves two main purposes in quantitative research. First and foremost, we examine the distributions of scores for a particular variable in order to see how it is 'behaving'. I study distributions to see if there is a lot of variability in the sample, or if there is practically no variability. In the first instance, this is exciting because it means there is something to explain, to account for in my research. If my students differ quite widely in their ability to run 100m, then I try to explain what might, dare we say, be causing the differences between them. Second, most of our basic and advanced statistical tests are based on core rules: among them are rules about what distributions *should look like* in observed data. Remember I mentioned that I could have forecasted what the distribution of scores in the class would look like before I ever measured them. Here is why.

Until this point in the discussion of distributions, we have been focused on what we might call raw or observed distributions. These are the actual distributions produced within the measurement process. In statistical theory (far too complex and detailed to engage with in this discussion), there is a probable range of scores for variables we measure. That is to say, we believe true scores will probably fall within a range of scores dictated by statistical theory. There are dozens and dozens of these theoretical distributions (popular ones in sport and exercise research are *Fisher's F* distribution and the *Student's t* distribution). Another way of thinking about a probability distribution is that it often takes shape in the research process as a table or an equation that links each outcome of a measurement process or statistical experiment with its probability of occurrence. So, for our example of 100m sprint times, there are actually statistical tables that predict what the distribution should look like, and how people should score. In many natural processes like running ability, random variation among people conforms to a particular probability distribution known as the *normal distribution*, which is the most commonly observed probability distribution.

French mathematicians Abraham de Moivre and Pierre-Simon Laplace pioneered and used the normal distribution in the late 1700s. The importance of the normal curve stems primarily from the fact that the distributions of many natural phenomena are (at least approximately) normally distributed. By the early 1800s, German mathematician and physicist Carl Friedrich Gauss independently 'discovered' and used the idea of the normal curve to analyse astronomical data, and it consequently became known as the *Gaussian distribution* among the scientific community. The shape of the normal distribution resembles that of a bell, so it is sometimes referred to as the 'bell curve'.

I am well and truly in love with the normal distribution curve. I often tell my students that if I could marry a statistical concept it would be the normal distribution. Why? Well, the normal distribution is a widely observed and respected distribution in statistics, arguably ushered into modern mathematics by the Russian statistician Andrey Kolmogonov in the early 1930s. Furthermore, it frequently can be applied to situations in which the observed data is distributed very differently than expected. This extended applicability is possible because of a wonderful theoretical idea called the *central limit theorem*, which states that regardless of the distribution of the population, the distribution of the means of random samples approaches a normal distribution for a large sample size.

The normal distribution or Gaussian distribution is a probability distribution that often gives a good description of how observed scores for a variable cluster around the mean. The graph of the associated 'probability density' function is bell-shaped, with a peak at the mean, and is known as the Gaussian function or bell curve. The bell curve has been so influential that even qualitative researchers accept it as an accurate way to estimate average and atypical behaviours. Hughes and Coakley (1991), for example, theorised that most athletes are norm-abiding participants of their respective sports. Some rare participants, however, commit violations of sports norms (which they call the Sport Ethic) in negative ways (showing no respect for sport or the values of sport cultures), or positive ways (showing nothing but a blind and total acceptance of sport culture such that they go too far in wanting to be great athletes). So, athlete behaviour falls into a normal curve – with some at the far left end of the curve's tail and others at the far right end, and most fitting nicely in the middle.

Rather than examining each and every point or score in the normal distribution, however, there are two basic statistics we use to summarise its properties: the mean, and the standard deviation. The mean is the numeric average of scores in the sample (e.g. for our sprint times) and the standard deviation is a numeric expression of the average distance of any one person in the sample from the mean. The mean tells us something roughly about the average score in the sample, and the standard deviation is a nice little statistic teaching us about the variability that exists in the data (our rule of thumb is: the more variability, the higher the standard deviation). If the mean and standard deviation are known, then one essentially knows as much as if one had access to every point in the data set. The *empirical rule* of distributions is a handy quick estimate of the spread of the data given the mean and standard deviation of a data set that follows the normal distribution. The empirical rule states that for a normal distribution:

distributions

- 68% of the data will fall within 1 standard deviation of the mean.
- 95% of the data will fall within 2 standard deviations of the mean.
- Almost all (99.7%) of the data will fall within 3 standard deviations of the mean.

For example, according to the normal curve probability density function, 95% of the data will fall within 1.96 standard deviations of the mean; 2 standard deviations is a convenient approximation. Why do we care about this? Well, because if we produce distributions in observed data that are not normally distributed or do not evidence the above properties, then we may have issues. It might signal error in our measurement, sampling, or even data analysis processes.

SHOW ME HOW IT'S USED!

If you analyse statistics, you are already knee deep in distributions. The applications of distributions are so wide-ranging and varied that any attempt to summarise them would be futile. There are very simple and straightforward ways of using a distribution as outlined above. Imagine you are a health researcher interested in the development of epilepsy among adults. While medical researchers have studied the illness for many decades, they still know relatively little about how and why it manifests among adults. Dominant arguments attribute late-stage epilepsy to be a product of a brain injury (from a blunt force trauma), brain infection, tumour or a stroke. A basic use of distributional analysis is to examine how the causes of epilepsy in adults is distributed in order to understand the main risk factors or conditions predicting its onset. Distributional analyses are similarly undertaken to study differences between males' and females' participation in sport in a country (i.e. how is participation in sport distributed by gender), what social classes elite athletes come from, and the maximum force generated by long-jumpers at takeoff.

An important part of conducting distributional analysis (with continuous variables) is examining their graphic shapes for what statisticians call *skewness* and *kurtosis*; both are bits of statistical information telling us how much sample data deviate from the expected normal distribution. Skewness is a measure of whether or not the 'fat' part of the distribution curve is shifted to the left or right (producing a long tail to the right or left respectively). Kurtosis is a measure of the 'peakedness' or 'flatness' a distribution of scores. We inspect skewness to assess whether or not the distribution tends to cluster around one end of the curve (for example, potentially telling us whether or not the mean is a poor estimate of average running ability in our 100m example). We examine kurtosis (usually in conjunction with the standard deviation) to assess the degree of variability in our observed scores (for example, are the 100m sprint scores tightly distributed around the mean – creating a very peaked curve – or widely distributed from the mean – creating a very flat curve?). There are statistical rules and regulations (statisticians love rules!) for how much skewness or kurtosis is acceptable in normally distributed data.

The distributions of individual variables are not too exciting. The story changes considerably when we start to compare the distributions for two or more variables. Most guys in my sport, physical activity and health classes argue that men are always stronger than women, full stop. We could take a sample of 100 (50 male, 50 female), competitive university cyclists with similar training histories and backgrounds and place them in a 10km time trial test. The guys argue that the mean time for the 50 males will always be higher than for the females. They are essentially arguing that the distribution of gender in the sample is directly related to the distribution of time trial scores. What? Think about it for a minute. Statistical tests involving a proposed relationship between two variables are fancy exercises in examining whether or not your score or placement in the distribution of one variable matches up with your score on the other variable. Does my knowledge of your gender score directly map onto your time trial score? Most of our advanced level statistics (inferential statistics) are based on this single principle. Statistical tests designed to examine the strength and direction of two variables start with the examination of how related their distributions are in a sample.

PROBLEMS, PITFALLS AND CONTROVERSIES

The concept of a distribution is probably among the least problematic or controversial of the ideas in this book. Nevertheless, there are several problems and pitfalls associated with distributions that can be considered.

First, while I encourage my students to develop an understanding of distributions via simple univariate analysis (i.e. where we spend time understanding a distribution of scores for a particular variable and its statistical properties), good old crosstabular analysis of two variables is a straightforward way to rapidly expand one's understanding of how quantitative researchers test hypotheses by examining if and how the distributions of two variables 'match' in one manner or another. Basic crosstabular work is, I think, fundamental for understanding how all of advanced statistics is based on the principles of distribution comparison. A logical progression to basic Chi-square testing then helps to solidify the concept. For anyone approaching statistics for the first time, a solid grasp of the principles of crosstabular analysis helps immensely.

Second, not all distributions are created equally. I have seen some ugly distributions in my time! I would wager that at least 7 times out of 10, bad (i.e. non-normally distributed) sets of scores for a variable are produced through poor sampling procedures. Unfortunately, reality can often get in the way of great research ideas and best sampling practice. Consider the following example. I wish to research VO_2 max rates among all university students. I advertise the study widely across my campus and, lo and behold, 67 people volunteer. Now, ideally, my sample would be representative of the normal distribution of scores I would expect in the university. But from what I know about VO_2 max testing, only a very special sub-population of the student body will likely volunteer – most likely sport, exercise and health students. If they are all pretty well-trained athletes (as our students often are), then I am in trouble. The distribution will not only be relatively platykurtic (very peaked), it will most likely be negatively skewed (the heart of the curve will be shifted way to the right). Not good. This level of sampling error provides me with an incredibly flawed and biased idea of how VO_2 max is distributed among university students.

Third, and finally, without an understanding of how distributions are dialogical with basic statistics like the mean, variance, standard deviation, range, skewness and kurtosis, we have not accomplished much. 'Eyeballing' a histogram to examine its central tendencies is a good start, but without benchmark descriptive statistics (we can think about these as the forensic evidence in distributional analysis), we do not have a true portrait of how a variability in the sample is behaving. What I well and truly admire about statistics is the interrelatedness of everything. Statistics are a beautiful and intricate web of relationships between measurements, scores, averages, tendencies, probabilities, and of course distributions. From an early phase in one's learning about statistics, the faster one begins to make these connections the better. Distributional analysis is the best place to start.

See also: *Descriptive Statistics: Populations and Samples; Representation.*

KEY READINGS

Fallowfield, J. (2005) *Statistics in Sport and Exercise Science*. Chichester: Lotus Publishing.

Field, A. (2009) *Discovering Statistics Using SPSS*. London: Sage.

Hughes, R. and Coakley, J. (1991) 'Positive deviance among athletes: the implications of overconformity to the sport ethic'. *Sociology of Sport Journal*, 8: 307–25.

Newell, J., Aitchison, T. and Grant, S. (2010) *Statistics for Sports & Exercise Science: A Practical Approach*. Toronto: Pearson Education.

Thomas, J. and Nelson, J. (2001) *Research Methods in Physical Activity*. Champaign: Human Kinetics.

Williams, C. and Wagg, C. (2003) *Data Analysis and Research for Sport and Exercise Science: A Student Guide*. London: Routledge.

Epistemology

From the very first day one becomes a researcher until the very last day one collects one or another form of evidence on a subject, issues in epistemology influence one's life. Methods are but a means to an end for better understanding the potential answers of a question we are interested in exploring. Why do so many guys watch sports? What are the most effective means of combating sedentary lifestyles? Does the emotional relationship between a coach and an athlete really affect the athlete's performance? All of these questions call for knowledge in the absence of, or critical reception of, available evidence. But at a much deeper level, before researchers are able to venture out somewhere into the world in a quest for knowledge (*qua* answers), we have to ask some very tough questions about what we feel can be known at all, and how we propose to know anything. Such questions deal with the foundational philosophical positions of all methodologies: epistemology.

WHAT IS THIS CONCEPT?

Epistemology is the branch of philosophy that studies the production of knowledge. In other terms, it is the study of the origin, nature, methods and limits of human knowledge. By definition then, a researcher, whether aware of it or not, is affected by epistemological theories and debates. When we study epistemology, we quickly learn that its focus is on answering a basic question: what distinguishes true (adequate and accepted) knowledge from false (inadequate) knowledge? Or, in other terms, what is it that we believe we can know, and how? Please remember that when we speak of 'true', methodologists tend to mean a statement about reality that has been supported by some form of systematically gathered and analysed evidence. To simplify matters considerably, one might argue that in the context of sport and exercise science research methods, a discussion of what counts as *empirical knowledge* is a direct way of understanding the subject of epistemology.

Most of us in sport and exercise science are one or another type of empiricist. We believe that something 'true' about the world can be known through close and meticulous observation. Empiricism focuses on a kind of knowledge that we derive from our sensory experience of the world. Many people conflate empiricism and science. That is an unfortunate mistake! The reason that empiricism is so closely tied in our minds to science is really more of a historically reproduced idea than anything else; over time scientists have claimed the loudest to be empiricists and we have come to associate empiricism with science. The simplest form of empirical truth is that based on nothing 'scientific' *per se*, but rather simple, direct observation – taking a good hard look. Now this is not the same as anecdotal evidence/knowledge, such as 'I heard about a high jumper from Sault St Marie who can clear 3.27m.' It's not really even the same as saying, 'I know of a high jumper from Sault St Marie …'. It means that there is an observation that I made that you can make, too, and that, were it possible, everyone should be able to make. In other words, 'Here's the guy from Sault St Marie … take a look for yourself!' In order to build a more complex body of knowledge from direct observations, we must make use of induction, also known as indirect empirical knowledge. We take the observations and carefully stretch them to cover more ground than we could actually cover directly. The basic form of this is called *generalisation*.

Now, as alluded to above, there are different styles of empiricism. In this case, we can give them some names. Most empirical approaches are forms of *epistemological realism*, which says that what the senses show us is reality, is the truth – objective, universal truth that cuts across time and space. The goal of empirical research is to discover these objective truths. The basic form of realism is *direct realism* (also known as simple realism, naïve realism or *objectivism*). Direct realism says that what you see is what you get: the senses are able to comprehend and portray the world accurately. This perspective informs the basis of scientific positivism (see the entry on Positivism in this book), and is the main reason why people tend to associate scientific methods with empiricism. If you think about it, this idea alone makes research possible and believable! The other kind of epistemological realism is called *critical realism*, which suggests that we see sensations, the images of the things in the real world, but not the things directly. Critical realists point out how often our eyes (and other senses) deceive us. One famous example is the way a stick jutting out of the water seems to be bent at the point it comes out. Take it out of the water, and you find it is straight.

The third main form of empiricism is called *subjectivism*. Subjectivism is the theory proposing that reality (and therefore knowledge) is what we perceive to be, and that there is no underlying true reality (and therefore knowledge) that exists independently of human perception. One can also hold that it is consciousness rather than perception that is reality (sometimes called subjective idealism). Subjectivism has been the dominant view of subjectivity in many fields of scholarship, including significant bands of socio-cultural researchers of sport and exercise. René Descartes and Bishop Berkeley expressed the core notion of subjectivism. Descartes proposed that mind is distinct from body and world and is a realm of its own. Berkeley expressed this in his classic statement that the world is 'as I see it'. My perception does not represent the world, rather, the world is an expression of my personal subjectivity. The processes and principles of my subjectivity determine how I see the world; the world does not influence my perception of it. But, what is interesting is how people come to see/know the world in agreed upon ways that we call *intersubjective*. If we didn't, no such thing as a society or a culture would be possible. On the other hand, *solipsism* is at the most extreme end of subjectivism. According to this hyper-subjectivist position, all people naturally see things differently … so differently that some say everyone experiences a different reality and there is no real way to verify if there an objective reality at all, aside from what is observed. Go as far as sub-jectivism takes you, and you arrive at solipsism. Not many of us in research methods go this far … but some do from time to time!

WHY IS THIS RELEVANT TO ME?

The relevance of epistemology, I would hope, is clear and concise based on all of the discussion about methods, evidence and knowledge in this book. One's belief in what can be known (see the entry in this book outlining Ontology) translates into a methods pathway for knowing empirically. Realists argue that through the correct application of (scientific) methods we can access objective truths about the world. Subjectivists argue that only through methods allowing for the inspection of how people construct the world will we ever grasp how reality is ordered by people. A major split in thinking, practice and knowledge production occurs here. 'Hard science' researchers in sport and exercise attempt to know objective, universal truths about bodies, minds and societies by studying them through (predominantly) experimental or survey/questionnaire-based techniques. Subjectivists balk at the idea of immutable, universal truths (and therefore knowledge), focusing instead on methods of knowing which tap into how people themselves understand things, such as ethnography or interviewing. While all of the methods stress the empirical basis of all knowledge, the nature of the knowledge produced through realist/objectivist versus subjectivist approaches are very, very different in practice.

SHOW ME HOW IT'S USED!

Knowledge obtained from realism/objectivism is based on systematic and standardised forms of observation (like experiments, questionnaires or scale items) and experimentation. The methodological standpoint of realism/objectivism is, then, one emphasising the need to examine patterns in the world that may be beyond human consciousness of them. Realism focuses on knowledge development through the deductively directed (i.e. by the theory and hypotheses) collection of quantified facts and patterns about the world extracted from those empirical methods alone. Because the knowledge to be conveyed is deemed objective and therefore factual and quantified, it is also said to be de-contextualised and exists independently of the knower. Therefore, the knowledge can be learned, tested and applied more or less independently of particular contexts. Isn't this, after all, the nature of lab-based experimentation, mass surveying and analytic epidemiology? Due to the independency of knowledge from the knower, realism/objectivism has become (to reiterate) commonly understood as the source of 'unbiased' or factual knowledge, and as such the most widespread and institutionally revered form of academic knowledge acquisition.

Subjectivism dominates qualitative methodology. It construes interactions between researcher and subjects (through interviews in particular) and the active, inductive interpretation of data – which are central features of qualitative research. The subject is free to express whatever subjective idea he or she desires, research is often conducted in social places and spaces where subjects' knowledge of the world is gained (i.e. in the places where they are living), and the researcher is granted an open licence to subjectively interpret data and build empirical knowledge by using people's collective knowledge of the world. In many ways, the position on knowledge development subjectivists take is that they seek to make sense of how people make sense of the world. Subjectivist qualitative researchers on sport and exercise thereby claim that the world is unknowable as a standard, universal thing with concrete meanings, causal determination of events and structure, and objective knowledge. Subjectivists favour instead methods that allow for analytic induction processes to unfold through the research act (i.e. the building up of conceptual and theoretical understandings of things by studying first how people make sense of them); and so open-ended, contextual techniques of data collection like interviewing, ethnography, narrative analysis and others are privileged.

PROBLEMS, PITFALLS AND CONTROVERSIES

Trying to explain the relevance of epistemology to even the most seasoned researcher is an unenviable task because it's like trying to convince someone who has driven a car for 30 years that they need to know the principles of internal combustion. Epistemology is a highly specialist and esoteric topic within methods courses, but a working understanding of its meaning goes a long way in developing an appreciation that not all 'empirical methods' are realist, and not all meaningful knowledge is gleaned through scientific experiment. I devote no more than 30 seconds to the discussion of epistemology in my methods modules, and some students argue that even that is too long! But since sport and exercise departments and faculties may contain faculty and students with such diverse disciplinary interests and backgrounds, it is an important 30 seconds.

The discussion of epistemology presented in this entry is also more than a touch ideal-typical in the sense that realism, critical realism and subjectivism are portrayed as three competing (or at least opposite) models of knowledge philosophy and production. Mixed methods research, in particular, blends qualitative and quantitative techniques, underlining the point that perhaps 'either/or' mentalities in the academy do little to help stimulate new and interesting ways of thinking about and knowing the world. Mixed methodologists quite rightly point out that a philosophy of what can be known (and how to know it) is just that, a human-created set of ideas and assumptions and not necessarily methodological gospel.

See also: Causality; Evidence-Based Research and Practice; Interpretivism; Ontology; Positivism; Theory.

KEY READINGS

BonJour, L. (2002) *Epistemology: Classic Problems and Contemporary Responses.* Lanham: Rowman & Littlefield.

Hay, C. (2008) *The Theory of Knowledge: A Coursebook.* Cambridge: Lutterworth Press.

Niiniluoto, I. (2002) *Critical Scientific Realism.* Oxford: Oxford University Press.

Rand, A. (1979) *Introduction to Objectivist Epistemology.* New York: Meridian.

Tomberlin, J. (1999) *Philosophical Perspectives 13, Epistemology.* Oxford: Blackwell Publishing.

Unger, R. (1985) 'Epistemological consistency and its scientific implications'. *American Psychologist* 40: 1413–1414.

Ethnography

Few topics simultaneously stir as much interest, bewilderment and criticism in research methods courses as ethnography. For students inclined to see the world from socio-cultural perspectives, ethnography not only makes immediate sense, it inspires them to get up, get out, and engage in the world of lived experience. For hardcore science types, ethnography is almost entirely unappealing as an academic venture. In basic terms, an ethnography provides a representational (usually written) account of a particular culture during a specified time period. The ethnographer learns the culture through immersion in it over a year or several years; the method is, on the surface, that simple. But how the ethnographic venture is conducted, how data are analysed, and the use of ethnographic data in the academy are far more complex matters.

WHAT IS THIS CONCEPT?

The term ethnography is quite loosely, and most of the time erroneously, applied to *any* qualitative research project where the purpose is to provide a detailed, in-depth description of the everyday life and practice of a group of people. This is sometimes referred to as 'thick description' (a term attributed to the cultural anthropologist Clifford Geertz). Ethnographers generate understandings of culture through the 'insider's point of view'. An ethnographer believes that in order to understand, translate and explain how cultures work, one needs to become a functioning member of that culture. Therefore, the ethnographic method is quite straightforward; one becomes a part of the cultural group, does what they do, goes where they go, lives where they live, and exists how they exist. Ethnographers adopt this approach in order to develop a nuanced and complex theoretical understanding of culture from the ground up; emphasis is thus placed on allowing abstract concepts and meanings to *emerge* from the ethnographic encounter rather than imposing these from existing theoretical models.

An ethnographic understanding of a culture is developed, then, through close exploration of several sources of data. First and foremost, long-term engagement in the field setting or place where people in the culture meet and interact daily is called *participant observation*. This is perhaps the primary source of ethnographic data. The term represents the dual role of the ethnographer in that one is both a participant in the culture, and at the same time an academic observer. To develop an understanding of what it is like to be a member of a culture, the researcher becomes a *participant* in the life of the settings wherein the culture operates, while also maintaining the stance of an *observer*, someone who can describes the experience with a measure of what we might call professional detachment. Note that this does not prevent ethnographers from becoming advocates for the people they study. Typically, ethnographers spend many months or even years in the places where they conduct their research, often forming lasting bonds with people. To be sure, many undergraduate students, graduate students and faculty members conduct ethnographies in the communities where they themselves live and work. However, the nature of participation in ethnography is not so easy to define in a single way. Gold (1958) describes four principal ways in which people perform ethnography. These participatory roles range along a continuum of involvement, from complete participant (one who is fully immersed and participates in the culture),

ethnography

to participant-as-observer (one who participates, but not in everything), to observer-as-participant (one who moderately participates, but principally watches the culture from the social periphery), to complete observer (one who observers the culture only, without ever participating in or interacting among its members).

At some point in time, most ethnographers will also interview members of the culture. Ethnographic interviews provide a context for 'targeted' data collection by asking specific but open-ended questions among key informants identified through the research process. There is a great variety of interview styles. Each ethnographer brings his or her own unique approach to the process. Regardless, the emphasis is on allowing the person or persons being interviewed to answer without being limited by pre-defined choices – something which clearly differentiates qualitative from more quantitative or demographic approaches. In most cases, an ethnographic interview looks and feels little different from an everyday conversation, and indeed in the course of long-term participant-observation most ethnographic conversations are in fact purely spontaneous and without any specific agenda. Researchers collect other sources of data that depend on the specific nature of the field setting. This may take the form of representative artefacts that embody characteristics of the topic of interest, government reports, and newspaper and magazine articles. Although often not tied to the site of study, secondary academic sources are utilised to locate the specific study within an existing body of literature.

WHY IS THIS RELEVANT TO ME?

A number of research questions are well suited for an ethnographic approach. By and large, though, research questions focusing on the ways in which specific cultures shape personal and collective sport, exercise and health behaviours are the most amenable to ethnography. For example, my first proper ethnographic venture homed in on the ticket scalping subculture in Toronto, Canada (Atkinson, 2000). I wanted to know how the subculture is produced, how members are brought in, how tickets were acquired and what this illegal subculture signifies with regard to the broader sports-entertainment complex in Canada. Such is a classic example of a *cultural ethnography*. The purpose of a cultural ethnography is to learn the inner workings of a culture and then explain how and why the culture operates as it does as a theoretical matter. Ethnographies that involve the study of two or more groups/cultures over time are often called *ethnologies*, while historical accounts of a culture arising from a study of them are referred to as *ethnohistories*. Although not a prerequisite of a cultural ethnography, researchers will occasionally strive to connect what is learned in a local cultural setting with broader trends and processes in a society. In my ticket scalping study I argued that the very subculture itself is partially produced by diffuse market capitalist trends in sport and elsewhere. How scalpers think, organise, interact and structure their styles of living is inexorably linked with ongoing commercialisation processes in sport and neo-liberal trends and ideologies in the larger market economic system.

Institutional ethnography is an approach to empirical inquiry associated with the feminist scholar Dorothy Smith (1987). The approach emphasises connections among the sites and situations of everyday life, professional practice and policy-making. Smith developed the approach initially in a feminist context, calling it a method that could produce a sociology for women; but yet she describes it as an approach with much wider application. In essence, an institutional ethnography (sometimes called a standpoint ethnography) is one striving to understand how people's everyday lives are structured by social forces working through and within institutions like the family, media, workplaces, schools, and others. Those following Smith in the development of institutional ethnographic methods have taken up a variety of substantive topics, including the organisation of health care, education, and social work practice, the regulation of sexuality, the police and the judicial processing of violence against women, employment and job training, economic and social restructuring, international development regimes, planning and environmental policy, the organisation of home and community life, and various kinds of activism. The method is ethnographic, but more concerned with political-economic contexts than most qualitative approaches. To date, and quite surprisingly, very few have explored the potential of institutional/standpoint ethnography in sport studies (though many have engaged a version of institutional ethnography more loosely described as feminist ethnography).

More recently, *auto-ethnographic* methods have mushroomed in popularity within the study of sport, physical activity and health. Auto-ethnography is a method in which the investigator develops a research question pertaining to a particular social process, experience, or reality and then creates an ethnographic description and analysis of his/her own behaviour, attempting to develop an objective understanding of the behaviours and work context under consideration by casting the

ethnography

investigator as both the informant 'insider' and the analyst 'outsider'. For example, a spate of auto-ethnographies about running has been published within the recent past (Hockey, 2006). These ethnographies, almost always written in a story or aesthetic narrative form rather than as a traditional academic/journal article, illustrate that by knowing one's own self and exploring how one's own life takes meaning (for instance, as a runner), we learn a great deal about the processes by which social life unfolds. Auto-ethnographies can be deeply personal, emotional and artistic in their written form, as part of the logic of the method is to 'open up' and personalise published research in order to help readers connect with academic arguments, theories and ideas.

Audience ethnography strives to understand how people actively receive, decode and use media texts. Audience ethnography might be designed as a one-shot case study, or be structured as a long-term panel study of how a group interprets media over the course of time. In the typical scenario, participants in an audience ethnographic project are asked to collectively or individually watch, read or listen to selected media and then respond to its content. A researcher acts as a facilitator in these scenarios, prompting questions among respondents about what the messages or symbols in the media might mean to them and how they actively decode them from a variety of cultural standpoints (age, race, sexuality, gender, class). The underpinning logic of doing audience ethnography is that by observing and questioning how people make sense of media data, 'live' and *in situ*, researchers compile a more valid understanding of the process of immediate reception and the cognitive processing of media content. Wilson and Sparks (1996), for example, illustrate how African-Canadian teenage boys fashion their own constructions of, and lived experiences with, Black masculinity to interpret mass mediations of 'Blackness' in basketball shoe advertisements. Wilson and Sparks discuss how the boys find humour, reality, and frequent inferential racism in the depictions of Black masculinity in the advertisements. They also attest to how the youth selectively take from the commercials what makes sense to them culturally, and how they negate or resist supposedly preferred images and constructions of 'Blackness' in the commercials.

Finally, with the rise of new online media the practice of *netnography* is gaining popularity as a technique of analysis. Netnography, or online ethnography, is an online ethnography of Internet sites wherein a researcher does not simply observe the content of websites, but often contributes to them as a registered or recognised member. Wilson and

Atkinson (2005), for example, studied the online recruiting and social connecting mechanisms provided by Rave and Straightedge blogs and chat forums/rooms. In both subcultures, young people use Internet sites as a performing community and a way of fostering bonds between members across great spaces. Both of the researchers participated and chatted with members online as a means of conducting quasi-interviews, but, more importantly, of gaining a first-hand understanding of how new media space is produced by groups in 'real time' as a vehicle for developing a sense of mutual identification and commitment.

SHOW ME HOW IT'S USED!

Ethnographies are not merely projects one participates in in a leisurely fashion, or in one's spare time. Proper ethnographies totally encompass one's life. Following the rhythms, activities and everyday goings-on in a culture is more of a style of life than a part of an exercise encapsulated neatly within the confines of one's office walls. Ethnographies require time, patience, energy, and the willingness to immerse. Any ethnographic instruction manual preaches a similar lesson. When one chooses to study the sport and exercise worlds ethnographically, one's modality of living shifts. For this reason alone, neophyte ethnographers must reflexively analyse their own enthusiasm for social interaction with strangers, their abilities to manage stage fright, their desire to spend copious amounts of time away from friends and family members, and their capability for sacrificing almost all of their free time.

Ethnographies, in any manifestation, thrive or fizzle out depending on the researcher's ability to gain access to the setting or culture of their choice. Consider the following example. About three years ago I decided I wanted to conduct an ethnographic field project on fell runners in the UK. There are hundreds, if not thousands of fell runners across the country and I wanted to explore the existential aspects of running off-road, and the cultural traditions associated with the practice. Easy one, right? Well, I have to find fell runners first. No problem there because I knew several from a local running club in which I participated in the English midlands. But knowing a few runners, then participating in a few races, is not an entrée into the culture of fell running. I needed to access and interact with people who lived, breathed and promoted the tradition. I needed to do what they do, see the sport how they see it, and understand how their culture makes sense to them as its core enthusiasts.

Access to the core networks of lifestyle participants in a sport culture is only the beginning. Several weeks or months may pass before one secures a role in the group. A basic sociological lesson instructs us that membership in a culture is framed by one's role, status and identity in the group. Why is this important in ethnography? Because one actually becomes what we call the 'instrument of data collection' (i.e. you are actually the recorder of data every day in the field), how you access the group, what roles you play therein and how other people position you as a person in the group substantially influences the volume and depth of the information you are able to gather over time. Who you are partially determines what you see, what you are told, and what you eventually know. I am fully convinced, for instance, that unless one fully immerses oneself in a culture, for example, fell running its members will maintain an arm's length cultural distance from you. The greater the depth and breadth of your role in fell running culture, the more its culture becomes real and your intersubjective connection with other enthusiasts sharpens. But still, not all ethnographic projects lend themselves to full immersion, for both practical and professional reasons.

The next 'stage' of data collection is the long haul in ethnographic projects. This involves the day-to-day collection of empirical data. Empirical data to an ethnographer could be everything and anything one hears, feels, sees and reads in the field. Most of the time, a researcher will only have a vague understanding of what is important at first (i.e. for answering one's initial research question) and so everything is noted, recorded and reflected upon until a dominant theoretical idea or set of main conceptual foci emerge in the study. Conversations with others, descriptions of interaction, artefacts gathered in the field and places visited need to be recorded with meticulous detail. Interviews with key informants provide the ethnographer with focused data on conceptual and substantive curiosities coming to the fore, and the research focus is narrowed further. What generally starts as a broad and overwhelming venture into the cultural dark transforms into a tightly defined research venture. There are no magic templates, tricks, tips or steps one might employ in order to develop conceptual clarity in a project. For example, whereas I started my project on fell running as an exploration of existentialism in outdoor sports, it turned into one on the rise of biomimicry in post-sport physical cultures.

The arduous part of ethnography commences with the processes of data interpretation and representation. Because anything and everything in an ethnographic project is data (at least at first), the process of whittling down one's study into a paper or even book-length report can be daunting. One commences the data analysis process from day one; reviewing and making interpretive/analytic notes about sociological 'things' one has heard, witnessed or discovered in the field with others. As time progresses, one learns to connect discoveries to conceptual ideas, and perhaps even to a new theoretical framework. Field notes, observations, interview data and artefacts gathered serve as partial indicators of broader sociological processes and structures. Thus, the lion's share of ethnographic research is interpretive and qualitative in orientation; that is to say, researchers are not so concerned with testing formal hypotheses derived from theory against data, in most cases. So, it is fair to suggest that ethnographic analysis is based more on the use of field data to generate, explore, probe and extend the empirical applicability of particular concepts, axioms or ideas.

PROBLEMS, PITFALLS AND CONTROVERSIES

Fervent advocates of more scientific methods question the reliability (repeatability) of ethnographic findings. Could another person have studied Ashtanga in Toronto and compiled the very same (or at least a similar) story of the setting? Probably not, because so much of ethnography relies upon, and is produced through, the intermixing of roles, relationships and personalities in the field. As a related concern, then, can an ethnographer ever represent the reality of everyday life in a valid manner? Can months or years in the field be reduced to an 8,000-word journal article or 200-page manuscript? The belief that ethnographic accounts can be 'realist' (i.e. textually represent the complexities of social life in an accurate manner) has come under considerable challenge over the past 40 years.

Finally, the social scientific point, value or outcome of ethnographies is questioned on a regular basis. Ethnographic accounts generally evolve in their written form as socio-cultural stories or narratives; their 'drivers' are theoretical concepts and their audiences are often very small groups of people within universities. But social science for the sake of esoteric storytelling now receives substantial scrutiny, and growing numbers of critiques are asking ethnographers to underline or tease out the social benefits or institutional policy implications of their research.

See also: Grounded Theory; Interpretivism; Media Analysis; Visual Methods.

ethnography

73

KEY READINGS

Andrews, D., Mason, D. and Silk, M. (2005) *Qualitative Methods in Sport Studies*. London: Berg.

Atkinson, M. (2000) 'Brother, can you spare a seat: Developing recipes of knowledge in the ticket scalping subculture'. *Sociology of Sport Journal* 17: 151–170.

Charmaz, K. (2006) *Constructing Grounded Theory: A Practical Guide Through Grounded Analysis*. London: Sage.

Gallagher, K. (2007) *The Methodological Dilemma: Critical, Creative, and Post-Positivist Approaches to Qualitative Research*. London: Routledge.

Gold, R. (1958) 'Roles in sociological field observation'. *Social Forces* 36: 217–223

Hockey, J. (2007) 'Sensing the run: Distance running and the senses'. *The Senses and Society* 1: 183–202.

Sands, R. (2001) *Sport Ethnography*. Champaign: Human Kinetics.

Smith, D. (1987) *The Everyday World as Problematic: A Feminist Sociology*. Boston: Northeastern University Press.

Sparkes, A. (2002) *Telling Tales in Sport and Physical Activity: A Qualitative Journey*. Champaign: Human Kinetics.

Wilson, B. and Atkinson, M. (2005) 'Rave and straightedge, the virtual and the real: Exploring online and offline experiences in Canadian youth subcultures'. *Youth & Society* 36: 276–311.

Wilson, B. and Sparks, B. (1996) 'It's gotta be the shoes: Youth, race, and sneaker commercials'. *Sociology of Sport Journal* 13: 398–427.

Evaluation Research

Research methodologists devote a great deal of time, money, energy and creative inspiration into developing techniques for the study of life. In both pure and applied ways, we try to hone particular skills for answering questions. Methodologists are like multi-skilled mechanics of the research process; engineering, building, testing and fixing research vehicles of one sort or another. From time to time researchers are called upon to deploy their methodological and analytic skills to help solve the problems of others. By this, I mean we are consulted with or hired to assess, evaluate or fix an institutional policy, programme or method of operation either in practice or one that is being proposed. For example, at the university where I teach (the University of Toronto), the Faculty of Physical Education and Health instituted a policy in 2009 establishing a women-only workout hour between 12:00pm and 1:00pm in one of the main fitness facilities. The Faculty's intention was to create a welcoming space to exercise for women who had previously felt uncomfortable in co-ed gym settings. A great idea within a university that promotes fitness and physical activity for all! But does the programme work? Does it encourage more women to come to the gym than before, does it attract women who would not otherwise come to the gym, and does the women-only workout hour create the desired atmosphere as stated in policy. When we are striving to assess whether or not a policy like this is effective, or simply how it creates effects, then we are on the methodological ground of evaluation research.

WHAT IS THIS CONCEPT?

Evaluation research is a type of applied research geared towards determining if a programme, policy, intervention or some intended plan is achieving its desired outcomes. In this scenario, we are evaluating something another group of people have developed and implemented in their organisation. In many cases, the research is conducted well after the programme or policy has been implemented (think of the case of the women-only hour at the gym). Still, we can also conceive evaluation research as classic experimental research where we actually conduct the analysis of the effectiveness of an organisation product, policy or programme before it is implemented 'live'. For example, researchers will evaluate the effectiveness of a new drug on an illness to determine its effectiveness, or examine the accuracy of a new software system for tracking student use of a campus gym. In these cases, evaluation research determines potency, reliability and effectiveness before an organisation policy or product is distributed. Further still, evaluation research could be conducted in order to help assess needs within an organisation and shape their future public policy. Just imagine if we were asked to study participation rates in the University of Toronto gyms as a way of informing the administration about who is or is not using the facility (they want to know, because they firmly believe in providing physical activity for all on campus). We conduct a usage study and find women are significantly under-represented in the gyms and conclude the university needs to amend policy or best practice to involve more women

The bottom line is that practically anything can be evaluated, and organisations usually have great needs for ongoing research on their products, programmes and policies. Common 'things' evaluated by sport, exercise and health researchers include:

- Public and private physical activity and fitness practices and policies;
- Pedagogy and coaching techniques;
- The effects of performance-enhancing drugs and ergogenics;
- Delivery of health services;
- Lifestyles of (un)healthy living;
- Sports marketing and management decisions;
- Legislation designed to eliminate inequality in sport participation.

The above is merely a small list of current evaluation research zones demarcated by researchers. To help expand ideas about what could be evaluated, a brief mention of the four most commonly cited purposes of evaluation research is probably worthwhile.

First, and as alluded to above, evaluation research may be designed as a programme of *needs-assessment*. Normally, needs-assessment research is sought after by an organisation when they feel that a major discrepancy exists between their existing policies and actual outcomes. What does the organisation need to do in order to adapt and change so that the desired results are achieved? Second, *formative evaluation* is akin to needs-assessment, but is slanted towards the evaluation of a programme/policy which is in place in order to determine its effectiveness as the programme/policy unfolds over time. So, formative evaluation may begin as soon as the policy or programme begins and tracks its effectiveness over time. Third, *summative evaluation* is generally undertaken after a programme, product or policy has been 'live' for quite some time, and people within the organisation desire a 'bottom line' summary of its effectiveness. From there, decisions are made about whether or not the organisation should continue with the policy/programme/product, amend its structure or desist with it entirely. Finally, *responsive evaluation* is a research venture intended to provide an assessment of the policy, programme or product from a variety of stakeholder perspectives; not just the designers or administrators if it! A responsive evaluation would, in the case of the women-only-hour programme at the University of Toronto, first gather information from administrators, students, faculty members, sports facility managers, programme co-ordinators and others to see the programme and its effectiveness from their eyes; and even, in many cases, to gather a sense of how they feel the programme should be evaluated and why. From there, our understanding of the women-only-hour policy's effectiveness is a composite of a variety of stakeholder interests and perspectives about the policy. Reports and communications should speak to all of these groups and address their perspectives on how and why the policy is or is not effective.

WHY IS THIS RELEVANT TO ME?

When my students groan and grumble about having to enrol in and sit through a research skills module, I am quick to remind them that there is a world 'out there' full of problems waiting to be solved. Skills in the methods of research design, implementation and presentation are a niche product a university offers students. Problem-solving is problem-solving, and those of us in the university stream should not fetishise academic research (designed to tackle broad, disciplinary-specific or highly theoretical issues) rather than looking at small-scale problems people strive to overcome in the here and now of everyday life.

SHOW ME HOW IT'S USED!

Bless celebrity chef and health activist Jamie Oliver. In 2008, the well-known British chef and television darling embarked on a school lunch revolution project designed to remove junk food from school cafeterias and replace it with fresh, wholefood options. He successfully convinced a handful of schools in the United Kingdom to exchange their (slightly above) fast-food lunch options with his balanced-diet options. Some of the children balked at the options (leaving school grounds to find fast-food nearby) while others immediately took to the new menus. Oliver's intentions are beyond well-placed and appropriate in light of consistent research pointing to the unhealthy food choices made by school-aged children and the nutritionally lacklustre menus they encounter at school. Yet Oliver has struggled to convince most educational policy-makers of the cost-effectiveness and long-term viability of his food revolution idea. If there is anything school board trustees hate to see it is thousands of dollars'/pounds' worth of uneaten health food in rubbish bins after every lunch. The idea of gastronomic overhaul in the cafeteria certainly has empirical merit, but a successful revolution might need careful planning, implementation and monitoring. It would be a prime context for evaluation research.

Evaluation research can be conducted through a range of data collection techniques and forms of analysis. Depending, of course, on the subject at hand, the purpose of the evaluation and the desired information needed to evaluate, experiments, surveys, interviews, focus groups and unobtrusive observation are readily employed. I would love to conduct an evaluation research project in one of Jamie Oliver's revolutionary schools. To examine audience reception of the new menu, we could easily send-out a survey to students asking them to rate the new menu, and could interview them over time to track their reactions to the junk food phase-out; or, we could sit in a range of cafeteria settings and observe eating behaviours. With respect to data analysis, because the intended audience for evaluation reports is not normally fellow academics, the techniques used may be relatively 'high level' but must be communicated in very straightforward ways. Easily readable charts, bulleted summaries of conceptual findings and statistical tables are always welcomed. Overly verbose, highly theoretical language and interpretation and standard academic templates of presentation are not appreciated.

How to structure an evaluation project is another matter entirely. Given the purpose of the evaluation and the intended audience, there can be any number of ways to structure one's investigation. Three stand out as very common methodological plans of attack in an evaluation project. First, an evaluation research will be frequently called upon to assess *behavioural outcomes* of a policy or programme. These projects revolve around the question of whether or not the policy or programme affects behaviour in the manner intended. Does the new menu actually encourage students to forgo junk food while on campus every day? Do they simply avoid the menu by bringing their own junk-filled lunches to school, and/or do they travel off campus to locate fast-food alternatives to the school's healthy menu. Studies examining the biophysical impacts of drugs or ergogenics operate similarly, focusing instead on changes (or not) in physical outcomes and performance abilities. Second, researchers may be called upon to evaluate whether or not the policy or programme achieves the desired behavioural results in the most efficient, cost-effective and maximally impacting manner. Such studies are referred to as *systems analyses*. If, for example, the food revolution programme is neither the most cost-effective nor maximally effective programme for encouraging healthy eating in the school, this will be noted in a systems analysis study. Finally, evaluation researchers are asked to provide information on a specific group's reception of the new programme or policy. These studies are referred to as *case studies* in evaluation. Here, the goal is to measure how a particular subgroup of those directly affected by the policy respond to it in everyday life.

I might, for example, wish to focus on the impact of the food revolution policy on eating behaviours within the oldest age group in a school to examine whether or not the policy affects those with the most entrenched and habituated eating.

PROBLEMS, PITFALLS AND CONTROVERSIES

The small-scale and esoteric nature of evaluation projects tends to raise criticisms regarding the broader merits of the research. With low levels of external validity (and to some degree reliability), and lack of emphasis on theoretical testing or development, evaluation projects garner little in the way of academic prestige. Partially a reflection of the low utility of the results (i.e. beyond the organisation or group commissioning the study) and partially a reflection of a belief that evaluation research is mainly 'extra-curricular' research, university and college faculties or departments may even place restrictions on how much of this type of research a faculty member may undertake during a given year. Again, these sentiments and conditions of employment tend to dissuade rather than encourage active researchers in universities from partaking in the practice of evaluation unless it is writ large in one's job description.

My personal experiences with evaluation research have been rewarding but yet frustrating across contexts because of one common factor. When one is accustomed to wielding full control over a research project and is able to devote large amounts of time to ensuring a proper test of one's theoretical ideas can be carried out, instances in which a policy has already been designed, implemented and partially monitored can be frustrating to encounter. Why? Because evaluation researchers are often called upon to extract meaningful data from programmes or policies that have been implemented or operated under less than ideal conditions. One may become immediately aware that measuring the policy's true effectiveness (i.e. if implemented in theoretically ideal conditions) is difficult. What if the University of Toronto decided to start the women-only gym hour at 6:00am? I would have no control over this decision and would simply collect data based on the evidence at hand. Now, based on my knowledge of workout patterns and gym attendance as a socio-cultural researcher I know the plan is less than ideal. But what can I do in this scenario?!

See also: Applied vs. Pure Research; Quantitative vs. Qualitative Research; Translation.

KEY READINGS

Brophy, S., Snooks, H. and Griffiths, L. (2008) *Small-Scale Evaluation in Health: A Practical Guide*. London: Sage.

Grembowski, D. (2001) *The Practice of Health Program Evaluation*. Thousand Oaks, CA: Sage.

Shaw, I., Greene, J. and Mark, M. (2006) *The Sage Handbook of Evaluation*. London. Sage.

Evidenced-Based Research and Practice

I help coach long-distance runners and triathletes from time to time. A hundred and one different variables factor into how training should unfold for individual endurance athletes, and among them is the degree to which one is affected by the process of teleoanticipation. Teleoanticipation is a very common and difficult to manage bio-psychological process. Ulmer (1996) outlined teleoanticipation by arguing that people possess a kind of 'central programmer' in the brain that focuses on the finishing point of a task (like the end of a triathlon or marathon) and works backward from that point to where one is presently in order to regulate body exertion. If the end point is unknown, or the body is not trained well to endure, the brain convinces the body to take it easy as a matter of self-protection. People feel fatigued, start to experience self-doubt and a drive to quit if the central programmer does not have enough information to assess whether or not a person is able to continue. Practically every 'distance' athlete I know has experienced teleoanticipation. The theory of teleoanticipation has been supported by dozens of experiments around the world, using runners, cyclists, swimmers and a range of other athletes as test subjects. Well-planned marathon or triathlon training should take into account existing research on teleoanticipation, how it unfolds, and how it can be managed. The case study of teleoanticipation illustrates not only the importance of finding evidence to support or discount complex theoretical ideas like teleoanticipation, but also how to best use *'evidenced-based' research* in practice.

WHAT IS THIS CONCEPT?

A convincing argument is one that carefully fits together like pieces of a jigsaw puzzle. From a distance, the mosaic is seamless, but upon close inspection of the puzzle one gains an appreciation of the intricacy of its connected parts. In research terms, our bits of evidence are our puzzle pieces. A smooth, flowing, convincing and acceptable argument is one in which evidence is so masterfully interwoven and presented it is difficult to resist or discount. Although there are any number of ways in which to define the nature of evidence and to describe its relevance in research, let's examine how gathered and analysed evidence is central in moving knowledge from *doxa* to *episteme*.

Practically every seasoned marathoner I know believes they alone have the secret for combating fatigue during the 'lonely' phases of the event (i.e. just around the half-way point). Essentially, they have certain tricks and techniques for combating the process of teleoanticipation which they learn through trial and error, from other runners or through a coach. Mind you, most of these techniques are not justified by anything other than personal or in-group belief. There may be little or no logic in the techniques at all (I know one runner who swears by the practice of concentrated/focused blinking as his method of mental distraction while struggling to continue), but they may develop as 'common sense' knowledge within running cultures. Now, my mind has been trained to work in exactly the opposite way, as a researcher and as a geek with a penchant for methods. These runners are operating under the basis of *doxa*; highly subjective, unverified knowledge or popular opinion about the world. The runners might be correct in some of their strategies for managing teleoanticipation, but they don't know why. There is no logical pattern or understood connection between the 'evidence' of their success in battling through the effects of teleoanticipation and the strategies they utilise.

Episteme, by contrast, is what we might call justified knowledge based on review, scrutiny and the application of systematic means of evaluating observable information about a phenomenon beyond local wisdom, ritual belief, conjecture or popular opinion. Episteme is knowledge we believe to be 'true' because it has been subjected to close evaluation through accepted standards and practices. Stated another way, this knowledge is understood to be 'legitimate' because evidence supporting the knowledge claims has been rigorously gathered, examined by experts, and mutually agreed upon as empirically verifiable. Scientists strive to produce, obviously, episteme over doxa.

The process of gathering and analysing evidence in a study is our opportunity to move from the realm of doxa to episteme. In academic research, we strive to collect empirical evidence about a phenomenon of interest. What is empirical evidence? This is where matters become a bit tricky. *Empirical evidence is most often described as something that can be observed through the senses; it can be seen, touched, heard, smelled, and/or tasted to some extent.* As such, empirical evidence can be measured and transformed into something numerical or quantifiable, according to positivist researchers (so, if teleoanticipation exists, it can be quantified precisely). In a given study, our evidence might be a measure of a thought, a belief, an event, a biological entity, a behaviour, a material object or representation that we use to help answer a research question of interest. So, empirical evidence commonly means objective evidence that appears 'the same' regardless of the observer – this is why some students see and treat evidence as fact. Now, qualitative researchers work with empirical evidence, but find occasion to argue that not all evidence is objective. While the process of teleoanticipation may very well be an 'objective' or at least common phenomenon, it is not experienced by everyone in the same manner. There is a subjective component to how people know and experience the process and so quantifications of how much teleoanticipation someone is suffering from may be impossible. Because of these contrasting viewpoints, quantitative and qualitative researchers have strong disagreements (from time to time) about episteme on a given subject.

WHY IS THIS RELEVANT TO ME?

Evidence is the basis of argument according to scores of academics and clinical researchers. Without evidence, there can be no argument beyond theory or philosophy (not that philosophy is a bad thing!). But without evidence there is no relevance for a research project; there is no end product, no set of answers for our questions. The nature of accepted evidence in research is quite another story entirely. Which kinds of evidence do we privilege in making claims as academic researchers? How much evidence do I require before I can be confident that I know something? What techniques are most appropriate for assembling my evidence? Here is an exercise. Consider the following two scenarios and ask yourself which study you would trust more than the other.

Still fascinated by teleoanticipation, I set out to test whether or not a group of 100 triathletes I pull into my lab are affected by this phenomenon. I take 50 of the triathletes and put them on a treadmill at a standardised, set speed and I measure their perceived rate of exertion using the Borg scale about two minutes into the run. Almost all of them are working at a fairly predictable, comfortable pace. I tell them to keep running until I tell them to stop. I measure their perceived rate of exertion again at 58 minutes. Wow, it's really high! Two minutes later, I tell them to stop running entirely and they are very thankful. The protocol is precisely the same for the second group of 50 triathletes with one major exception. Even before they step onto the treadmill, they are told that they will be running for 60 minutes in total. I find something very interesting in the process: while their first perceived rate of exertion scores are similar to the first group, their second scores are much lower than the first group's! The theory of teleoanticipation predicts this will happen – knowledge of the end point of an endurance event greatly impacts one's perceived rate of exertion toward the end. My evidence of the process is, of course, the measurement of perceived exertion using the Borg scale.

A colleague of mine takes an entirely different approach to the question. Because he has some experience in triathlons and knows triathletes, he decides to interview 15 of them about their experiences with mental and physical fatigue during distance events. He speaks to them about their strategies for training, what techniques within races they use to combat mental and physical low points during the races and what it feels like to mentally and physically suffer during these races. What does he learn? He gathers descriptive accounts of mental and physical endurance work while racing, learns how the athletes understand their bodies as tools to be honed and perfected, and conceptualises the different mental/physical/social strategies they employ to manage self-doubt in a race. His evidence, then, is the words, phrases and stories contained in their individual/group accounts of how fatigue is experienced.

SHOW ME HOW IT'S USED!

In the early 1970s, an epidemiologist named Archie Cochrane wrote a book called *Effectiveness and Efficiency: Random Reflections on Health Services*. Cochrane argued that best practice in medical circles is to apply the best available evidence gained from the scientific method to clinical decision-making. This means that proper health care follows whichever interventions, techniques and strategies to improve health and wellness are shown to be effective across many studies (episteme, right!). Cochrane maintained that the most reliable and valid evidence comes from randomised controlled trials (RCTs) that have been replicated across contexts.

So, Cochrane's statements define acceptable evidence in this sphere as numeric and produced through particular experimental protocols. That is, proper knowledge and medical practice should stand on the shoulders of replicated, quantified knowledge. Within the realm of evidenced-based research and practice in the medical professions, there is now a generally accepted Cochrane Systematic Review process for examining RCTs.

Evidence-based practice, then, refers to the use of research and scientific studies as a base for determining the best thinking, policy suggestions, intervention, or treatment strategies in a field. The movement began in the 1990s with a focus on the medical profession, but it has since crossed the line into other professions, including health studies more broadly (and sport and exercise research). Evidence-based practices ostensibly eliminate subjective professional judgement when developing appropriate plans of action (doxa, right!), and, by association, forms of subjective knowledge used as evidence in qualitative research. Current thinking is that best practice for rehabilitating athletes, training better coaches, mobilising immobile populations, improving equity policies in sports organisations, perfecting athletic movements, or eliminating problem thoughts from athletes' minds, flows from systematic review of all the 'objective' information on hand (Cochrane, 1971).

PROBLEMS, PITFALLS AND CONTROVERSIES

One wonders if the push towards evidenced-based research and practice in the past two decades merely coincides with the 'discovery' of qualitative ways of knowing health and wellness in nursing, sport psychology, medicine, sport management and pedagogy, health studies and epidemiology. In a recent editorial in *Qualitative Health Research*, Sally Thorne indicts the majority of non-quantitative-based approaches as antithetical to research or serious academic scholarship. Drawing explicitly on the language of evidenced-based truth claims, Thorne laments the recent trend in physical culture and health scholarship towards the consideration of more subjective ways of gaining knowledge about health and physical activity. This trend is also evident in the sociology of sport, as exemplified by past special issues in this journal (e.g. volume 17, issue 1), and Bob Rinehart's Presidential Address at the 2009 NASSS conference in Ottawa (since published in *Quest*). Critical articles detailing the pressure for sport, health and exercise to pursue more quantitative evidence-based forms of empirical research reveal a rhizomatic tendency within universities to discount innovative forms of (qualitative) scholarship like storytelling as simply decorative, inconsequential or pragmatically pointless (Denzin et al., 2006; Holmes et al., 2006; Rojek and Turner, 2000). From the perspective of those seeking to push the boundaries of academic research and explore alternative ways of knowing, writing and representing physical culture(s), it is not only that these decorative approaches have something to offer substantively, theoretically and methodologically; they also seek to critically interrogate our understandings of reflexivity, objectivity, and the science/art of (qualitative) scholarship. Given the recent rebirth of 'evidence' discourses in the academy, however, these approaches are at serious risk of being pushed beyond the boundaries of legitimate academic research.

See also: *Applied vs. Pure Research; Epistemology; Validity.*

KEY READINGS

Cochrane, A. (1971) *Effectiveness and Efficiency: Random Reflections on Health Services.* London: Nuffield Provincial Hospitals Trust.

Denzin, N., Lincoln Y. and Giardina, M. (2006) 'Disciplining qualitative research'. *International Journal of Qualitative Studies in Education* 19: 769–782.

Holmes, D., Murray, S., Perron, A. and Rail, G. (2006) 'Deconstructing the evidence-based discourse in health sciences: truth, power, and fascism'. *International Journal of Evidence-Based Healthcare* 4: 180–186.

Rojek, C. and Turner, B. (2000) 'Decorative sociology: towards a critique of the cultural turn'. *The Sociological Review* 48: 629–648.

Ulmer, H. (1996) 'Concept of an extracellular regulation of muscular metabolic rate during heavy exercise in humans by psychophysiological feedback'. *Experientia* 52: 416–420.

experiments

Experiments

85

My 'running friends' tell me ice bathing is a wonderful recovery method for managing the effects of long bouts of intensive exercise. I hate ice bathing. I cannot imagine a pursuit less pleasurable than lying in a pool of frigid water for 10–20 minutes. But does it really work? If it did, why wouldn't every serious athlete ice bathe on a regular basis? In fact, most of the people I know finish their workout routines by immediately jumping into a hot shower rather than an ice bath! Tips, tricks, techniques and suggestions for training and recovery abound in sport and exercise subcultures. The scientific basis for many of these tips and regimens is practically non-existent or founded on the weakest of empirical grounds. So how do we sort out the rubbish from the sage advice? One of the ways is through the scientific method of experimentation. Consider this example. To test the theory that ice bathing reduces recovery time after long-duration (120 minutes and over) training at a minimum of 75% VO_2 max, I get an idea for research. If the ice bathing theory is correct, then we should find significant improvement in 5km time trial times 48 hours after ice bathing. We could test that out! We have people run in my lab on treadmills on Friday for two hours at 75%, rest Saturday, and then come in for a 5km time trial on a treadmill on Sunday. We do this twice. In the first trial, they have no ice bath, and in the second they have an ice bath. When research is conducted in this manner, we have adopted the thinking and practice of an experimenter.

WHAT IS THIS CONCEPT?

Experiments are a collection of research designs preferred by sport and exercise physiologists, nutritionists, biomechanists, behaviouralists and many psychologists that use the manipulation and controlled testing of variables to potentially better understand causal processes between them as predicted by theory and stated by research hypotheses. In an experimental research design, one or more variables are manipulated (also called 'treatment' variables) and examined in controlled conditions to determine their effect on a dependent variable (also called 'outcome' variables). Experiments are part of the measurement phase in the scientific method that arbitrates between competing models or hypotheses about a given phenomenon. But where do our ideas for experiments come from? That's very easy to answer … from theoretical ideas, past research, or previous findings. As described by innovators and proponents of experimental protocols including Galileo, Francis Bacon and Louis Pasteur, experimentation is generally used to test existing theories that purport to explain the causally determined nature of events, entities or processes in the world through the process of deduction. Students need to learn and remember that while we often become caught up in the substantive topics under investigation, the real aim of conducting experiments is to test hypotheses derived from theories.

The most valued kinds of experiments scientists run are called *controlled experiments* (versus 'natural' experiments that occur haphazardly in the world outside of the laboratory). A controlled experiment generally compares the results of a test we design and carry out among an experimental sample against a control sample, which is practically identical to the experimental sample except for the one aspect whose effect is being tested (the independent variable). A good example would be an ice bath experimental trial to see if the method actually works at improving time to full recovery! There are many biological theories justifying why intense cold helps the body to recover after long bouts of exercise. We could organise a simple experiment to test the effectiveness of ice baths. In our experiment, the sample or group receiving ice baths after a 20-mile run would be called the experimental group – they receive the treatment. In order to test whether or not the ice baths are better than no treatment at all, we would need to compare their time to recovery (let's not worry about how to measure this right now) with a group of people who ran the same distance but who did not receive an ice bath afterwards (a smelly group, for sure). The second group would be called our control group. This simple but powerful research design is the basis for practically all experiment protocols and the benchmark design of the scientific method.

The nature of 'control' in experimental designs refers to another matter entirely. Imagine that we actually seek to test the ice bath theory. The very first consideration I need to have in designing the experiment is whether or not any variables I am not measuring or interested in could potentially influence my data if left unaccounted for in the experiment. What if I accidentally included all the young runners in the first group and the veterans in the second? What if one group ran 20 miles of hills and the other 20 miles of a flat course? What if one group ate and drank as recommended for runners during training, and the other starved themselves? Any systematic differences (variables) unaccounted for and unmeasured by experimenters wreak havoc in our studies. We call these pesky variables *confounds* or *extraneous* variables. So, a second aspect of control refers to making sure each of the two groups (in this case) under investigation 'look like' one another in every possible variable we can control other than the treatment variable. This occurs through the process of *randomisation of subjects*.

Randomisation is a process that assigns research participants by 'chance', rather than by choice, to either the treatment group or the control group of all experiments. That is, each study participant has a fair and equal chance of being placed in the treatment group, or being placed in the control group. The goal of randomisation in our example is to produce comparable groups in terms of general participant characteristics, such as age, gender, career history with running, injury background, training volume per week … and other key factors that affect the probable course of recovery for the runners. In this way, the two groups are as similar as possible at the start of the study. At the end of the study, if one group has a better outcome than the other, the investigators will be able to conclude with some confidence that one intervention is better than the other. A randomised, controlled experiment is considered the most reliable and impartial method of determining what treatments or interventions work the best. Randomisation is normally undertaken in one of two manners:

- *Single-blinded* experiments are those in which participants do not know which group they are in – and therefore which intervention they are receiving until the conclusion of the study.
- *Double-blinded* experiments are those in which neither the participants nor the investigators know to which group the participants have been assigned until the conclusion of the study.

In sum, then, controlled experiments are valued because they must be performed when it is difficult to exactly control all the conditions or variables potentially affecting the outcome of an experiment. Double-blinding, in particular, helps to ensure that the experiment begins by creating two or more sample groups that are *probabilistically equivalent*, which means that measurements of traits should be similar among the groups and that the groups should respond in the same manner if given the same treatment. This equivalency is determined by statistical methods that take into account the amount of variation between individuals and the number of individuals in each group (too complex to cover in this entry). Once equivalent groups have been formed, the experimenter tries to treat them identically except for the one treatment *variable* that he or she wishes to isolate.

WHY IS THIS RELEVANT TO ME?

Asking a scientist why experiments are important in the research process is like asking an ice hockey player why it is important to skate, or swimmers about the importance of water in their sport. But, if an experimenter is pressed to answer the question of relevance, one might expect several of the following answers (aside from their ubiquity across all 'science' disciplines in the university):

- Experiments are very powerful research designs, because if controls are undertaken properly, we can potentially observe cause and effect relationships unfold before our eyes.
- Experiments can be (in most cases) easily replicated by others.
- If experimental findings are replicated across time and space, it adds to the external validity of the findings.
- If the above is true, the method is perfectly suited for testing theory and developing stronger empirical claims regarding causality.

Amongst the 'unwritten' cultural reasons as to why experiments are so fundamental in academic inquiry is that in the modern research-oriented university, the method is practically synonymous with science, research and knowledge. Experiment-based studies command much attention, respect, and indeed funding, if they take as their aim a major problem, theory or dominant belief.

SHOW ME HOW IT'S USED!

What can be overwhelming about experimental designs is that there are so many from which to choose when conducting research. Experiments vary in accordance, for example, with how many hypotheses are being tested, the number of variables involved, how many times the variables are measured before, during and after the treatment is administered, the number of groups and sub-groups in the study, and the duration of the experiment. Phew, that sounds complicated. For the sake of ease, the common types of laboratory experiments employed in sport, health and exercise sciences are outlined below.

Pre-experimental designs – the distinguishing feature of this first category of designs is that it contains no randomly assigned control group, and so extraneous variables pose serious threats to validity. Examples of pre-experimental designs include:

- *One-shot case study*: A treatment is given to one group (an ice bath after 20 miles of running) and we measure time to recovery … that's it!

- *One-group pre-test, post-test design*: Identical to the above, except that we would have measured time to recovery for the group following a no ice bath scenario on one occasion after a 20-mile run a few weeks before the run/ice bath test in order to get 'baseline' data on the group.
- *Static comparison design*: A design wherein there is a treatment and control group (but not randomly assigned) and each are measured 'post-test' only.

True experimental designs – in these designs, treatment and control groups are employed, and there is random assignment across both groups. Examples include:

- *Post-test only*: Like the static comparison design described above, but with random assignment.
- *Pre-test, post-test, control group design*: The flagship of the experimental protocol. Here, there is a control and treatment group, both are randomly assigned, and measurements are taken on both groups before and after the treatment is administered to the experimental group.
- *Solomon four group design* – An amalgamation of the post-test only and pre-test, post-test designs leading to four groups being involved in the study.

Quasi-experimental designs – these designs are characterised by a lack of random assignment to both the treatment and control groups. Examples of quasi-experimental designs include:

- *Interrupted time series design* – multiple measurements are taken on a dependent variable (time to recovery, for example) over a set period of time, both before and after a treatment is introduced to the experimental group. In this scenario, for example, we might study runners over nine months, asking them each to run 20 miles on the last Sunday of each month. For the first four months the participants do nothing after their runs, but at month five we administer the ice bath to the treatment group. Then for the next four months, no further treatment is administered.
- *Non-equivalent control group design* – this looks and 'feels' like the gold standard pre-test, and post-test design, but there is no random assignment of subjects to either group. This occurs quite frequently

when researchers have not been able to gather their entire sample group before the study commences.

Whatever the experimental design one selects (and the above are not all of the experimental designs available, only the most common), several steps in the experiment process are worth undertaking before one actually conducts the study.

First, to avoid being forced into performing a quasi-experimental design, one should attempt to obtain a full sample before the research commences. Such is not always feasible due to time constraints, competition for lab space, worries about participant schedules and needs, and a host of other factors. Second, it may be wise to first conduct a very small-scale pilot or test study or two before you do the real experiment. Pilot studies help ensure that the experiment measures what it should, and that everything is set up right in the lab setting. Minor errors, which could potentially destroy the experiment, are often found during the pilot test process. Are my thermometers measuring water temperature accurate? If I am using several ice baths in the lab, and one of the thermometers is off, this translates into systematic error in my design. With a pilot study, you can gather information about potential errors and problems, and improve the design, before putting a lot of effort into the 'main event'. If the experiments involve humans, a common strategy is to first have a pilot study with someone involved in the research protocol itself (good luck getting a volunteer from the research team to run 20 miles and then jump in an ice bath), and then arrange a pilot with a person who resembles the subject(s). Those two different pilots are likely to give the researcher important information about any problems in the experiment.

PROBLEMS, PITFALLS AND CONTROVERSIES

The most consistently voiced criticisms of experimental designs focus on threats to internal validity brought about by problems in the design or practice of the method. While staunch defenders of experiments claim internal validity (am I really measuring what I think I am measuring?) as among the strongest selling points of the method, critics are accurate in mentioning a lengthy list of serious threats to internal validity. Researchers undertaking lengthy trials are often unable to control for the *maturation effect*: the condition in which subjects 'naturally' change in their abilities or characteristics due to factors beyond experimental manipulation. Runners get injured outside of the lab, or they might progress and improve their physical conditioning over the course of a year and thus are not affected in the same way by ice bathing. Both situations might dramatically impact the findings in our study. More potentially damaging than maturation effects are *test effects*, in which participants become accustomed to being tested and adjust their behaviours accordingly (perhaps they run very hard in the first test, and then take it easier in the second test). *Experimental attrition* (subjects withdrawing from the study) can alter the balance of equality between the two groups (as established by randomisation) and thus weakens our ability to be sure extraneous variables have been managed sufficiently in the study.

More damning challenges to the integrity of experimental designs come from attacks on the *external validity* of the findings. While the external (population) significance of sample data can be examined and argued through inferential statistical tests, unless sampling has been carried out through a sufficiently random fashion from the theoretical population, there are scant reasons to believe the data represent the population (thus, there is poor *population validity*). If in my test of ice bathing, only very novice runners volunteer, can I make legitimate claims about ice bathing's impact on runners in general? In a related way, if there is little confidence in the *ecological validity* of the experimental protocol, then researchers are in quite a quandary. Questions of ecological validity focus on whether findings in the lab would hold true in other contexts. If our experimental results can only be obtained in the lab using treadmills and specially constructed baths, but not where people actually live, interact, and do things like running or bathing, then what is the use of the study?

See also: Causality; Evaluation Research; Evidence-Based Research and Practice; Inferential Statistics; Meta-Analysis; Populations and Samples; Positivism; Variables.

KEY READINGS

Field, A. and Hole, G. (2006) *How to Design and Report Experiments*. Thousand Oaks, CA: Sage.

Freedman, D. (2009) *Statistical Models: Theory and Practice*. Cambridge: Cambridge University Press.

Thomas, J. and Nelson, J. (2001) *Research Methods in Physical Activity*. Champaign: Human Kinetics.

Grounded Theory

When I discovered grounded theory as an undergraduate student, I thought it had to be the coolest academic idea on the planet. Today, I'm not so sure about the tenability of doing grounded theoretical work in active research, or its place in qualitative methodologies. Grounded theory is a term much bandied about in qualitative/interpretivist research circles, but probably one of the least understood. Common understandings and applications of the concept manifest like an end product of a 'broken telephone' game; where the originally communicated message is lost almost completely and replaced with an utterly garbled and nonsensical message. In what follows, we will briefly review the general principles underpinning grounded theory and discuss common applications of grounded theoretical methodology.

WHAT IS THIS CONCEPT?

I am fascinated by the use of football (soccer) programmes in countries like Zambia, Kenya, South Africa and elsewhere as a tool for cultural, social and economic rebuilding (especially for youth). In the spirit of this interest, I design a four-year ethnography of two programmes: one in Kenya and one in Zambia. True to the spirit of inductive, qualitative ethnography, I start the endeavour with a general research question; such as, 'How are "football for development" programmes experienced by youth in Africa?' Now, there is smallish literature on sport-development but the subject is not very well theorised. What do I mean by that? Simply, that extant theories of behaviour, organisation, cognition, or community development are either ill-equipped to explain how youth experience sport-for-development programmes, or have not as yet been applied to the area. If we remember that the goal of academic research is to account theoretically for how and why the world operates in a particular manner, then this is an issue! But the scenario is perfect for me because I might argue that since the phenomenon is so new and poorly understood as an academic matter, we need to conduct grounded theoretical research on the subject.

Grounded theory is most accurately described as a research method in which the eventual theory one 'discovers' about the nature of life is developed from the data, rather than the other way around. I would need to go to Africa, get a qualitative sense or feel for how football programmes are received and experienced by youth there, and then explain how and why reality seems to unfold in such a manner. That process makes grounded theory a classically inductive approach; meaning that it moves from the specific (observations in the real world of events) to the more general (conceptual and theoretical generalisations about how life operates). Grounded theory is often perceived as a method which separates theory and data, but others insist that the method actually combines the two from the very first day of data collection. Data collection, analysis and theory formulation are undeniably connected in a reciprocal sense, and the grounded theory approach incorporates explicit procedures to guide this process (see Charmaz, 2006: Glaser, 2001; Strauss and Corbin, 1998). Given the above, doing grounded theory is, at once, a process of collecting data, interpreting data, developing conceptual ideas and eventually developing formal hypotheses about the nature of social reality.

The above sounds fine and laudable, but this is where matters become a bit more problematic. Grounded theory contains many unique characteristics that are designed to maintain the conceptual 'groundedness' of the approach. Data collection and analysis are consciously combined, and initial data analysis is used to shape continuing data collection. What does this mean? Quite simply, the minute one starts collecting data (usually in the form of ethnographic observation, qualitative interviewing, discourse analysis or archival/media research), one starts to analyse data and recalibrate the emerging form, content and focus of one's study. Think about the question I posed earlier regarding the experience of football-for-development programmes. After several days, weeks and months in the field, my study would most likely narrow down to a much more tightly defined focus given my observations and interpretations in the field. For instance, I might come to understand the movement as another instance of White colonialism in Africa. Such would be a conceptual generalisation I made based on disparate bits of data I gathered over time while observing the football programmes and speaking with participants. I might also conclude that, given the corporate involvement and sponsorship in most football-for-development programmes, participants come to develop a common scepticism of the philanthropy supposedly buttressing them. So, my study then might shift to the exploration of the relationship between corporate sponsorship, alienation from the programmes and colonialism ... a far more theoretically directed thrust than at the outset! At the end of the study, the goal is to generate a series of empirically testable hypotheses (for instance, about the relationship between corporate involvement in sport and colonialisation).

WHY IS THIS RELEVANT TO ME?

A grounded theoretical approach to qualitative research has the potential to shed new, innovative, challenging and paradigm-directing insights on the nature of social reality. While there are debates regarding the proper application of the method, there is no other method of data analysis as well suited for generating creative theoretical insight on world, full stop. But academics are funny, and in many ways very predictable creatures of habit. I have spent the better part of the last 20 years developing my own theoretical tastes and preferences for reading social reality – these are not, technically, allowed to surface in a 'grounded' study of mine. I am supposed to encounter the world as a tabula rasa, and allow the rhythms, flows and currents of everyday life to direct my theorising. Will I ever succeed? Like most of my colleagues, probably not. But why do we still call so much research grounded theoretical?

Grounded theory is a term that has become rather lazily applied to a full range of qualitative/interpretive studies. Indeed, the term is at once generally conflated with the notion of interpreting qualitative data and employed as a default slogan describing data collection methods in a qualitative study. I argue that the vast majority of research projects flying under the banner of grounded theory across sport, exercise and health (including epidemiological and nursing) literatures are most likely ventures in what we might call *concept elaboration*. Here, a researcher commences with pre-configured conceptual ideas in mind (or their preferred theoretical explanations of the world – which we all develop as researchers despite protests to the contrary!), and then 'applies' them to emergent qualitative data. Such a method is a 'light' or Frankenstein version of traditional science; it is hypothesis testing without the hypothesis, and theoretical application in disguise. It is research produced, directed, represented and received through the lens of pre-existing concepts. Our concepts might be expanded, contracted, tightened, or partially redefined through qualitative inquiry, but very rarely are new theoretical systems or sets of interconnected hypotheses produced.

SHOW ME HOW IT'S USED!

First and foremost, 'traditional' grounded theory is a *general* research method (and thus is not owned by any one school or discipline), which guides researchers on matters of data collection (where you can use data of any type, for example, video, images, text, observations, spoken word, etc.) and details strict procedures for data analysis. In a much more 'academic' sounding definition, grounded theory is a research tool which enables one to seek out and conceptualise the latent social patterns and structures of an area of interest through the process of 'constant comparison' (a fancy term describing the 'constant' interpretation and reinterpretation of emerging data in a study with every bit of data collected beforehand). How does the method unfold in practice? The generally accepted methodological stages of grounded theory as constant comparison are:

1. Identify your substantive area – your area of interest. Your study will be about the perspective of one (or more) of the groups of people from the substantive area who will comprise your substantive population – for instance, the participants in two separate football-for-development programmes in Africa.

2. Collect data pertaining to the substantive area/general research question. A grounded theory approach may use qualitative data, quantitative data or a mixture of the two. Thus data types include but are not restricted to:

   - collecting observations of the substantive area itself and activities occurring within the substantive area;
   - accessing public or private records irrespective of form (e.g. photographs, diaries, paintings, sculpture, biographies, television broadcasts, news reports, surveys, government or organisational documents, etc.);
   - conversing with individuals or a group of individuals, face-to-face or remotely (synchronously [e.g. telephone, text chat] or asynchronously [e.g. email]).

3. 'Open code' your data as you collect it in small waves. Open coding and data collection are integrated activities, thus the data collection stage and open coding stage occur simultaneously and continue until the core category is recognised and selected. (Note: there may be more than one potential core category.) Open coding simply means code everything for everything. Eventually the core category and the

main concern become apparent – where the core category explains the behaviour in the substantive area (i.e. it explains how the main concern is resolved or processed).

4. Write 'interpretive memos' throughout the entire process. Memos are theoretical ideas, hunches or spotted interpretations you are making as the data collection process unfolds. They may be very innovative, risky, 'out there' ideas at first. The development of your theory is captured in your memos; few memos = thin theory. Most importantly, theoretical memos are written about codes and their (potential) relationships with other codes.

5. Conduct selective coding and theoretical sampling. Now that the core category and main concern are recognised, open coding stops and selective coding – coding only for the core category and related categories – begins. Further sampling is directed by the developing theory (who do I need to ask to learn more about these issues?) and used to saturate the core category and related categories. When your categories are saturated …

6. Sort your memos and find the theoretical code(s) which best organises your substantive codes.

7. Read the literature and integrate with your theory through selective coding.

8. Write up your theory. Job done!

If you follow the above method – as outlined by Glaser (2001) – you end up with a theory, or at least of set of concepts related to one another in a 'theoretical' manner!

PROBLEMS, PITFALLS AND CONTROVERSIES

Traditional grounded theory is more of an art rather than a science. I know of no template, manual, set of tactical procedures or foolproof steps for conducting grounded theory. There are recommendations, canons and principles but one simply cannot be taught how to code, interpret and generate theory with the requisite degree of creativity needed to flourish in practice. University courses, seminars and workshops abound as means of exposing researchers to the principles of grounded theory, but analytic flair cannot be learned in the classroom. Neophytes to the approach, then, often find the entire procedure vexing and inaccessible as a data collection and analysis technique. Perhaps this alone accounts for the routine use of concept elaboration in qualitative research efforts. Advocates of the grounded theoretical method also have a curious tendency to rarely venture beyond the concept development stage of research. That is to say, qualitative researchers tend to avoid developing formal hypotheses out of 'grounded' research projects. Perhaps the offshoot of a common tendency to disavow or distrust positivistic research in general, grounded theoreticians are reluctant to progress with the methodology to its logical (and instructed) end point. Without advancing general, testable theoretical principles from grounded research, qualitative research runs the inevitable risk of being classified as esoteric, non-generalisable and unreliable.

See also: *Ethnography; Interpretivism; Interviewing.*

KEY READINGS

Charmaz, K. (2006) *Constructing Grounded Theory. A Practical Guide Through Qualitative Analysis.* London: Sage.

Glaser, B. (1992) *Emergence vs. Forcing: Basics of Grounded Theory Analysis.* Mill Valley: Sociology Press.

Glaser, B. (2001) *The Grounded Theory Perspective: Conceptualisation Contrasted with Description.* Mill Valley: Sociology Press.

Glaser, B. and Holton, J. (2007) *The Grounded Theory Seminar Reader.* Mill Valley: Sociology Press.

Glaser, B. and Strauss, A. (1967) *The Discovery of Grounded Theory: Strategies for Qualitative Research.* Chicago: Aldine Publishing.

Morse, J., Stern, P., Corbin, J., Bowers, B. and Clarke, A. (2009) *Developing Grounded Theory: The Second Generation.* Walnut Creek: University of Arizona Press.

Strauss, A. and Corbin, J. (1998) *Basics of Qualitative Research: Grounded Theory Procedures and Techniques.* Newbury Park, CA: Sage.

Hypotheses

The processes of creating and testing hypotheses are the backbone of scientific research. Scientific research commences from a deductive standpoint. We have many, many theories about why bodies work they way they do, why our minds function in particular manners, and about the observable patterns in social structures and cultures across the planet.

Whenever we set out in a research process to test a theory, or component of a theory, to see if it actually predicts and explains the world in the way it states, we will need to construct hypotheses. A working understanding of where hypotheses come from and their centrality in science is crucial for connecting the various stages in the scientific process.

WHAT IS THIS CONCEPT?

I very rarely encourage students to memorise a definition of anything, but the definition of hypotheses is one exception. An hypothesis is a *testable statement of relationship between two or more variables*. Let's take a closer look at the three essential features of an hypothesis: testability, relationship and variables. For the sake of ease, I discuss them in reverse order from how they appear in the definition of an hypothesis. But before we do that, let's consider an actual example of research from sport and exercise science.

Professor of physiology Tim Noakes is sort of a hero of mine. Not only is he a gifted runner, he is also a brilliant academic. I have read his book, *Lore of Running*, countless times. Noakes (2001) is a strong supporter of a theory called the central governor theory. What is the theory all about? It's basically a theory about why endurance athletes fatigue when they do in a race. Scientists and athletes have always thought that your muscles tire because they reach some kind of physical limit. Either they run out of fuel, or they drown in toxic by-products. Nasty stuff, really. In the past few years, Noakes (along with his colleague Alan Gibson) has begun to question the standard theory. They are convinced that athlete fatigue simply is not the same as a car running out of petrol. Fatigue, they argue, is an *emotional response* that begins in your brain. The essence of the 'central governor' theory is that your brain paces your muscles to keep them back from the brink of exhaustion. When the brain decides it's time to quit, it creates the distressing sensations you interpret as muscle fatigue and imminent system shutdown (based on an old physiological theory called 'catastrophe theory'). So, your mind quits before your body, and convinces the body to give up lest it dies! What athletes need to do then, is train their bodies and brains to perceive exertion as less threatening to the system. This will then push them through their current threshold/exhaustion barriers. One method of doing this, based on the theoretical logic of Noakes's (2001) research is interval training. Interval training is a technique where repeated bouts of high-intensity exercise are separated by short to medium length recovery periods. In physiological and cognitive theory regular bouts of interval training teach your system to push through, and be comfortable with, the pain.

Running legend Bart Yasso would agree with Noakes. Yasso developed a training system of interval work for marathon runners. Yasso argued that if marathon runners regularly incorporated sessions of 10 x 800m all-intensity interval sessions into their training regimens, not only would they improve their marathon performance, they would also be able to almost exactly predict their marathon times from work in these sessions! He argued that if you averaged, say 3:18 per 800m in your interval sessions, you could run a 3:18:00 marathon. All of Yasso's method is based on, for all intents and purposes, the theory of the central governor and its relationship to athlete performance. The sessions are intended to push the body through the central governor threshold. This is such an interesting idea to me as a marathon runner. I've used the method on several occasions. Each time, I posted a personal best for the marathon. A coincidence? Perhaps, but we could test it!

Let's illustrate how to write hypotheses using the example above. I wager there is a relationship between interval training and marathon performance. Note right away that I'm not saying a thing about the central governor at all. We will come back to that in a while. I intend to conduct an experiment with novice marathon runners. One group I will train with tempo, long and hill sessions (pretty standard in marathon training), and the other with tempo, long, hill and Yasso 800 interval sessions. My bet, based on Noakes's theory, is that the interval-trained athletes will fare better than the other group. Now, how do I summarise all of this as a testable hypothesis?

Hypotheses can be stated in a number of ways. For example:

- **As a negative relationship between two variables**. *Negative* means the values for the variables included move in opposite directions – as one variable increases the other decreases. In terms of the research on interval training, a negative relationship exists between the amount of interval work during training and finishing time in a marathon: that is, the higher the amount of interval training during one's marathon preparation time, the lower the marathon time. The words *inverse* or *indirect* are also used to describe a negative relationship.
- **In the form of a positive relationship between variables**. *Positive* means the variables move in the same direction – as one increases so does the other (or by contrast, as one goes down, the other goes down as well). The word *direct* is also used to describe a positive

relationship. A positive or direct hypothesis can be expressed in several ways, such as: 'As one's Yasso 800m average time per session decreases, one's rate of perceived exertion at mile 20 in a marathon decreases.' Or you could simply write (but this is not preferred), 'There is a positive (or direct) relationship between Yasso 800m average times in training and rate of perceived exertion in the marathon.'

- **Some group (A) is different from another group (B)**. This form of hypothesis occurs when the purpose of research is to find out if two groups are different with respect to some variable. Generally, however, we can go beyond just saying we expect to find some difference. Usually, a hypothesis specifies the direction of the difference by saying that the variable for one group is larger or smaller than for another group. To illustrate, we could hypothesise that marathon runners who train using Yasso 800 interval sessions have lower marathon times than individuals who do not interval train with the method.

None of the above hypotheses is preferable to the others from a researcher's perspective. However, they are all hypotheses. How? First, hypotheses contain two well-identified variables. Remember that a variable is something that can be changed, such as a characteristic or value. Or, stated differently, it is a 'thing' that can take on different values for people. Every research hypothesis contains two variables, an independent variable and a dependent variable (see the entry on Variables as a reminder). As a quick reminder, the independent variable is assumed to be the one responsible for changes in the dependent variable. In our running example, interval training is the independent variable and marathon time is the dependent variable. Hypotheses express an expected relationship between an independent and dependent variable. As a matter of syntax, think of an hypothesis as a single sentence with three parts:

1. The subject, which generally is the independent variable;
2. A connecting verb, which defines the relationship between the independent and dependent variables;
3. The object, which is the dependent variable.

Try to express any hypothesis you write in the same way – as a single sentence with a subject, a connecting verb and an object. Also, since most hypotheses deal with the actions of groups of persons, plural forms are generally used. In addition, because you want to generalise to empirical conditions as they currently exist, hypotheses are generally expressed in the present tense.

The crux of an hypothesis is the proposed, directional statement (positive or inverse) of relationship between the two variables. Embedded in the statement of directionality is a causal and not just a correlational assertion. An hypothesis is a statement derived from a theory predicting how one variables changes another variable. Finally, an hypothesis must be testable: it cannot be dogma, ideology or faith alone. The variables must be measurable (we have to be able to score interval training and marathon performance in quantifiable, reliable and valid ways) through the use of empirical indicators.

WHY IS THIS RELEVANT TO ME?

The development of research hypotheses needs to be sorted out well before any piece of empirical evidence is gathered, as the form and content of the hypotheses dictate everything about the data collection and interpretation process. Hypotheses rather narrowly prescribe the focus of the data collection process.

In order to state a hypothesis we have to have a sound set of theoretical reasons for saying why we think the hypothesis will be supported by some body of data. I often tell students that hypothesis testing is really theory testing. A study with a shaky theoretical basis does not explain very much to us in the end. A good theory teaches us how and why the two variables are related. It proposes a detailed explanation of a causal relationship by specifying the mechanism of change associated between the two variables. In the world of academic knowledge production, it is not enough to state: 'Interval training seems to improve marathon time, if my data are correct.' We need to be able to tell people, using a blend of physiological and psychological theory what changes in the body and mind result through interval training to produce better marathon times. The data allow us to empirically see (or not) theories in action. Researchers refer to this rationale as the theoretical framework underlying the hypothesis. Without theory, we are simply shooting arrows in the dark at targets we cannot see.

SHOW ME HOW IT'S USED!

As outlined above, a *research hypothesis* is a statement of prediction between two variables. It describes in concrete (rather than theoretical) terms what you expect will happen in your study. Not all studies have hypotheses.

Sometimes a study is designed to be exploratory. There is no formal hypothesis, and perhaps the purpose of the study is to explore some area more thoroughly in order to develop some specific hypothesis or prediction that can be tested in future research. Nevertheless, so far we have covered how to generate research hypotheses. Students and non-quantitative researchers almost always get tripped up when we introduce a different kind of hypothesis into the research mix: the statistical hypothesis.

A statistical hypothesis (test) is a method of making statistical decisions about the results of our research. In statistics, results from a study are said to be 'statistically significant' *if they are unlikely to have occurred by chance alone in our research process*. Say I find in my experiment with a sample of runners that, indeed, there is a huge difference in times between people who have interval trained and those who have not (the latter being far slower). How do I know whether the results were atypical – for instance, caused by a strange sample of people? In research we are interested in whether or not the relationships in my sample could be generalised to the level of the population (say, all marathon runners, everywhere). So, our sample statistics are hopefully very good representatives of the true 'population parameters' (i.e. the actual relationships we would see if we sampled all marathon runners, everywhere). This assumption may or may not be true. The best way to determine whether results are 'statistically true' would be to examine the entire population. Since that is often impractical or impossible, researchers typically examine a sample from the population. To test whether or not the results from the sample are likely to be observed at the level of the population, we engage in statistical hypothesis testing.

Research hypothesis: The statement of relationship between two variables driving your study and/or the statement of expected relationship tested within a sample of people.

Statistical hypotheses testing: A processes in which we test whether or not the observed relationships between variables in our sample are likely to be observed at the level of the population.

Actually, whenever we talk about a statistical hypothesis, we are really thinking simultaneously about *two* hypotheses. Let's say that you predict that there will be a relationship between two variables in your study, like interval training and performance. We conduct the study and observe a relationship. Now, can we trust this relationship from the sample at the level of the population? We need statistical hypotheses. The way we would formally set up the statistical hypothesis test is to formulate *two hypothesis statements*, one that describes your prediction and one that describes all the other possible outcomes with respect to the hypothesised relationship. Your prediction is that variable A and variable B will be related (in statistical hypothesis testing, you don't care whether it's a positive or negative relationship). Then the only other possible outcome would be that variable A and variable B are *not* related. Usually, we call the hypothesis that you support (your prediction) the *alternative* hypothesis, and we call the hypothesis that describes the remaining possible outcomes as the *null* hypothesis. Sometimes we use a notation like H_A to represent the alternative hypothesis or your prediction, and H_0 to represent the null.

If your prediction specifies a direction, we call this a *one-tailed hypothesis*. For instance, a one-tailed test in our running study would be written as follows:

The null hypothesis for this study is:

H_0: There is no relationship between interval training and marathon times.

Which is tested against the alternative hypothesis:

H_A: Interval training produces a significant *decrease* in marathon times.

When your prediction does *not* specify a direction, we say you have a *two-tailed hypothesis*. In this case, you might state the two hypotheses like this:

The null hypothesis for this study is:

H_0: There is no relationship between interval training and marathon times.

Which is tested against the alternative hypothesis:

H_A: There is a statistically significant relationship between interval training and marathon times.

Remember, hypothesis testing is the use of (inferential) statistics to determine the probability that a given null hypothesis is true at the level of the population and *not just* the sample (see the entries on Inferential Statistics, and Populations and Samples). The usual process of statistical hypothesis testing consists of four steps. All of these occur after we have collected the data in our study:

1. Formulate the null hypothesis and the alternative hypothesis;
2. Identify a test statistic (*t-test*, *F-test*, etc.) that can be used to assess the truth of the null hypothesis;
3. Compute the *P*-value (probability value) using a computer program like STATA, R or SPSS, which is the probability that a test statistic at least as significant as the one observed would be obtained assuming that the null hypothesis was true. The smaller the *P*-value, the stronger the evidence against the null hypothesis;
4. Compare the *P*-value to an acceptable significance value (sometimes called an alpha value). If the observed effect is statistically significant, the null hypothesis is ruled out and the alternative hypothesis is accepted.

At the beginning of the research process, it is important for students to understand the generic and specific differences between research and statistical hypothesis. Each is unique and has its own role in the research process: one is essentially oriented towards measurement and data collection, while the other is for statistical analysis.

PROBLEMS, PITFALLS AND CONTROVERSIES

Is a single study ever enough to test a theoretical idea? I could run my little experiment on Yasso 800 interval training, but is this study enough to test the central governor theory? What Noakes and others are proposing is an incredibly complex rendering of how body/mind systems work in a complementary fashion in situated environments to regulate behaviour. No single study could ever test all of its dimensions adequately. When we inspect the theory closely, we realise that even central concepts in the theory, like perceived exertion levels, are difficult to measure at all – the standard use of the Borg RPE scale aside. Therefore, we never fully test many of our theories, but instead test fractions or principles from them. If our research efforts are partial, then our explanations of the world are only ever partial, tentative and probable.

Students also love to speak and think in languages of proof and cause. Maybe this stems from the impact of crime shows like *Law & Order* and *CSI* or medical dramas like *House* where cause and effect are slickly and tidily packaged into 60-minute snippets of contrived life. While hypotheses are built on the pursuit of such lofty concepts as proof and cause, our research results never come close to either. Hypothesis-based research is excellent at revealing tentative relationships, probable associations and supported patterns. These results provide better understandings of if and how our theories operate. But do not be misled by the tone and content of hypotheses! Scientists tend to be a conservative lot, and only until survey or experimental data have been replicated many times does even quasi-confidence in demonstrated empirical relationships develop. I plead with students to remove the word 'proof' from their lexicons, and every year it is a tough task.

See also: *Causality; Experiments; Positivism; Questionnaires; Variables.*

KEY READINGS

Creswell, J. (2008) *Research Design: Qualitative, Quantitative and Mixed Methods Approaches*. Thousand Oaks, CA: Sage.

Neutens, J. and Rubinson, L. (2010) *Research Techniques for the Health Sciences*. Toronto: Pearson.

Noakes, T. (2001) *Lore of Running*. Champaign: Human Kinetics.

Inferential Statistics

Lab researchers in sport and exercise sciences never proclaim to me, 'Mike, I want to do a study of people that has absolutely no value outside of this lab.' The exercise physiologists, motor skills specialists, and behaviouralists I know hope that their small studies might have a large impact. Scientific research is predicated on the need for theory-based hypothesis testing with applicability of findings (hopefully) beyond the confines of the lab. But ensuring that sample data have meaning beyond the limitations of one study is not the easiest of tasks in all cases. There are, however, designed-based ways of shoring up the external generalisability of scientific research, and statistical ways of testing whether or not one's sample data are indicating something about the 'big picture' to researchers. In this entry, we will focus on the latter.

WHAT IS THIS CONCEPT?

Quantitative researchers seek to make meaningful, reliable and generalisable conclusions about their hypotheses from observed data. To do this, they require a set of statistical techniques to give us a sense of what is 'going on' in the data with respect to the research hypotheses, and how likely or probable it is that any observed patterns in the sample data exist in the same magnitude at the level of the population. Again, though, why? Simply because in practically all of our research efforts, it is impossible to study every member of a 'population' for whom our hypotheses are relevant. Therefore, we gather a sample from the big population and test our hypotheses. I have to know whether or not the statistical data in my sample (our sample *estimates*) well represent what is going on at the level of the population (our true population *parameters*). How reasonable would my study of health and wellness of university students be if the sample (of 100 students on my campus) data illustrated that their average weight was 40kg? Does this seem reasonable? Do you think this would be an unbiased estimate of the true population? (The average adult weight, I might add, in Canada and the United States is roughly 68–70kg.)

If our sample values are estimates of the true population parameters, then we can never be 100% confident that the values we produce in our studies are truly perfect representations of reality. Therefore, the hypotheses we test via sample data are only partially tested and we can never be entirely confident that we have definitely proven or entirely discounted anything in a single study alone. Consider this example. I am interested in the relationship between the Faculty a student is enrolled in at the University of Toronto and their health behaviours (specifically, how many cigarettes they smoke per week). I hypothesise (a basic one, I realise!) that the higher the average anxiety score in the Faculty, the higher the rates of smoking we will observe. Between 2009 and 2010, there were roughly 47,000 full-time undergraduate students in the university. If I wanted to devote the next decade of my life to the study, try to find a multi-million-dollar grant for operating expenses, and employ two or three dozen researchers in the process, I could theoretically send out a health survey to every undergraduate. This never happens, however, and so I would determine a method for randomly sampling perhaps 1,000 students (in total) cutting across the 13 faculties and would ask them to fill in an online survey. Magically, all of the 1,000 students fill in the online survey, and so I have my data regarding their levels of anxiety and smoking habits. Hooray! Informed hypothesis testing time, right? Well, here is the proverbial kicker, as they say. How do I know those 1,000 students will represent the range of student anxieties experienced across the Faculties and the range of smoking habits amongst the students? What if, by total chance alone, I managed to sample all of the non-smokers or those who only smoked every once in a while? Or, what if I managed to sample the most extremely mellow or highly stressed and anxious students in the university?

WHY IS THIS RELEVANT TO ME?

The use of inferential statistics is a cornerstone of research on populations because it is difficult, and sometimes impossible, to survey or experiment on every member of a population or to observe every empirical piece of data required to make definitive, conclusive statements about our hypotheses. Instead, researchers attempt to get a representative sample and use that as a basis for their claims. A number of things can go wrong in the process of quantitative research and hypothesis testing, such as sampling error. For this reason, researchers tend to be very careful about how inferential statistics are used, and they take care to test their data and survey sample to confirm that the information is accurate. The goal is to demonstrate that an observed difference between groups in a sample (say observed differences between one's Faculty membership and smoking habits) is not a simple fluke of the data or the peculiarities of the researcher's study design.

SHOW ME HOW IT'S USED!

There is a massive amount of statistical theory and mathematical 'proof' underpinning inferential statistics … far too much in fact for this book. A good course or text in statistical analysis will systematically outline these theories and principles. But not all is lost, because the steps in performing inferential statistical analysis are general enough to gain a preliminary understanding of what is involved in determining whether empirical relationships observed in a sample are likely to be representative of trends at the level of the population. The steps in inferential statistic testing are as follows.

Step 1 – State the statistical hypotheses: This is where much confusion arises in inferential statistics. Statistical hypotheses are not the same, exactly, as the hypotheses informing the research process. These hypotheses are statements predicting whether or not any observed differences in our sample (around the variables under analysis) are probably observable or 'true' at the population level or have been produced in our sample by chance alone. There are two statistical hypotheses to state at the beginning of a test:

- *The 'null hypothesis'* (H_0): A statement predicting no relationship between the variables (any difference observed in the sample data is due to error sampling chance alone);
- *The 'alternative hypothesis'* (H_A): A statement predicting there is a significant relationship between the variables in our study (any observed differences between groups in the study – like undergraduate students from different Faculties – on an outcome variable like smoking habits is likely or probably representative of the true population relationships).

Step 2 – Set the level of 'significance': We often refer to the significance value as the probability value (p) or level of confidence in a study. To determine whether or not, statistically speaking, sample results are 'flukey' or produced by chance alone in our study, quantitative researchers set critical numeric benchmarks for 'how much' chance can be tolerated – called the level of significance. Quantitative researchers ask a computer program like SPSS or STATA to tell us how many times out of 100 the data/relationships we have observed in the study/sample would be produced by chance alone – that is, if we drew 100 similar samples from the population how likely it is that similar results would be observed. Convention has established that we need to believe that in at least 95 times out of 100 we would see similar results to our sample. So, that means if there is a greater than 5% chance that our results are atypical, SPSS or STATA can tell us that immediately, and thus the sample data are poor estimates of the true population parameters. How do we read this on a statistical chart or table? If the critical *p-value* (please do not get confused, but convention is to call this the *'alpha value'* as well) falls below 0.05 (meaning that there is less than a 5% chance these data are 'rare' at the level of the population – or stated another way, that I am 95% confident that the sample values represent the true population parameters), then the results are said to be 'statistically significant'.

Step 3 – Compute the test statistic: Depending on the type of hypothesis one is testing, the levels of measurement of the variables, and the statistical model for the variable relationships being explored, one or another test of difference or relationship is involved. Most of the major inferential test statistics come from a general family of statistical models known as the 'General Linear Model' (GLM). This includes the t-test, Analysis of Variance (ANOVA), Analysis of Covariance (ANCOVA), regression analysis, and many of the multivariate methods like factor analysis, multi-dimensional scaling, cluster analysis, discriminant function analysis, and others. Given the importance of the General Linear Model, it's a good idea for aspiring quantitative researchers to become familiar with its workings. These tests allow researchers to examine the strength and direction of relationship between two variables, and to examine whether or not observed differences in their sample distributions are meaningful (in our example, are there actual and meaningful 'linear' differences between how you score on your Faculty of enrolment and how much you smoke?).

Step 4 – Examine the computed 'significance value': After running the appropriate statistical test of inference in Step 3 above, examine the computed significance value the computer program provides for the test. Every inferential statistical test of relationship or difference (such as a t-test or ANOVA) provides us with a significance value in a table of results. It is the program's assessment (given sample size and standard deviation observed in the sample – or, the estimate of sampling error in the study) of how likely these data are produced by chance alone. Again, the reading of this value is straightforward. If the computed value is lower than the level of significance we set as reasonable in Step 2, then we would say the results are likely not due to chance alone.

Step 5 – Conclusions: Using the results from Step 4, make a conclusion as to whether or not we are able to reject the null hypothesis and accept the alternative hypothesis. If the results of our observations are deemed to be statistically significant then we fail to accept the null hypothesis and must accept the alternative hypothesis.

PROBLEMS, PITFALLS AND CONTROVERSIES

The establishment of 95% as the gold standard of significance values (alpha levels) is absolutely arbitrary. People sometimes think that the 95% level is sacred when looking at significance levels. But if a test shows a .06 probability that there is an observed relationship between smoking and Faculty-based anxiety, it means that it has a 94% chance of being true at the level of the population! You can't be quite as sure about it as if it had a 95% chance of being true, but the odds still are that it is true! The 95% level comes from *subjective* researcher convention and reproduction in academic publications, where a theory usually has to have at least a 95% chance of being true to be considered worth telling people about. Elsewhere in the world if something has a 90%, 80% or 70% chance of being true, it can't be considered proven as a fact, but it is probably better to act as if it were true rather than false.

Second, any non-randomness in the sampling procedure casts significant doubts on the representativeness of the data. If the population is poorly defined, if there are no accurate or inclusive sampling frames from which to draw samples, or there are systematic biases or flaws in the sampling procedure (and thus sampling becomes a non-probability exercise), then high degrees of sampling error will exist in the study. Statistical 'power' analyses alone (i.e. that instruct researchers as to how many people should be included in a study in order to make meaningful claims) do not correct for poorly defined populations or systemic problems related to who is selected for inclusion. Third, and finally, there are real differences between statistical significance and substantive meaning. In normal language, when something is described as significant it is important or widely relevant (declining rates of participation in school sport, world hunger, or the rise in cardiovascular disease is significant). In statistics significant means probably true and not due to (sampling) chance. A research finding, by definition, may be very true without being important at all. When statisticians say a result is 'highly significant' they mean it is very probably true in a numeric sense. They do not (necessarily) mean it is highly important.

See also: Descriptive Statistics; Hypotheses; Reliability; Variables: Validity.

KEY READINGS

Fallowfield, J. (2005) *Statistics in Sport and Exercise Science*. Chichester: Lotus Publishing.

Field, A. (2009) *Discovering Statistics Using SPSS*. London: Sage.

Newell, J., Aitchison, T. and Grant, S. (2010) *Statistics for Sports & Exercise Science: A Practical Approach*. Toronto: Pearson Education.

Thomas, J. and Nelson, J. (2001) *Research Methods in Physical Activity*. Champaign: Human Kinetics.

Williams, C. and Wagg, C. (2003) *Data Analysis and Research for Sport and Exercise Science: A Student Guide*. London: Routledge.

inferential statistics

Interdisciplinary Research

Departments or Faculties called Sport and Exercise Sciences, Physical Education and Health, Kinesiology, Movement Sciences, Human Kinetics, Public Health or Epidemiology all have one thing in common; they are diverse academic spaces with members from disciplines such as physiology, sociology, psychology, economics, biology, ergonomics, political science, women's studies, biomechanics, pedagogy, and others. Undergraduate and graduate degrees offered in these schools are varied and specialised but tend to emphasise multi-disciplinary learning. Bodies, health and physical activity are taught as complex subjects requiring study from a range of perspectives and methods. The ostensible ethos in the majority of our Departments and Faculties thus places emphasis on learning about health/exercise/sport from 'cell to society'. Any 'problem' we study, such as performance enhancement, motivation to exercise, illness prevention, social integration through play, has bio-physical, cognitive and behavioural, socio-cultural and historical elements worthy of study. The structuring and performance of rounded learning about the body/health is part of a trend toward interdisciplinarity in the contemporary university.

WHAT IS THIS CONCEPT?

Interdisciplinary research involves the interaction among two or more different disciplines, and is said to occur at the 'interface' between disciplines. This may range from the sharing of ideas between colleagues with different academic specialisations and backgrounds to the full integration of different disciplinary concepts, methodology, procedures, theory, terminology, data, and the organisation of research and training within single research projects. Interdisciplinary research draws on knowledge from different disciplines, but stays within the boundary of one primary field. Health research, for example, traditionally has been organised much like a series of cottage industries, lumping researchers into speciality areas, where their efforts remain disconnected from the greater whole by artificial barriers constructed by technical and language differences between different disciplines and departmentally based specialities. But, as science has advanced over the past decade, two fundamental themes are apparent: the study of human biology and behaviour is a wonderfully dynamic process, and the traditional divisions within health research may in some instances impede the pace of scientific discovery. The broad goal in interdisciplinary research groups is to change academic research culture. Not an easy task! While very traditional academic departments and specialisations continue to thrive in universities and colleges, there has been a rise in the value of the concept and practice of interdisciplinary research and teaching and a growth in the number of bachelors degrees awarded. In the United States alone, the number of interdisciplinary bachelors degrees awarded annually rose from 7,000 in 1973 to 33,000 a year by 2008, according to data from the National Center of Educational Statistics.

WHY IS THIS RELEVANT TO ME?

HIV/AIDS is a disease knowing no borders, barriers or limitations. It does not discriminate, it does not care about one's cultural background, and it is insensitive to race, gender or one's sexual identity. For more than four decades, pathologists and immunologists have conducted thousands of clinical studies of HIV/AIDS and its transmission, and scientists have made important, life-saving discoveries in the battle against the disease. Research on the aetiology of illness and its impact on public health is critical. But knowing HIV/AIDS demands that we understand more than the condition as a biological disease. Recommendations for the prevention of HIV/AIDS, for example, are largely based on medical understandings of transmission, but not on the cultural contexts of risk that expose people to the virus in the first place. To effectively combat an illness we need to understand its dimensions 'in the round'; to uncloak how the illness attacks the body, how social and cultural contexts place people at bio-risk, and how living with HIV/AIDS impacts one's overall sense of biological, psychological and social wellness. To effectively problem-solve, university and college researchers are increasingly voicing the opinion that unless we pool knowledge about problem-solving on a given subject, we will never totally solve our problems.

interdisciplinary research

113

SHOW ME HOW IT'S USED!

I am fascinated by Developmental Coordination Disorder (DCD) and its effects on youth. DCD is a motor skills disorder that affects roughly 5–6%

of all school-aged children in countries like Canada. DCD occurs when a delay in the development of motor skills, or difficulty coordinating movements, results in a child being unable to perform common, everyday tasks. What is especially intriguing about the condition is that children with DCD do not have an identifiable medical or neurological condition that explains their coordination problems. Frequently described as clumsy or awkward by their parents and teachers, children with DCD have difficulty mastering simple activities, such as tying shoes or going down stairs, and are unable to perform age-appropriate academic and self-care tasks. Children with DCD usually have normal or above average intellectual abilities but their motor coordination difficulties may impact their academic progress, social integration and emotional development. DCD is commonly associated with other developmental conditions, including attention deficit hyperactivity disorder (ADHD), learning disabilities (LD), speech-language delays and emotional and behavioural problems. I am interested in DCD because of the effects the condition has on children within the context of physical education and sport. Children suffering from DCD tend to develop aversions to gym class, avoid the playground and organised sport because each context reveals them as different from others. So, there are clearly biological issues to be studied and understood with respect to DCD, psychological components to the illness, and socio-cultural dimensions to how it is experienced.

DCD is a subject begging for interdisciplinary research. There is no way one discipline alone is equipped with the theories and methods required to completely understand the dimensions and implications of the disorder. Take, for instance, the basic research question, 'What is the impact of DCD on affected children's involvement in scholastic physical education?' Given my personal disciplinary expertise, I have the knowledge required to address socio-cultural aspects of the disorder for children but not knowledge of motor skill disorders themselves, therapy interventions, or the psychological and behavioural aspects of the condition – each of which is crucial for figuring out how to help children at school who become terrified of physical education. One strategy would be to assemble an *interdisciplinary team* to address the subject. Interdisciplinary teams are comprised of researchers from two or more different disciplinary areas, who work together on a project in order to examine it from a range of 'knowledge angles'. The separate researchers would work under the same umbrella project, and either examine the subject together on one focused project (the true spirit of interdisciplinary research) or might work 'alone together' – conducting their own individual sub-studies of the subject. Imagine the team I assemble to study DCD is comprised of a psychologist, a motor skills specialist, and a physical culture specialist (me). We set out to investigate what might be accomplished in elementary school physical education pedagogy to provide children with DCD with a more inclusive space to learn and develop physical literacy. The motor skills specialist might propose and experiment with new forms of physical education games and movement catering to DCD children; the psychologist might survey children with DCD to measure how the intervention affects their sense of self; and the physical culture specialist might observe and interview the children to determine what else the children would like to see with regard to new policy and intervention in physical education. Three separate backgrounds, three separate methods, three complementary sets of data to answer the research question.

Another entirely different way of pursuing interdisciplinarity is through making connections with researchers at interdisciplinary centres (IDCs). A single university will organise and house an interdisciplinary centre on a subject of concern (such as movement disorders or physical education policy) and encourage or invite researchers from around the world working within that area to connect through the centre, share research findings, attend sponsored conferences, or publish in a journal together as a means of stimulating interdisciplinary thought. IDCs are knowledge centres within universities that serve as key beacons or reference points for anyone interested in knowing more about the subject.

PROBLEMS, PITFALLS AND CONTROVERSIES

The notion of interdisciplinary research sounds wonderful in theory and paints a portrait of research in the contemporary university as one of unproblematic collegial exchange. But the idea of interdisciplinary research is something with centuries-old roots in both philosophy and 'academic' thought. Why has it taken so long for interdisciplinarity to find a permanent role and place within universities and colleges, and what are some of the enduring barriers to interdisciplinary research? Interdisciplinary work is encouraged and supported by major grant councils, governmental departments and private organisations in North America and Europe. There is already sufficient financial incentive to build interdisciplinary teams to study physical activity and health topics. But financial incentive alone is not enough to change the culture of 'silo research'. Teams can be rather easily assembled on the pages of a grant application to make a project appear interdisciplinary, but the research team may never actually conduct research together, exchange ideas, or produce a truly interdisciplinary set of conclusions about the subject of interest. The grant application may be, then, nothing more than a strategy for several researchers working within a similar area (like DCD) to procure funding for their own research interests and projects.

See also: Translation; Triangulation.

KEY READINGS

Klein, J. (1990) *Interdisciplinarity: History, Theory and Practice*. Detroit: Wayne State University Press.
Lattuca, L. (2001) *Creating Interdisciplinarity*. Nashville: Vanderbilt University Press.
Metzger, N. and Zare, R. (1999) 'Interdisciplinary research: From belief to reality'. *Science* 29: 642–643.

Interpretivism

To students in human movement studies, health sciences, kinesiology or physical education, the concept of interpretivism can be foreign and wildly confusing. At least 75–80% of our undergraduate students in sport, exercise and health studies come to methods class possessing minds brimming with the idea that science = research = true knowledge. The notion and practice of interpretivism in research challenges such an assumption at its very roots. Interpretivism champions a divergent way of knowing and understanding the realities of human movement, and as an overall paradigm in the academy, destabilises the sentiment that science is always the best approach for asking and answering important questions.

WHAT IS THIS CONCEPT?

The precise nature of interpretivism, like all of our concepts, is debated by researchers but can be classified as a major paradigm. A paradigm is a set of views and related practices that serves to organise how one sees and understands the world. Paradigms provide guide maps for how we think and correspondingly act based on those perspectives. In academies, paradigms direct us to choose subjects as worthy of investigation, structure particular questions about those subjects, interpret findings from research, and determine how we speak about our results. Interpretivism has its roots in the social sciences and humanities, and is most often associated with German sociological traditions of the late nineteenth and early twentieth centuries. Key figures, including, Max Weber, Georg Simmel, Wilhelm Dilthey, Ludwig Wittgenstein, Alfred Schutz, and American behaviouralist researchers including George Herbert Mead and Herbert Blumer, championed the interpretivist message. Interpretivism emerged as an alternative to traditional understandings of science, based on the positivism paradigm. As such, interpretivism is regularly called an anti-positivism paradigm.

Okay, so what does the term interpretivism mean, and what is the nature of the paradigm? Let's refer to interpretivism as the study of the meaning of human (inter)action. Now, do not think about 'meaning' as a grand, cosmic or transcendental thing at all! Interpretivists are interested in understanding how people define, interpret and act upon individual, small group or bigger collective definitions of what 'things' mean in the here and now of everyday life. Interpretivism as a perspective is predicated on the ontological assumption that reality is a messy, complicated matter. Human beings do not merely encounter a world of objective truth or reality (and neither is this objective, law-like reality 'out there' waiting for researchers to discover it), but by contrast people actively construct and then act upon the realities they assign to events, thoughts, actions, processes, bodies, places, ideologies, spaces and conditions in the world. The interpretivist perspective on the nature of reality, and the need to understand how human beings make reality, is well captured by W.I. Thomas's theorem: 'If men define situations as real, they are real in their consequences.' A game or form of social interaction is only sport because we call it that, and act towards it regularly as if it is a sport. The reality of the social to an interpretivist is only such because we say so, and others confirm the statement.

In sum, then, interpretivism is a paradigm that provides an organised set of assumptions about the nature of reality and how to study that reality through empirical methods. It focuses on how people make sense of the world around them, and over the course of time how collective definitions of reality shape and direct human thought and behaviour.

interpretivism

WHY IS THIS RELEVANT TO ME?

There are many questions a person could ask regarding the nature of sport, physical activity and health from interpretivist orientations. Indeed, many research questions or subjects of interest are not necessarily suited to traditional scientific modes of thinking or methods of inquiry. Interpretivists stress that since so much of our daily lives is rooted in the subjective rather than objective perception or experience of reality, there is good cause to examine the processes of reality definition and experience. If humans accumulate knowledge in a range of ways, then so should researchers. Interpretivist approaches to the study of life are most likely relevant to researchers interested in questions pertaining to the nature of how human subjectivities organise our thoughts and actions. If I set a course of study designed to investigate the best healing strategies following a ligament tear in the lower leg, I probably would not pursue interpretivism as a guiding framework. But if I wanted to know how athletes construct pain and injury, and if, for example, they valorise abilities to play through pain as markers of distinction, personal accomplishment or dedication in sport worlds, then interpretivism might be the way forward! Each approach provides critical information on the problem of pain and injury in sport.

SHOW ME HOW IT'S USED!

Kevin Young, Phil White and Bill McTeer (1994) conducted a study of how athletes come to talk about pain in and around sports settings. Through interviews with elite athletes, they examined the patterns in athletes' descriptions of pain and injury experiences, and how both men and women athletes tend to frame pain in a range of ways – which Young, White and McTeer refer to as 'body talk'. For instance, athletes may come to depersonalise pain as a way of distancing their sense of self from the injury, reframe it as proof one's masculinity or describe how pain is unwelcome as a dangerous signifier of weakness in a physical cultural setting that associates strength with character. At the basis of their study is an interpretivist position emphasising the need to understand how pain is defined as 'real'. Studies of pain and injury focusing on the ways in which athletes make sense out of pain and injury through interpretive perspectives or worldviews shared in sports settings, teaches us a great deal about the importance of subjectivity in everyday life. By asking athletes how they describe the relevance of pain and injury, and what it is like for them to be injured as an athlete in a sports culture, researchers gain insight into a great deal of risk-taking in sports. We also learn how athletes make sense out of injury, how athletes develop common or unique strategies to deal with pain, and we learn about the need to develop better policies to protect athletes from feeling the need to play while seriously injured.

Among the most personally influential books I have read since my early days as an undergraduate student was Arthur Frank's (1994), *The Wounded Storyteller*. The very same year Young, White and McTeer published their research on athletes' constructions of injuries, my friend Art Frank published one of the most poignant analyses of how people learn to manage illness through the act of storytelling. Frank's book draws attention to how illness is traumatic not only because it invades the physical body, but also because it radically restructures the nature of one's social identity and subjective sense of self. Through qualitative fieldwork with patients and reflection on his own illness processes, Art weaves together a subjective account of how people learn to manage illness, in part by narrating it as storytellers – taking back a portion of control in the illness process in the act of offering different claims (i.e. other than medical) about what it is like to be ill. Art's research is significant beyond academic circles, and has challenged more than our theoretical notions of illness as a 'real' thing. His work has inspired people living with illness to publicly speak about disease as a way of combating stigmas about illness. It has also changed policy and practice in hospitals with respect to the treatment of patients and driven a need to examine the bioethics of contemporary care practices. All of his research commences from a paradigmatic emphasis on the need to learn about the world, and to potentially effect change, by first examining how life is experienced and understood in a range of ways.

PROBLEMS, PITFALLS AND CONTROVERSIES

Well, there are many debates about the role and purpose of interpretivism in sport, physical activity and health research. Among the first problems students encounter with the notion of interpretivism is that the paradigm is so broad in sport, exercise and health studies that its essence is difficult to comprehend. For example, theory and methods textbooks regularly fail to cite the difference between interpretivism in general and the theories influenced by interpretivism, including symbolic interactionism, dramaturgy, critical race theories, queer theories, feminist theories, (new) media theories, post-colonial theories, post-structuralist theories, (neo)Marxist and other political economic theories, existentialist theories, actor-network theories, critical pedagogy theories, identity crisis theories, theories of intersectionality, globalisation and cultural fragmentation theories, risk theories, new social movement theories, environmentalist theories, victimologies, postmodern theories, figurational theory, theories of consumption, and a swathe of theories loosely collated as cultural studies.

Questions concerning the generalisability of research on the essentially subjective nature of life are at the forefront of such criticism. If interpretivist inspired research attends to subjectivity and the ways in which people commonly define 'things' as real (what we call the process of achieving *inter-subjectivity*), then ultimately one set of findings in an interpretivist study may be relative only to that group. If we interviewed 25 children in a PE class about their social constructions of 'fatness', for example, there is no guarantee we will produce similar subjective understandings of fatness in other classes. So, then, what is the use of the case-specific data? Even more problematic is that if I went back and re-interviewed the children a month, six months or a year later, their understandings of the reality of fatness might have changed considerably. The hyper-subjectivism and emphasis on the locally constructed nature of reality in interpretivist research is off-putting for researchers committed to the discovery of objective, standard and generalisable patterns across time and space. Interpretivists may fuel these criticisms further by failing to articulate the importance of understanding the relevance of multiple subjectivities in the practice of everyday life, or by ignoring the role of translating important ideas gleaned from research efforts into public practice.

See also: Critical Theory; Ethnography; Interviewing; Media Analysis; Ontology.

KEY READINGS

Frank, A. (1994) *The Wounded Storyteller: Body, Illness and Ethics*. Chicago: University of Chicago Press.

Guba, E. and Lincoln, Y. (1994) 'Competing paradigms in qualitative research'. In N. Denzin and Y. Lincoln, *Handbook of Qualitative Research* (pp. 105–117). Thousand Oaks, CA: Sage.

Prus, R. (1996) *Symbolic Interaction and Ethnographic Research: Intersubjectivity and the Study of Human Lived Experience*. Albany: SUNY Press.

Willis, J. (2007) *Foundations of Qualitative Research: Interpretive and Qualitative Approaches*. London: Sage.

Young, K., White, P. and McTeer, W. (1994) 'Body talk: male athletes reflect on sport, injury, and pain'. *Sociology of Sport Journal*, 11: 175–195.

Zammito, J. (2004) *A Nice Derangement of Epistemes: Post-Positivism in the Study of Science from Quine to Latour*. Chicago: University of Chicago Press.

Interviewing

Qualitative researchers of sport, exercise and health prefer interviewing methods to any other interpretivist technique of data collection. Without question, interviewing is the methodological *lingua franca* for researchers who are qualitatively oriented. Today, there are many different interviewing techniques, styles and approaches. Thus, there is no standard definition of, or set of procedural templates guiding, the interviewing process. Further still, while methodologists often describe how a proto-typical interviewing process should unfold, the lived practice of research instructs differently. Researchers spend their entire careers becoming experts in specific styles of interviewing, and use the techniques fluidly and creatively to answer a full range of research into socio-cultural or social psychological questions about sport, physical activity and health. There is an old adage in research methods classes that interviewing is more of an art than a science, and this is certainly true.

WHAT IS THIS CONCEPT?

Interviewing is a method predicated on a few important beliefs and perspectives. First, interviewers feel that knowledge about the world is gained by asking people about how they view, experience and see the world. Quite simply, how could we ever believe people experience pain and injury in sport in precisely the same ways? Interviewing is a technique informed by German philosopher Wilhelm Dilthey and German sociologist Max Weber's notion of *verstehen* (roughly translated from German as 'meaningful or sympathetic understanding'), and the social science tradition of interpretivism. Basically, these schools of thought argue that to understand others' behaviours, researchers need to see the world from people's varied points of view. This idea has been recently discovered by psychologists of sport who have developed a method of interviewing called 'interpretive phenomenological analysis' (Smith, 2007). The reality of pain and injury in sport is, for example, not fixed or immutable, as it is subject to situated personal and group interpretation. To know how to encourage safe play among athletes, I first need to know how people in an athletic culture interpret pain and injury differently and commonly. Interviewers, then, do not understand human behaviour in a standard way, structured by biological, psychological or social forces, but rather argue that it unfolds and is understood relatively by people. This is a huge assumption and it underpins the logic of all interviewing-based studies!

Second, and based on the above, interviews are most appropriately used as a technique of data collection when researchers require knowledge of how human beings assign meaning to their thoughts and actions within cultural contexts. If I wanted to know the best mechanisms for treating a broken femur, I would not interview athletes. If I wanted to know about the role of neuropeptides in the healing processes, interviewing is out of the question. But if I want to know what it is like to be pressured by a coach to play through pain and how particular sports cultures might demand athletes to 'suck it up' and take risks, I would want to talk to many athletes. Why? Because they could teach me (provide first-hand knowledge) about the lived experiences of injury, how it is defined by people in their sports culture, the norms of play dictating how pain is to be defined, and what social influences help shape an athlete's mindset when they play through pain and injury. In brief, I need to see injury and pain in all the ways athletes do; would programmes and policies designed to improve conditions of safe play start out from any better point of departure?

Third, and finally, students often ask how and why interviewing is more appropriate in a given study than face-to-face surveys. One simple word will suffice: standardisation. Consider the research topic, 'Athletes with low self-efficacy will play through injury more than athletes with high self-efficacy scores.' By contrast, consider the following question: 'Does one's sense of self as an athlete play a role in the sports injury process?' In the first instance, I would survey: we need to measure efficacy levels in athletes and their 'playing through injury' behaviours. In the second case, I would interview athletes. I need to explore, or discover, what playing through injury means to them as athletes with different identities and perspectives on who they are as athletes. Surveys, in practically all of their manifestations, are built upon the principles of respondent similarity rather than difference. Questions are by and large standardised through surveying (that is, everyone is asked the same question in the same manner) to generate comparable, quantifiable data across the participant sample in the effort of testing tightly defined hypotheses. The interviewing process is, as described by Glaser and Strauss (1967), oriented towards maximising potential difference and variability in respondents' answers. Stated in another way, survey researchers normally speak *to* respondents, asking them to provide answers within narrowly defined parameters. Interviews seek to speak *with* subjects in order to generate a wide and deep knowledge base about their topic.

WHY IS THIS RELEVANT TO ME?

Interviewing is by design an open method of data collection. We routinely call interviews 'guided conversations', directed by an ostensible research topic at hand but flexible like a run of the mill conversation between two people – yet with a slight twist. Most of our interviews take the form of a conversation, ranging from 30 minutes to several hours, about a series of topics germane to a research question. An interview-based research project is best employed when a researcher wishes to gather a large amount of biographical, experiential or attitudinal information on a relatively small group of respondents. Respondents are identified from a non-probability sampling pool, usually because they have been identified as having special, typical, or particularly relevant knowledge about the subject at hand. Snowball sampling, convenience sampling and theoretical/purposive sampling are regularly employed.

Defining the type of and approaches to interviewing is a bit of a challenge, but methodologists tend to assign interviewing approaches to one of seven categories:

- **Structured, face-to-face interview**: A structured interview is one in which the researcher asks respondents to answer a series of standardised questions. In truth, I am always a bit puzzled as to why we include structured interviews in discussions of the technique, because these are essentially mock-surveys.
- **Semi-structured, face-to-face interview**: The semi-structured interview is the gold standard. Essentially, the researcher comes to the interview with a list of 10–30 questions to be covered (called an 'interview schedule') in one manner or another during the conversation. I tell students that the interview schedule is like a prop or a prompting sheet, reminding us what we would like to ask the respondent in general, but it is not a script! The interviewer and respondent dialogue back and forth, with the researcher picking up on and asking for elaboration regarding new, exciting, important, ambiguous or conceptually intriguing information that emerges during the conversation.

interviewing

- **Open, face-to-face interview**: The exciting, wild west of interviewing approaches. An interviewer has only a brief list of topics to be included in the discussion, and approaches the exchange like a brainstorming session rather than a led conversation. Here, the goal is to remove research bias from the interview (that is, interview schedules always tend to reflect what the researcher thinks about the subject already!). Unless you have a lot of experience in doing interviews and feel comfortable in the process, this approach should probably be avoided.
- **Life history interview**: The life history interview is a blend of semi-structured and open interviewing. These interviews are highly detailed explorations of people's biographies. In many cases, researchers might interview a subject on several occasions in order to draw on and further explore themes and events emerging from previous interviews.
- **Collaborative interviewing**: A rather recent development within the social sciences, collaborative interviewing grew in popularity quite rapidly following Gubrium and Holstein's (1997) call for more participatory forms of interviewing. A collaborative or 'active' interview is one in which the researcher encourages the interviewee to co-direct the interview, and in which the researcher's interpretations of emerging data are openly discussed in the interview context. The goal is to stimulate creative and open dialogue between the interviewer and interviewee in an effort to tease out the many ways a person might make sense of the subject at hand.
- **Focus groups**: Born out of ethnomethodology and conversation analysis, focus group interviewing is a situation in which several participants (normally 6–12) are interviewed together, at one time. Focus groups are a strategic and efficient way of gathering a mass of data, and are especially relevant when a researcher wishes to witness how people speak about and culturally negotiate a subject of interest (just imagine getting a group of young men together to speak about sexism in sport – the answers you might hear from men in private could differ considerably from how they answer in public in front of their peers!). A specialist form of focus group interviewing is 'collective memory work' (Haug, 1999), wherein subjects co-operatively discuss past experiences (like pain and injury in sport as a youth) in order to make sense of them.
- **Computer mediated interviews**: Forms of instant communication online have partially changed the terrain of interviewing. For research participants who are difficult to reach spatially, or who have busy schedules, interviewing them over time through posted weblogs, instant messaging

and other forms of virtual interface is common. Additionally, many young people are more comfortable communicating via the Internet (as it is so common for them within their peer groups), and people with either learning or communicative disabilities might be far more comfortable with online interviewing at their own pace.

In all the cases above (perhaps with the exception of structured interviewing), the aim of the interviewing process is to gain a preliminary empirical understanding of the topic you are researching, to potentially break new ground in a subject area or take a research topic in a new direction.

SHOW ME HOW IT'S USED!

At the beginning of this chapter I alluded to the difference between a textbook definition of interviewing and how interviews are engaged in practice. There is nothing like conducting your first set of interviews in your first qualitative research project. It is amazing how different and unpredictable the interview process is 'in the flesh' than as routinely described in textbooks. Anyone can ask a question; really, honestly, anyone can do it. The tricky part is asking questions as a researcher, and knowing how and why you will use the data you gather from respondents. It might be relatively straightforward to design an interview, but its application is another matter entirely. Trust my claim (or test it for yourself with a review of the literature) that there are three main applications of the interview method. One is the so-called ideal type, and the other two dominate in actual practice.

- **Concept development or grounded theory**: If I could exorcise one concept or idea from our interviewing canon, it would be grounded theory. As developed by Glaser and Strauss (1967), and elaborated by Charmaz (2006), grounded theory is like the Holy Grail of the interviewing process. This application of interviewing methodology is a classic analytic-inductive approach to knowledge gathering and theory development, where the data collected through interviewing are used to develop *sui generis* theories. In its traditional manifestation, the grounded analysis of interview data is a concept and theory-building process emerging from a programme of knowledge collection not fuelled or directed by preconceived theoretical ideas. Such emergent theoretical understandings are then to be used in developing general, testable propositions and hypotheses about human behaviour.

An impossible practice, to say the least. Grounded theory is now, more or less, used as a conflated buzzword among sport, exercise and health researchers referring to a process of open coding or reflexive analysis. Translation: it is a lazy term for an interpretive reading of interview data. A review of literature claiming to be informed by a grounded theoretical approach will reveal few, if any, new theoretical or conceptual ideas emerging from the research process; or, for that matter, developed, testable hypotheses generated from an inductive approach to data analysis. Most people claiming a grounded theoretical approach to the interviewing process are actually practising concept elaboration.

- **Concept elaboration**: This is the garden-variety application of the interviewing method, and partly represents what Anselm Strauss envisioned as the role of qualitative analysis through interviewing. All researchers have conceptual ideas in their heads when planning a research process, implementing a method of data collection and then analysing the data. Let's be honest, we have them! I have theoretical tastes and preferences like everyone else; certain theoretical ways of seeing the world make sense to me more than others and I explore their academic worth through interviewing processes. We frame research questions from these perspectives and import conceptual ideas into a plan of interview attack. As a fan of theories in cultural studies, for example, I am heavily influenced by particular post-structuralist and neo-Marxist concepts. My interview-based research efforts are essentially programmes designed to explore the boundaries of the concepts contained in the theories I utilise, and examinations of whether the concepts actually can help to explain the interview data I collect. So, I read my interview data through the lens of fancy sounding theoretical concepts like habitus, signification, articulation, implosion, heterotopia, simulation, and so on, during an interview – the very questions I ask are designed to facilitate this from the outset. The goal of using interview data to elaborate concepts is simple. The data are examined to see if our collective understanding of the concept seems to apply to a wide range of empirical situations and cases, and, if not, whether the concept could be modified or expanded/contracted. The concepts we bring to the research table are, then, what Blumer (1969) refers to as 'sensitising concepts'. The concepts are used in a directive way, but we aim to show no outright loyalty to them or their current definition. For example, the concept of habitus has been well used in the socio-cultural study of sport for some time, but progressively debated and expanded over the last decade by a core set of researchers on both sides of the Atlantic.

- **Theory application**: Here is a test you can conduct at your leisure. Select a scholar in sport, exercise and health sciences who regularly conducts interviews with people. Select one of their published papers and develop a sense of their theoretical and conceptual preferences in that paper. From there, read other articles they have published. How many times do the same, unchanged theoretical ideas and concepts pop up across their writing – even across a potentially wide range of topics they have researched? Researchers often develop special expertise in, or very loyal commitment to, a single theory, axioms or set of concepts. Interview data are collected in separate studies by the researcher to simply extend the validity or relevance of the concept or theory to new empirical terrain. The practice is, in methodological terms, a violation of the interpretive and inductive essence of the interviewing process. If the theoretical outcome is already known, interview data are required only to breathe a whisper of empiricism into the research process.

PROBLEMS, PITFALLS AND CONTROVERSIES

There are many problems to consider with interviewing; too many to list in a small chapter on the technique. A brief mention of three concerns is worthwhile.

Interviews are performed rather than straightforwardly conducted. A respondent reacts not only to the questions posed, but also to the person posing the questions. As a result, an interview is a complex form of social interchange wherein emerging data reflect how people respond to one another on an interpersonal level. It is a performative event where identities are expressed as a matter of ritual and social self-protection. Interviewees will give answers to questions when they have no real answer, stories might be embellished, memories imperfectly recounted, details selectively edited as part of looking good in front of an interviewer (all an offshoot of the social desirability effect). On the other side of the table, if an interviewer dresses inappropriately, phrases questions awkwardly or uses a lot of academic jargon, asks people to be interviewed in a socially uncomfortable setting, or seems uninterested in a person, then the interview is equally affected. The best skill a neophyte interviewer can practise in this regard is the art of listening. If a respondent feels as if an interviewer is not attending to responses, the communication flow will inevitably break down.

The issue of sampling respondents always comes up for students as well. How many people do I need to interview? What sorts of people should I include? Most of these types of questions stem from an enduring feeling in sport, health and exercise science that 'good research' must have a massive sample and produce generalisable (externally valid) conclusions. But excellent empirical and theoretically informative interview studies might revolve around only one or two subjects interviewed several times. Or, a handful of interviews might produce a treasure-trove of empirical data. The sample size is also largely reflective of how much time one has to complete a project. I would not expect a student to interview dozens of people for a research paper assigned in an undergraduate methods class, but a doctoral thesis or granted research study has completely different quantity expectations. Moreover, depending on the application of the method discussed above, one may need more or fewer respondents: in theory, we interview people in a grounded approach until we reach a point of data saturation – a point when we are learning very little, if anything, new from each new respondent in the sample.

Questions about the reliability (consistency) of interview data constantly surround the method. If the interview context is beset with dramaturgy and interpersonal factors affecting data collection processes, it is indeed difficult to claim that further interviews with a respondent by other researchers would produce precisely similar results. Gubrium and Holstein (1997) accept the criticism and concur that no two interviews on the same topic with a respondent will produce identical data. Techniques used to check the reliability of interview data can include team interviewing of respondents, inter-coder reliability checks of interview data, and multiple interviews with a respondent. Richardson (1999), however, argues that reliability is a scientific criterion and concern, developed to assess quantitative or positivist methodology. To her, qualitative researchers should pursue other understandings of 'reliability' in their research: such as, whether or not the analysis of the data is socially, emotionally or psychologically compelling and trans-contextually relevant for audiences.

See also: *Grounded Theory; Interpretivism; Research Questions.*

KEY READINGS

Arksey, H. and Knight, P. (1999) *Interviewing for Social Scientists: An Introductory Resource with Examples.* London: Sage.

Blumer, H. (1969) *Symbolic Interactionism: Perspective and Method.* Berkeley, CA: University of California Press.

Charmaz, K. (2006) *Constructing Grounded Theory. A Practical Guide Through Qualitative Analysis*. London: Sage.

Glaser, B. and Strauss, A. (1967) *The Discovery of Grounded Theory: Strategies for Qualitative Research*. Chicago: Aldine Publishing.

Gubrium, J. and Holstein, J. (1997) *The New Language of Qualitative Method*. New York: Oxford University Press.

Haug, F. (1999) *Female Sexualization: A Collective Work of Memory*. London: Verso.

Richardson, L. (1999) 'Feathers in our CAP'. *Journal of Contemporary Ethnography* 28: 660–668.

Seale, C. (2004) *Social Research Methods: A Reader*. London: Routledge.

Smith, J. (2007) 'Hermeneutics, human sciences and health: Linking theory and practice'. *International Journal of Qualitative Studies on Health and Well-Being* 2: 3–11.

Wengraf, T. (2001) *Qualitative Research Interviewing*. London: Sage.

Literature Reviews

I have graded or reviewed hundreds of undergraduate and postgraduate research proposals in the past few years. Because I teach in a very diverse sport and physical activity department, the proposals are substantively and methodologically varied – which makes my life far more interesting as an instructor. I am also fortunate enough to review for a range of academic journals, frequently participate on ethics review boards, and routinely sit on university or governmental grant adjudication committees. So I see a full panorama of research proposals! One of the most common areas for, let's say, improvement, in so many proposals, papers, articles, and essays, is the literature review. A good literature review is critical in the research process for a number of reasons. The literature review frames our thinking through all stages of the research process, it shapes our arguments, and it provides an intellectual context for our claims. It is a focal point in our dialogue with other researchers and illustrates our understanding of why a specific research project is important as an evidence-seeking, or claims-making, venture. My students often view the literature review as a necessary evil, and colleagues see it as a way of demonstrating one's intense familiarity with a subject. But it is so much more.

There are blueprinted, textbook-defined, ideal-type ways of conducting an interview, and then there are literature reviews conducted by people in the trenches of lived research. But a working, textbook definition is a place to begin, nevertheless. A literature review is, basically, an excavation and discussion of the *relevant* literature in a given area of study. Stated differently, it is like a topographical analysis of traditional, contemporary or state-of-the-art thinking/knowledge on a topic at hand. As such, it is a concise (or very long, in the case of graduate level theses) and directed overview of the major studies, arguments and established empirical findings about a topic. What counts as the 'literature' is another story entirely. Academic journals and books are the gold standard sources of information for university and college researchers, but, depending on your subject at hand, informative literature might also come from non-academic published reports, government or other institutional documents, historical archives and special collections in libraries, documentaries, Internet postings, non-academic books, and even anecdotes. Depending on your field of study and the subject of your research, do not be surprised if someone sternly scrutinises the quality of your reviewed literature as the first step in assessing the quality of your research.

Literature reviews can have different types of audiences, depending on the purpose of our research, so we must always consider why and for whom we are writing a review. For example, a lot of literature reviews are written as a chapter for a thesis or dissertation, so the audience will want to know why your research is important and original – why it should count as a worthwhile exercise in the production of knowledge. As a colleague and mentor once said to me a long, long time ago, it has to answer the 'so what?' question for people. While my or your research might be inherently interesting or relevant to us as individuals, it is not so to others (at least immediately). Two of the most well-worn methods of illustrating importance is either to cite the statistical commonality or demographic relevance of your topic (e.g. 'over 27% of people in the UK experience body dysmorphic disorder'), or highlight the gap in knowledge which your research aims to fill (e.g. 'to date, no academic has studied the potential relationship between watching the Olympic games and cancer'). In the former instance, one convinces the reader that one's topic is relevant to a swathe of people, while the latter is designed to convince the reader that there is an opening for new knowledge in the area of study. A literature review will, therefore, attempt to illustrate the academic (and in the best cases the applied social or personal) significance and worthiness of the proposed project. In contrast, when students are writing a literature review for a course assignment, a professor may want you to show that you simply *understand* what research has been done, giving you a base of knowledge. There is a method to our madness here, in that your professors are encouraging you to become an expert in a subject of your choice.

In sum, a literature review has a clear organisational pattern and combines both summary and synthesis. A summary is a recap of the important information of the articles or sources one reviews, but a synthesis is your personal re-organisation, or a reshuffling, of that information into a narrative whole.

WHY IS THIS RELEVANT TO ME?

If we think about any research paper as a statement of knowledge and our production of such knowledge in our study (i.e. this is what I did, what I found and what we now know about my topic), then the literature review is fundamental in *defining* that field of knowledge for the readers. It should outline what we knew (or thought we knew) about the subject prior to our research process. The information/literature included in the literature review will instruct the reader about what existing ideas we are speaking to in our research, and how the reader should see the current status of knowledge about our subject (e.g. is it dated, gap-filled, partial, theoretically dry, and so forth). I cannot over-emphasise the last point enough. The literature review is a *selective* process in that we often cannot include every piece of published information about a subject into our review (think about trying to cite everything published on the relationship between gender and sport participation or all studies on the relationship between exercise and heart disease!). By selecting particular studies to cite and synthesise in the literature review, we are literally framing the specific focus of our studies, their relevance in the field, and the purpose of our work as a knowledge developing enterprise. The literature review, if tactically written as a framing exercise, establishes the framework of significance for the question and evaluation, illustrates the empirical relevance of the subject, and makes disconnected articles, findings, statistics, and arguments or theories connected. By the end of the literature review section in our papers, a reader should not only be able to predict the question driving a study, but clearly understand why someone would ask this question to begin with.

SHOW ME HOW IT'S USED!

The first step in conducting a literature review is, of course, finding literature. No kidding, right? In the old days, before computers and when I had to walk 10 miles to school in the snow (even in July), we would do a traditional 'stacks' search in the library. Today, most of us will commence a literature review in several ways. Online searches through university library portals and search engines are perhaps the most common. Practically every university library hosts or subscribes to an online means of searching for articles across thousands of journals worldwide to retrieve articles on a subject/topic of choice. Google has replicated this idea through their 'Google Scholar' engine. These tools provide access to pdf files of published articles for people with access to academic journals. A major issue with this search method is that many quality or new journals are not included in many of the common search indexes. The indexes are also notoriously sensitive to the terms one uses in a search, and are not entirely systematic in a number of ways. As a supplement, researchers will often consult literature reviews published in existing studies, and students often utilise bibliographies in academic books or general course textbooks as points of departure.

Among the most common questions students ask methods instructors is what literature to search for as part of their review. What terms, categories or words should be searched? I conduct quite a bit of research on young men with eating disorders. (Yes, it is true, there are young men who experience disordered eating, despite many of our preconceived notions about the gendered nature of the subject.) A logical place to start with an online literature review would be to do an advanced search, using the terms eating disorders and sport to start. Then, I might search the terms men and anorexia. Then I could type in body disorders, and the list goes on and on. As frustrating as this might sound – because of the infinite semiological possibilities – searching as many key terms and phrases as possible is best practice. We experience initial frustration in many cases because practically nothing has been published on a subject of our interest. In these instances, we can 'read around' a subject. While very little had ever been published on men and eating disorders in sport, there is quite a bit on the relationship between masculinity and body image, masculinity and bodybuilding, men and risk-taking activities (in sport and elsewhere), and men and body alienation. Literature in each of these areas helped me to frame my theoretical and substantive understanding of why a male might engage in self-injurious behaviour as part of the sports process.

With respect to how literature reviews are structured, we tend to approach the analysis of each article or book's contribution to our study in a number of ways. Asking questions such as the following will help you sift through your sources and organise your literature review. Remember, the literature review organises the previous research in the light of what you are planning to do in your own project:

- What's been done in this topic area to date? What are the significant discoveries, key concepts, arguments, and/or theories that scholars have put forward? Which are the important works?
- On which particular areas of the topic has previous research concentrated? Have there been developments over time? What methodologies have been used?
- Are there any gaps in the research? Are there areas that haven't been looked at closely yet, but which should be? Are there new ways of looking at the topic?
- Are there improved methodologies for researching this subject?
- What future directions should research in this subject take?
- How will research build on or depart from current and previous research on the topic? What contribution will your research make to the field?

The length of a literature review varies depending on its purpose and audience. In a thesis or dissertation, the review is usually a full chapter (about 20–40 pages), but for a course assignment it may only be 3–4 pages.

The ways to organise and structure a literature review are practically endless. There are four common ways literature reviews are organised. First, a simple and effective manner of organising one's literature review is *chronologically*. I could easily trace out the genesis of research on athletes with eating disorders, and how the literature has developed over time. Selected studies are highlighted within a set time period (up to the present) in order to trace the development of knowledge related to the subject. Second, reviews are organised according to the *definitive studies*, or the progressively most important pieces published in terms of impact or new ways of thinking. In this instance, I could cite the most dominant ways of thinking about eating disorders and athletes and the benchmark studies. Third, literature reviews are occasionally structured by a *trend* analysis. Here, our review attempts to categorise or document dominant shifts in academic thinking about a subject, chart the kinds of questions asked over time, or suggest key moments in theoretically re-conceptualising the subject. I could, for example, structure my review around how we have research which individually pathologises the problem, to challenges from research on sports environments, and rebuttals by feminist scholars who study the problem as an aspect of patriarchy. Finally, *thematic* literature reviews identify key conceptual ideas dominant in an area of research, or identifies connections between seemingly disparate studies. In my research on males with eating disorders, I have actually clustered my review as such: sequentially reviewing the literature on athletes with eating disorders, male body problems, body ethics in sport, and then the literature on habituating body practices in sport.

A special case worth mentioning is the meta-analysis. Meta-analyses, if you can find one for a study you are pursuing, are wonderful things to discover! A meta-analysis is a published review of literature on an identified subject, designed to summarise what we know about a subject in total. That's it, that's the article. For example, Hader and Chima (2008) published a meta-analysis of the benefits of physically active commuting in the *British Journal of Sports Medicine*. Their aim was to examine published research on the cardiovascular benefits of walking to work, sift through all of the published findings, and quantify the association between walking and risk of cardiovascular disease (CVD) in healthy men and women. They collated and examined data from 4,295 articles published between 1997 and 2007, focusing on the benefits of walking, running and biking to work. Their reading and summary of literature produces something very important: the current consensus is that death from coronary causes, myocardial infarction, angina pectoris, stroke, congestive heart failure, and coronary revascularisation procedures may be reduced, on average, by around 11% if people simply walk 30 minutes to work daily at a vigorous pace.

PROBLEMS, PITFALLS AND CONTROVERSIES

Because there are no templates for conducting a literature review or commonly accepted frameworks for writing one, producing a literature review for the first, second, tenth or even fiftieth time can be a confusing process. The fatal error we all make at some point or another is turning the literature review into a bland series of unconnected and uninformative abstract-like summaries of the articles we reviewed. Many quotes, findings, fancy sampling terms and statistical ideas, esoteric concepts and generally scattered ideas fill these sorts of literature reviews. Literature reviews in this manifestation reveal no purpose or point; they do not 'set up' your study, nor are the works therein ever mentioned again in the research paper. These reviews tend to be islands unto themselves in the report, and generally illustrate that one has hurried through the literature review process at the beginning (or even very end) of the research process. They also hint at the fact that the researcher might not be able to articulate, as yet, the exact point of the research.

Students also struggle with the idea of quantity in a literature review. Are three studies enough to cite, or 10, or 20? Again, there are no standards or measures for quantity, but the size of a literature review should be (roughly) proportionate to the size of the research task at hand. Even more relevant to inclusion and exclusion criteria are the use of *directly pertinent* studies to the task at hand, and the inclusion of at least some very contemporary materials. In our current interdisciplinary research world, much can be learned by reading outside of one's discipline and drawing on ideas from other scholars. My research on athletes with eating disorders has been deeply influenced by published research in psychology, physiology, sociology, nutrition, anthropology, human geography and history.

See also: Academic Journals; Analytic Epidemiology; Research Proposals; Research Questions.

KEY READINGS

Hader, M. and Chima, Y. (2008) 'Walking and primary prevention: A meta-analysis of prospective cohort studies'. *British Journal of Sports Medicine* 42: 238–243.

Lipsey, M. and Wilson, D. (2000) *Practical Meta-Analysis*. Thousand Oaks, CA: Sage.

Media Analysis

The analysis of (mass) media production, the meaning of its content and its varied effects on audiences as 'interpretive communities' (Fish, 1980) has mushroomed in popularity within the academy over the last three decades. The burgeoning interest is due, in part, to the growth and proliferation of media technology, the shrinking of cultural space between groups through ongoing globalisation process, and the nature of everyday life within information obsessed and consumer driven late market capitalist societies. Quite some time ago, Stuart Hall (1980) pointed to the power of the media in constructing and disseminating social knowledge in late modern societies, commenting on how the media deliberately assemble (or *encode*) information and then how audiences are encouraged to receive (decode) the information in a narrow range of manners. Today, the media function as more than a one-way assemblage of cultural information distribution and education portals in our societies. When it comes to sport, health and exercise, few social institutions have the ability to shape public consciousness and practice about them like the media. As a result, scholars around the world now meticulously study media content pertaining to sport and health in order to understand the link between physical cultures and their mass representations.

WHAT IS THIS CONCEPT?

Media analysis is, in simple terms, the systematic analysis of how images, words, video, and a host of other 'texts' are distributed to and received by people through print or electronic mediums. Cutting across differences of opinion regarding the social functions and impacts of the media are, nevertheless, a series of core questions or substantive concerns driving most research:

- What are people exposed to by the media (i.e. the *encoded* messages)?
- How do audiences actively interpret media content (i.e. how are interpretive communities constituted)?
- How are media messages actively used by people and when do they become incorporated into (popular) cultural practice?
- Are cultural differences and spaces eroding between groups as a result of the mass mediation of cultures in an increasingly global society?
- What systems of representation, ideology or discourse dominate in the media?
- How and why are people (especially youth) producing their own media, and exploring the link between new social media and human agency?

The analysis of media forms, their content and impacts is not one methodology but rather a host of interrelated techniques. Whilst researchers grant, in varying degrees, baseline attention to the encoding–decoding–usage process in most active research on media, no one style of, or approach to, media analysis reigns supreme as proto-typical. There are quantitative, qualitative, historical, semiotic, structural, post-structural, feminist, critical realist, post-positivist, existential and a full range of other ways of performing media research. Whatever the orientation, those conducting media research strive to better understand how the mass circulation of images, messages, discourses and symbols through societies creates, disrupts, reflects, reproduces, distributes and aligns collective definitions of reality (or simply, knowledge) for people. In this pursuit, media research ranges from very politically and ideologically passionate efforts to quasi-neutral and purely descriptive reports. Students often complain that media research is densely theoretical and conceptually labyrinth-like at times. This is unfortunate, as much media research sheds considerable light on the real-world influence of media on human groups, cultural practices and social structures.

WHY IS THIS RELEVANT TO ME?

Media analysis has boomed in popularity among academics because the media have a massive impact on everyday life and how knowledge about the social world is generated. Pierre Bourdieu (1993) notes that the media constitute, to all intents and purposes, an 'autonomous [popular] cultural' field; endowed with the ability to entertain, provoke, distract, produce, connect and, of course, educate people in unique manners. Today, few social practices or concerns (save, perhaps for crime or international politics) are as globally mass mediated as sport or health matters. From the Olympic Games to global health pandemics like H1N1 to the World Cup to obesity, the representation of the active/sporting body is a universally 'weighty' cultural matter. Most of us know someone who attends to sports or health media on a daily basis as an avid consumer, and many of us derive a significant percentage of our accumulated sports and health knowledge from media content. Sports, exercise and health researchers find good cause, then, to question what people are producing and consuming through sport and health media, and what are the impacts.

SHOW ME HOW IT'S USED!

Among the most straightforward media analytic designs is *manifest content analysis*. Here, the goal of the research is to examine the overt or surface level characteristics of media texts. For example, one might be interested in studying whether patriarchal ideologies still dominate in media representations of amateur or professional sport. To investigate the question further, a researcher could sample 10 years of Summer and Winter Olympic Games television coverage in Britain as the case study data. Before analysing any of the television content, the researcher would have to decide what would be examined in the broadcasts, and how to 'count' the presence of patriarchy. One might suggest that the percentage of men's versus women's sports coverage, the gender of athletes interviewed or showcased in special stories, whether one gender is featured in more 'primetime' events than the other are all empirical indicators of patriarchal attitudes. These are easily recognised by a researcher, and could be tallied quite quickly across the broadcasts. At the end of the study, basic descriptive statistical and impressionistic analysis could be offered to conclude whether, on the surface, Olympic television broadcasts in Britain seemed to privilege men over women; potentially indicating the enduring face of patriarchy in the representation of Olympic sport. A number of studies have conducted such an analysis of patriarchy and sport media, and found vast discrepancies in the media coverage of men and women in organised sport (see Coakley and Pike, 2009).

Discourse analysis is a technique inspired by French structuralists including Ferdinand de Saussure, Jacques Lacan and Roland Barthes; and critical post-structuralists including Judith Butler, Julia Kristeva and Michel Foucault. Discourse analysis is not a single method, but rather a series of complementary techniques focusing on the interpretive 'reading' of a sample of media texts in order to expose the dominant *episteme* (knowledge), assumptions, ideologies or values underwriting them. Another way of describing discourse analysis is to call it the study of the 'dominant languages' or ideologies in media texts that frame how audiences are supposed to understand and use them. Hall (1980) refers to this process as the encoding of 'preferred' meanings in a text that limit alternative (or 'resistive') readings and understandings of a represented subject. For discourse analysts, the exposure of dominant discourses in texts is critically important; as those who tend to control how something is spoken about (and thus thought about and known) have immense social power to frame reality and dictate policy. Discourse analysts see mass circulated media texts as connected through and composed by socially diffuse systems of language encoded with dominant ideologies. Discourse analysts assert that no media text is ever 'neutral' or outside the trappings of language/ideology. Rich and Miah's (2009) research on the medicalisation of cyberspace illustrates how governmental ideologies of self-surveillance and associated neo-liberal discourses of healthism abound online. Rich and Miah (2009) highlight how the Internet has become a zone for spreading dominant, conservative and self-blaming health messages, and, as such, how they systematically blur and eschew real material differences in people's access to quality, state-provided health care schemes and styles of healthy living. Giroux's (2005) work on discourses of neo-liberalism in stories about education cutbacks in the United States and Canada exposes how the slashing of public school budgets (including portions devoted to physical education and health) is largely framed by late modern, supply-side economics mantras and principles.

Narrative analysis is similar to, and yet importantly different from, discourse analysis. Narrative analysis – the examination of how stories are told through the media, or a specific set of media texts – looks and feels like discourse analysis, but their respective emphases on how power is related to discourse/narrations in the media are quite different. Narrative analysis tends to focus on how and why individuals, groups, organisations, or others choose specific language and symbols to represent something about themselves. Whereas the approach in discourse analysis tends to be rather top-down (that is, focusing on how discourses wrapped in ideologies are spread through society by powerful or elite groups), narrative analysis tends to home in on how media may be used to create and disseminate a wide range of cultural identities, images and opportunities for social storytelling. Gillett (2003), for example, argues that the media are a critical cultural context where gay men are able to write their social selves in empowering ways; especially in the case of telling different (that is non-medically pathological) stories about life with HIV/AIDS. Gillett's examination of how men narrate gay identities through magazines and websites attests to the emancipatory potential of public storytelling as a form of claims-making and knowledge production for socially marginalised communities.

While the techniques of media analysis listed above, emphasise by and large, how media produce or shape cultural meaning and social practices, *audience ethnography* strives to understand how people actively receive, decode and use media texts. An audience ethnography might be designed as a one-shot case study, or be structured as a long-term panel study of how a group interprets media over the course of time. In the typical scenario, participants in an audience ethnographic project are asked to collectively or individually watch, read or listen to select media and then respond to its content. A researcher acts as a facilitator in these scenarios, prompting questions among respondents about what the messages or symbols in the media might mean to them and how they actively decode them from a variety of cultural standpoints (age, race, sexuality, gender, class). The underpinning logic of doing audience ethnography is that by observing and questioning how people make sense of media data 'live' and *in situ*, researchers compile a more valid understanding of the process of immediate reception and the cognitive processing of media content. Wilson and Sparkes (1996), for example, illustrate how African-Canadian teenage boys fashion their own constructions of, and lived experiences with, Black masculinity to interpret mass mediations of 'Blackness' in basketball shoe advertisements. Wilson and Sparkes discuss how the boys find humour, reality, and frequent inferential racism in the depictions of Black masculinity in the advertisements. They also attest to how youth selectively take from the commercials what makes sense to them culturally, and how they negate or resist supposedly preferred images and constructions of 'Blackness' in the commercials.

Bennett's (2008) book, *Civic Life Online* presents a series of chapters detailing the emancipatory potential of new media forms such as personal websites, blogs, social networking sites and other forms of computer mediated communication (CMC) for youth in particular. The separate chapters in the book attest to how the development of online space provides an opportunity for people to be their own media producers, and thus become public knowledge producers and cultural claims-makers. To date, very few inside the academy have rigorously attended to the study of how, why and when youth choose to become media encoders and how this may impact systems of ideological production and dissemination within popular culture. Ohler (2008) has extended the study of new media into the classroom. His work advocates the use of computer programs and Internet space as a means of teaching students how to create and publish *avant-garde* digital stories. Ohler's emphasis is on the creation of dynamic texts, embedded with movies, images, digital interviews, and other visual-spoken forms of knowing. Ohler further emphasises the creative and knowledge-production capabilities of new, digital stories in that they all require the producers to play around with sound, speed, camera angles and other cinematic techniques in order to create desired feels, moods or atmospheres in stories. New media analytic methods advocated by

Bennett (2008) and Ohler (2008) establish exciting ways of knowing and seeing subjects of interest, and illustrate the potential for knowledge production and translation once representations of lived experience and human condition are liberated from one-dimensional written/ textual ways of knowing.

PROBLEMS, PITFALLS AND CONTROVERSIES

Media analysis receives substantial criticism from academics who consider themselves dyed-in-the-wool scientists. Due in large part to the extensive amount of reflexively interpretive analysis in most media studies projects, the overall methodology is prone to contestation from researchers searching robustly objective, reliable and generalisable data. Whilst there are many criticisms of media analysis studies, five are especially common. First, quarrels about the rigors of sampling in media projects are practically inevitable. The sampling approach underpinning many media-based projects is almost always non-probability based, but researchers nevertheless tend to make grand claims about the generalisability of their data and theoretical conclusions. Second, the question of how theory guides media research looms large. Even though many researchers purport to conduct 'grounded theory' through the data analysis process, their studies read as if the theoretical reading had been determined well in advance (see above). In this instance, one is led to question whether or not media studies are simply vehicles for reifying, rather than testing, expanding or amending, extant theories of cultures, individuals and societies.

Third, questions of the internal validity and reliability of researchers' readings of media texts, or interpretations of audience interpretations of texts, chase practically all media based studies. If, as semioticians instruct, media texts are indeed polysemic or 'floating' and thus open for countless cultural interpretations, then how is one researcher's set of conclusions any more reality-congruent than another's? If a thousand media researchers might decode the significance of, say, media accounts of the obesity epidemic in the London broadsheets in a thousand different ways, what is the legitimate role of media analysis in the academy? What trustworthy, usable, intersubjectively agreed upon or definitive knowledge does it generate? Fourth, new questions of best ethical practice (especially around participant anonymity and confidentiality) surround media projects in which photographs, film, blogs, websites, and other Internet spaces are employed as data. Whilst the use of new media and their forms of representation well and truly opens up representational practice in our research efforts, the 'public' nature (and therefore 'free to use' nature) of online material and our ability to 'invade' personal webspace for our research purposes, remain grey areas in research ethics debates. Fifth, even the most ardent defenders of media analysis struggle with how best to represent visual, spoken, moving, ambiguous and mass distributed media texts in academic papers. Thrift (2007) like Richardson (1999) challenges all qualitative researchers to seek new forms of moving, emotional, aesthetic and personally compelling forms of academic writing/representation that bring audiences 'closer' to that which has been studied in the here and now of everyday life. Their criticism is based on the idea that researchers take very complex, visceral and sensuous practices like media reception and usage, and then transform/represent them, as theoretically obtusely written, textual analysis.

See also: Archival Research; Critical Theory; Ethnography; Visual Methods.

KEY READINGS

Bennett, W. (2008) *Civic Life Online: Learning How Digital Media Can Engage Youth.* Cambridge, MA: MIT Press.

Bourdieu, P. (1993) *The Field of Cultural Production.* New York: Columbia University Press.

Coakley, J. and Pike, L. (2009) *Sports in Society: Issues and Controversies.* London: McGraw-Hill.

Gillett, J. (2003) 'Media activism and internet use by people with HIV/AIDS'. *Sociology of Health and Illness* 25: 608–624.

Giroux, H. (2005) 'The politics of public pedagogy', in Jeffrey Di Leo (ed.), *If Classrooms Matter: Place, Pedagogy and Politics.* New York: Routledge. pp.15–36.

Hall, S. (1980) 'Encoding/decoding', in S. Hall, D. Hobson, A. Lowe and P. Willis (eds), *Culture, Media, Language: Working Papers in Cultural Studies, 1972–79.* Centre for Contemporary Cultural Studies. London: Hutchinson. pp. 128–238.

Ohler, J. (2008) *Digital Storytelling in the Classroom.* Thousand Oaks, CA: Corwin Press.

Rich, E. and Miah, A. (2009) *The Medicalization of Cyberspace.* London: Routledge.

Richardson, L. (1999) 'Feathers in our CAP'. *Journal of Contemporary Ethnography* 28: 660–668.

Thrift, N. (2007) *Non-Representational Theory: Space, Politics, Affect.* London: Routledge.

Wilson, B. and Sparkes, R. (1996) 'It's gotta be the shoes: Youth, race, and sneaker commercials'. *Sociology of Sport Journal* 13: 398–427.

Meta-Analysis

Among the most luxurious aspects of life as a graduate student is the sheer amount of time one is given to simply read and learn. Reviewing literature never seemed like an onerous task. Today, I struggle at great length to find an hour or two during the week to sit and read; to direct attention towards what others in my field are saying, proposing and advancing. But all is not lost! What if students and colleagues publish systematic reviews of literature they have undertaken? Could this be possible? Indeed it is, and we call them meta-analyses. In the past decade I have come to cherish reviews of literature published as meta-analyses of a subject. A meta-analysis on a topic of one's interest is a gift sent from the divine. There are differences in how meta-analyses are constructed or utilised in separate sub-disciplines, but their popularity is growing quickly.

WHAT IS THIS CONCEPT?

The short, definitional answer is that a meta-analysis is an expansive literature review designed to collate, synthesise and summarise extant evidence or theory on a very narrow subject of interest. Normally, meta-analyses are performed using quantitative findings on a subject. By far the most common use of meta-analysis has been in *quantitative literature reviews*. These are review articles where the researcher selects a research finding or statistical effect that has been investigated in primary research under a large number of different circumstances – say, for example, important studies documenting the statistical effects of walking for 30–45 minutes per day on the risk of contracting a cardiovascular disease (CVD). They then use meta-analysis to help them describe the overall strength of the effect (the impact of walking on CVD), and under what empirical circumstances it is stronger or weaker. Recently, as knowledge of meta-analytic techniques has become more widespread, researchers have begun to use *meta-analytic summaries* within primary research papers. In this case, meta-analysis is used to provide information supporting a special theoretical statement or hypothesis being tested by a researcher, usually about the overall strength or consistency of a relationship within the studies being conducted. We therefore use previously published meta-analysis to justify our own research project's hypotheses.

The two most often noted approaches to qualitative meta-analysis are the 'metaphoric translation' approach within the field of ethnography (Noblit and Hare, 1988) and a thematic synthesis approach most often associated with grounded theory development (Patterson et al., 2001). These approaches fall within traditional qualitative inquiry, highlight the importance of context, and both tend to focus on research questions that seek the meaning of 'lived experiences' of groups and individuals. For example, the research questions have often been in regard to the exploration of the meaning of illness or health. The work of Shao (1991) and the application of his work by Patterson, Thorne, Canam and Jillings (2001) suggest that a qualitative meta-synthesis should include an analysis of theory (meta-theory), an analysis of method (meta-method) and an analysis of findings (meta-analysis). What a lot of analyses! This means we summarise what we know theoretically, how we tend to know this, and what, specifically, about a subject we think we know. When someone conducts a meta-analysis using this tactic, there is a tendency to call the approach a 'triangulated' meta-analysis.

WHY IS THIS RELEVANT TO ME?

The answer pertaining to a meta-analysis's relevance is somewhat of a methodological no-brainer. If I set out on a course of quantitative, experimental research to examine the effects of 45 minutes of brisk walking (daily, over three months) on one's health, the very first thing I would do is consult the literature in search of a meta-analysis on the subject. Meta-analyses are not replacements for one's own reading or familiarity with a body of knowledge, but they do provide a useful starting point to examine the aggregate effect of walking on health. The meta-analysis could suggest the need for alternative hypotheses than those studied to date, along with alternative protocols and alternative samples. But quantitative meta-analyses serve additional purposes. As 'diagnostic' papers, they cull diverse studies with (often) small sample sizes into a larger pool of subjects. Rather than examining the impact of walking on a group of 25, 129, or 13, or 67, when the separate studies are pooled together, the people included in the analysis might range in the hundreds or thousands. The problem of extracting meaningful statistical inferences from small sample sizes is then partly solved. If the goal of quantitative research is to produce generalised statements of relationship between two or more variables, then pooled and aggregately analysed data provide a step in the right direction. With respect to qualitative research, meta-analyses (or meta-syntheses) are invaluable for their summary of both the main theoretical ways of seeing a field of study, but also for their systematic review of what is known about a topic of interest. Qualitative meta-analyses are more than summaries of effects and dominant theories tested, they are attempts to define the body of knowledge pertaining to a subject. The path-breaking meta-analytic work on chronic illness by Patterson, Thorne, Canam and Jillings (2001) illustrates how patterns of thinking about a subject can be shifted when researchers perform a meta-analysis well.

SHOW ME HOW IT'S USED!

Unlike many of the concepts and techniques discussed in this book, the process of performing a meta-analysis is fairly prescribed. For example, two main sources provide information and guidance on how to conduct a quantitative meta-analysis. First, the CONSORT (Consolidated Standards of Reporting Trials) Group is an international group of medical journal editors, clinical trialists, epidemiologists and methodologists who provide advice on how to report and analyse clinical trial research. The CONSORT group's endorsement of the PRISMA (Preferred Reporting Items for Systematic Reviews and Meta-Analyses) statement on how to conduct a meta-analysis has been influential in creating an international set of standards for conducting and publishing meta-analyses. The aim of the PRISMA Statement is to help authors improve the reporting of systematic reviews and meta-analyses. We have focused on randomised trials, but PRISMA can also be used as a basis for reporting systematic reviews of other types of research, particularly evaluations of interventions. PRISMA may also be useful for critical appraisal of published systematic reviews, although it is not a quality assessment instrument, to gauge the quality of a systematic review. The PRISMA Statement (formerly QUOROM Statement) consists of a 27-item checklist and a four-phase flow diagram that researchers should use when selecting studies to be included in a meta-review, and gives advice as to how the data should be interpreted.

Second, perhaps the best-known source for meta-analyses is called 'The Cochrane Collaboration', a group of over 18,000 specialists in health care who systematically review randomised control trials on the effects of prevention, treatments and rehabilitation as well as health systems interventions. When appropriate, they also include the results of other types of research. Cochrane reviews are published in *The Cochrane Database of Systematic Reviews* section of the Cochrane Library, which to date includes 6,244 articles: 4,130 reviews; and 1,911 protocols for additional reviews being conducted. The Cochrane Group provides a handbook for systematic reviewers of interventions, where they suggest that each systematic review should contain the following main sections:

- Background;
- Objectives;
- Methods of the review;
- Results;
- Conclusion and discussion.

According to the Cochrane group, there are seven steps for preparing and maintaining a systematic review:

1. Formulating a problem;
2. Locating and selecting studies;
3. Critical appraisal of studies;
4. Collecting data;
5. Analysing and presenting results;
6. Interpreting results;
7. Improving and updating reviews.

Although less frequently cited than the PRISMA Statement or the Cochrane method, the MOOSE (Meta-Analysis of Observation Studies in Epidemiology) is another template for performing meta-reviews.

The method of conducting qualitative meta-analyses is not nearly as delineated and collectively agreed upon as in the quantitative scenario. Qualitative meta-analysis is a set of techniques analogous to the comparative analysis method favoured by grounded theorists for synthesising qualitative studies. Qualitative meta-analysis was most notably championed by Noblit and Hare (1988), as a technique for deriving higher-order theoretical understandings of a subject from multiple qualitative studies. The overall aim of meta-ethnography is to achieve greater understanding of a subject by attaining a level of conceptual or theoretical development beyond that achieved in any individual empirical study alone. There are four general stages of a qualitative meta-analysis: the development of a search strategy to locate studies; the application of inclusion/exclusion criteria to studies (criteria generally include how to detect a 'sound' versus a poor qualitative study); quality appraisal of each study; and the integration/synthesis of study findings (which may or may not include a review of dominant theories and methods employed). The qualitative meta-analysis method itself involves selecting relevant empirical studies to be synthesised, then reading them repeatedly and noting down key themes or concepts running across the studies.

PROBLEMS, PITFALLS AND CONTROVERSIES

Several main criticisms apply to both quantitative and qualitative meta-analyses, and others to one group alone. First, decisions about which studies are included or excluded in a meta-analysis are neither clear nor objective in many cases. Second, meta-analysts are criticised for lumping chalk and cheese together for comparison. When studies of the same subject vary considerably in their shape, content and production, can they be legitimately standardised and aggregated? Third, there is a perceived bias in meta-analysis for published research – which has a tendency to only report statistically (quantitative) or conceptually (qualitative) 'significant' results'; and therefore totally ignores findings that might be important but do not meet rigidly applied methodological criteria and conventions.) Fourth, all published data has already been reduced in scope, volume and content from the 'raw' data collected in studies.

Perhaps the most consequential criticism of quantitative meta-analysis is that the study itself is not 'scientific' *per se*. While statistical techniques are employed to analyse effect sizes, the study itself is not based on traditional scientific, controlled, double-blind designs. Biases in sample inclusion, comparisons of non-standardised data and the inclusion of methodologically weak or suspect studies in a meta-analysis are equally problematic. On these grounds, based on the vested interests of a particular researcher conducting a meta-analysis (say, to illustrate no difference in walking every day and the reduction of CVD) one or another way to select the appropriate studies for inclusion could be devised to determine the results in advance. With respect to qualitative meta-analysis, one major problem stands out as a potential Achilles heel of the approach. If qualitative research itself is openly criticised for losing a bit of 'reality' or everyday meaning through the interpretation filtration process undertaken by researchers in the field (as I interpret other people's interpretations of reality and then summarise them conceptually!), then meta-analysis presumes one can unproblematically interpret people's (researchers') interpretations of people's (subjects') interpretations of reality. Try saying that one 10 times fast.

See also: *Causality; Translation.*

meta-analysis

Borenstein, M. (2009) *Introduction to Meta-Analysis*. New York: Wiley.

Cooper, H. (2009) *Research Synthesis and Meta-Analysis*. London: Sage.

Lipsey, M. and Wilson, D. (2001) *Practical Meta-Analysis*. London: Sage.

Noblit, G. and Hare, R. (1988) *Meta-Ethnography: Synthesising Qualitative Studies*. Newbury Park, CA: Sage Publications.

Patterson, B., Thorne, S., Canam, C. and Jillings, C. (2001) *Meta-Study of Qualitative Health Research: A Practical Guide to Meta-Analysis and Meta-Synthesis*. Thousand Oaks, CA: Sage.

Rosenthal, R. (1991) *Meta-Analytic Procedures for Social Research*. London: Sage.

Shao, S. (1991) 'Meta-theory, meta-method, meta-data analysis. What, why, and how?' *Sociological Perspectives* 34: 377–390.

Sutton, A., Jones, D., Abrams, K., Sheldon, T. and Song, F. (2000) *Methods for Meta-Analysis in Medical Research*. London: John Wiley.

·················· Ontology ··················

I could devote pages and pages to the complex philosophical discussion of ontology and academic research, but I will not. Ontological questions have preoccupied academic thinking and modern disciplines for ages. Disciplines in the humanities, social science, physical sciences and the arts all weigh in on a variety of ontological perspectives and positions. I could be wrong, but I firmly believe one's ontological stance is the very cornerstone of one's entire research career, let alone the foundation of a single research project in one's subject of interest. Ontological questions and positions are no laughing matter, and before anyone can embark on a quest to know something, they must possess an idea about what can be known at all. Determining the latter is the beginning of one's relationship with the idea of ontology

WHAT IS THIS CONCEPT?

Ontology may be defined as a special branch of philosophy pertaining to central metaphysical questions about the world. Okay, I know that is probably a very confusing set of ideas to manage at once. Metaphysics is the study of the fundamental nature of existence and being in the world. While metaphysics is often discussed at the level of 'theoretical possibility' or philosophy, ontology is a type of metaphysics geared towards the study of empirical being and existence. Stated in another way, one's *ontology* is a position one adopts about the nature of empirical, lived reality. That is to say, it specifies what is real and what are the nature and properties of what is real that we can observe?

WHY IS THIS RELEVANT TO ME?

Ontology is an important concept to grasp because you are already operating under a definition of reality and it shapes your own disciplinary, let alone research, interests. Imagine you are a population health researcher or epidemiologist tracking melanoma rates among young adults. You would most likely want to ask questions such as: who is at risk of developing a melanoma? where do they come from? is there anything about their biographies or family histories predisposing them to the condition? where do they work? what are their medical histories? how is their nutrition? and, based on all of the evidence, are there geographic, ethnic, sex, age, occupational or other commonalities in people with a 'high risk' of developing one? Yours would be a language of variables and factors and causes. To you, disease transmission in a society is patterned, ordered and predictable if we ask the right questions, study the right groups and perform the appropriate analysis. There is a biological/cultural formula that places someone at risk of contracting a melanoma, and our job is to problem-solve until we find the cause–incidence–solution link. Students in sport, exercise and health research who favour biomechanics, physiology, nutrition, population health and psychology see the world as *objectivists*; or, as people who believe in the law-like operation of biological, psychological and social-cultural aspects of life. Bodies, minds and selves are knowable through the scientific method of careful observation, data comparison and analysis.

Students of mine who believe the world, including our knowledge of the world, is socially constructed acknowledge the place of objectivist research in the academy, but see the subject of disease as far more complicated than cause and effect relationships. We call these people *constructivists* (or subjectivists) – people who believe in the social construction of reality. Here, I am reminded of the carving Sarah Connor (Linda Hamilton) makes in the picnic bench in the movie *Terminator 3*, 'No fate [but what we make]'. For example, while there may be an objective component to disease and risk of disease, the reality of illness does not end with risk or the condition itself. There are other ways of seeing disease as a subject that is not contingent on treating it as a law-like, factorial phenomenon. Disease is as much a social construction as a condition bound by factors. Skin cancer means something different to people. It might be only a minor bump in one's life, affecting little who the person is, how s/he lives or how s/he comes to see themselves in society.

SHOW ME HOW IT'S USED!

I cannot run very fast over short distances at all. I'm totally rubbish at it, in fact. But, I can run for a long, long time at a moderate pace. I have friends who run quickly in short distances but burn out even at the 10k mark. Why can some people run faster than others? When I ask this question in a research methods class, student hands quite quickly shoot up and I hear a range of explanations; amount of training time, age, gender, if they have been coached, basic skeletal or muscle shape, and so on. Without question, a student will offer race as the explanatory variable. They cite winners of the 100m dash (of the top 200 best times across the world in the 100m dash, not one of them is owned by a White athlete), the speed of players in sports like baseball and football, and the overall dominance of Black athletes in a full range of athletic events. Let's stick with the idea of 'race' as a key determinant of running speed. Authors in the physical and indeed social sciences of sport and exercise have pointed to the connection between race/ethnicity and sports performance for more than 50 years, but how to explain the reality of the connection is another matter entirely!

Let's recap just a bit. Our first major ontological camp is the *objectivists*. To objectivists, there is a world of reality 'out there' just waiting to be known by researchers. Reality operates in a law-like, observable and pretty consistent manner independent of human will. Laws of human thought and social behaviour operate with the same law-like patterns as the laws of physics, biology and human movement. Objectivists would say something like the perceived connection between racial (genetic) background and running speed is based on a truism regarding universal differences between racial groups. Running speed is governed by laws and rules influenced by muscle-mass (or concentration of muscle-fibres), testosterone produced in the body, amount of fat stored, and biomechanically determined gait. Why? Because each of these factors, as theories teach, governs speed, velocity and force generated by the body. So, if certain racial groups have the 'advantage' with respect to genes that produce more muscle, less fat, more testosterone and wider gaits, then they will have the advantage over all others. Now, guess what sport and exercise scientists have discovered all over the world? Yes, 'Black' athletes tend to be more biologically blessed than their White colleagues (Hoberman, 1997). Running speed is easy to figure out, then. Determine the bio-physical laws that govern running speed. Then, isolate which groups possess more of the raw materials (from the genetic level up) to be universally better runners than others. Then see if the theory matches the empirical evidence.

Another perspective entirely on the race-running success debate comes from the camp of people we refer to as *constructivists*. Constructivists argue there is *no universal reality* in a given domain or topic of study, only cultural constructions of reality. Football is only a sport (and is different from rugby) because people say it is different. Biological structures and systems in the body are only true by definition alone – they are only one way of seeing the body as an entity predicated on a whole series of abstract ideas and thoughts (let alone existing ways of seeing, measuring and documenting the body). Speed is only an idea. More importantly, race and ethnicity are only ideas. Just as a quick question for consideration: what classifies someone as a racially grouped person? Skin colour? Hair colour and texture? Place of birth or ancestral lineage? Race is a notoriously problematic concept to define and measure with any empirical consistency or universal acceptance.

PROBLEMS, PITFALLS AND CONTROVERSIES

A little over a year ago, a colleague of mine argued that students have neither a pressing need nor concern for the study of ontology within a research methods class. I see the point today as I did then – but only, from my perspective, because undergraduate methods classes tend to be jam-packed with so many ideas that students become conceptually lost very early on in the semester. So at a level of practical pedagogy I completely concur. But when should practical pedagogy (that is, time-based efficiency) dictate intellectual development for students. Without a basic understanding of the differences between ontological positions, there are scant grounds to believe students will be able to fully appreciate the fundamental philosophical positions underwriting everything we do as 'disciplined' academics, researchers and knowledge-producers.

My colleague's point has merit, though, when we consider how many undergraduate students in a kinesiology, health or physical education programme will actually end up with research roles or occupations after graduation. Introductory or advanced dissections of ontology may be superfluous to their eventual career choices and the skills sets required to thrive in them. But on these same grounds, discussions of standard deviations, experimental randomisation, inter-coder reliability, and concept mapping in inductive analysis are equally irrelevant. From an entirely different perspective, lessons about ontology instruct students about the beliefs which underline much social health policy and practice, sport and exercise experiences, and the chances for physical activity (and its expression) in our lives.

See also: *Epistemology; Theory.*

KEY READINGS

Browning, D. (1990) *Ontology and the Practical Arena.* Penn State University Park: Pennsylvania State University Press.

Grossmann, R. (1992) *The Existence of the World: An Introduction to Ontology.* London: Routledge.

Heil, J. (2003) *From an Ontological Point of View.* Oxford: Oxford University Press.

Hoberman, J. (1997) *Darwin's Athletes: How Sport Has Damaged Black America and Preserved the Myth of Race.* Boston: Houghton Mifflin.

Kaipayil, J. 2008. *An Essay on Ontology.* Kochi: Karunikan Books.

Populations and Samples

A series of recent media reports, widely disseminated anecdotes and academic studies have pointed to the growing problem of child trafficking in global football (soccer) cultures. Stories about the illegal transfer of children (aged 8–16) from Africa and South America to Europe for the purposes of 'talent development' raise serious questions regarding international youth talent identification and youth academy systems in the sport. Knowing more about the ways in which children become illegally brokered across international boundaries might prove monumental in curbing the exploitation of vulnerable youth within the sport. For example, based on the empirical evidence to date, I find that Kenya, the Ivory Coast and Uruguay are the three main countries of origin of 'trafficked' children in European football. I decide I want to examine the social and cultural conditions in these countries that place youth footballers at risk of being trafficked. Before I could begin the research (and let's not even tackle the associated issues in research ethics for now!), I need to consider one major factor: what children am I researching, specifically? Who is the bigger group that I consider to be 'at risk', and how is it that I am going to access them for my research? How many of them do I need to study, and who would be ideal participants for my study? This stage of the research process is about defining the nature of the *population* under study, and how many people from this group you are able to *sample*.

WHAT IS THIS CONCEPT?

Both populations and the samples derived from populations are theoretical concepts. Technically, populations do not exist in any undefined or natural state. A *population* is simply a discrete set of entities that researchers want to know something about. When we use the term 'population', I'm sure most people immediately think of a demographic population of people living within a geographic region (e.g. the population of Australia, New York City or Vancouver Island). Normally, the 'population' in a study refers to a group of people (usually from one or a series of interrelated geographic areas) who share some important characteristic we are interested in studying – such as their involvement in elite rugby, their experience of fibromyalgia, or their sexual identity. Still, a population could be a cluster of inanimate objects we wish to study and compare; for example, the population of all television broadcasts of the 2010 Winter Olympic Games, UK Sport policy documents regarding 'sport for all', or newspapers articles about the relationship between fast food consumption and obesity since 1990. In all cases, a population refers to each and every single person or artefact we wish to study. The number of units in a population might be a very small number or an incredibly large one. Consider the example I introduced at the beginning of this entry; the children in the three counties 'at risk' of being trafficked would be my population of interest. In the vast majority of cases, we will not be able to collect information on each and every unit in the population (personal time, money, geographic dispersion, and the sheer number of people are all constraints to full population sampling) so we take a *sample* from the population and study it intensively.

Samples are identified, gathered and analysed differently according to the purpose or nature of the inquiry driving one's study. Sampling is the process of selecting a group of units from the population. Traditional scientists who operate via deductive modes of inquiry strive to sample in such a way that the group of units they select 'represents' the population as closely as possible – so that results from their research are generalisable to all members of the population. Other researchers do not stress the need to produce generalisable data, so sampling procedures can be considerably more flexible and not necessarily representative.

The sampling procedure is greatly facilitated when some form of master list of the population exists. In methods terms, this list is called a *sampling frame*. If I wanted to study knee injury rates among Olympic athletes (say two weeks after an Olympic games), this is would be an easy venture because any country's Olympic Committee should have a master list of athletes who competed. Now think about my proposed study of child trafficking. No chance of a sampling frame there! The great majority of studies I have ever read, conducted, supervised or heard about, operated with a definitive or perfectly complete sampling frame itemising all units in the relevant population. The lack of a 'perfect' sampling frame at the outset will not immobilise a study, but will place parameters and limitations on the breadth, depth and scope of the claims we will be able to make about our results.

WHY IS THIS RELEVANT TO ME?

Research methods colleagues may disagree with me on this point, but I consider the sampling process to be the 'make or break' aspect of most studies. A sample must be cobbled together that will produce 'quality' information pertaining to the research question(s) being posed. What good would it be to sample 500 children in my proposed study who are only facing moderate, or no, risk of being trafficked? The quality of our answers to our research questions, and therefore the knowledge our research produces, directly reflects what we observe. In my study, I would need to sample a full panorama of children at risk of being trafficked in order to understand what places children at risk in these countries. A methods professor of mine once stated, in relation to the sampling issue, that 'garbage in (a bad sample), means garbage out (poor conclusions)'. A sample is always assessed, first and foremost, by the units' relevance to our research question at hand. If an entire sample is atypical of the larger population, or consists only of 'peripheral' units in the theoretical population, we are off on the wrong methodological foot!

Among the most important considerations in the sampling process is one's access to the sampling units. If one is sampling people for inclusion in the research, one must be able to access them, of course. Are people able to participate, what is the nature of their involvement, and what are the potential ethical issues associated with their involvement? How many people to include in a sample is another of the preliminary questions tackled by researchers, and a source of confusion for many students engaged in the research process. As a crude rule of thumb in quantitative-deductive research, the greater the sample size in relation to the population, the more generalisable and representative the results; this makes intuitive sense. But because we rarely ever sample huge numbers from a population, quantitative researchers rely on mathematical theories (like the central limit theorem) and 'power tests' to determine (before the study begins) how many people must be included in the sample (given the number of variables being analysed in the research) in order to achieve significant results at a particular level of statistical confidence. Qualitative researchers rarely rely on mathematical formulae for determining sample size; indeed, many qualitative samples are numerically ambiguous at the onset of the research, and the final number in the sample is realised only at the study's termination. Qualitative researchers often emphasise that the quality and depth of empirical information from a smaller number of people than typically seen in quantitative research is justifiable because qualitative studies focus more on conceptual development than hypothesis testing.

SHOW ME HOW IT'S USED!

There are two main styles of sampling from a population: *probability sampling* (typically associated with quantitative research) and *non-probability sampling* (typically associated with qualitative research). A *probability sampling* method is any method of sampling that utilises some form of *random selection process*. In order to have a random selection method, you must set up some process or procedure that ensures that the different units in your population have known and equal probabilities of being chosen for the eventual sampling. Basically, sampling theory holds that if we sample via probability methods, and if our samples are large enough, the sample will *probably* be representative of the population. The simplest form of random sampling is called *simple random sampling*. In simple random sampling, every unit in the sampling frame is assigned a number. If we wish to sample 100 units from the frame, we would ask a random sampling computer program to generate a list of 100 random units from the list. Because simple random sampling is a fair way to select a sample, it is reasonable to generalise the results from the sample back to the population.

More complex forms of probability sampling include *stratified random sampling, cluster sampling* and *multi-stage random sampling*. Stratified random sampling involves dividing your population into homogeneous sub-groups and then taking a simple random sample in each sub-group. Cluster sampling is somewhat like simple random sampling and stratified sampling, but here a researcher will random sample from a series of pre-determined geographic areas. Multi-stage sampling is a rather common technique in research, and it is a pastiche of the probability methods discussed above. Consider the idea of sampling children in Montevideo for the child trafficking study and administering a 56-item questionnaire among them. Clearly we would want to do some type of cluster sampling as the first stage of the process. Why? Well, we might sample neighbourhoods throughout the city in order to explore whether or not geographic region plays a role in risk exposure. Rather than sample everyone in the neighbourhoods, then, we might set up a stratified sampling process within each of the neighbourhoods; perhaps creating strata based on level of sports participation, age of children and gender. We would then take a random sample from each of the strata we have identified. By combining different sampling methods we are able to achieve a rich variety of probabilistic sampling methods that can be used in a wide range of research contexts.

The difference between non-probability and probability sampling is that *non-probability* sampling does not involve *random* selection of units. Does that mean that non-probability samples aren't representative of the population? Not necessarily. But it does mean that non-probability samples cannot depend upon the rationale of probability theory. In general, researchers prefer probabilistic or random sampling methods over non-probabilistic ones, and consider them to be more accurate and rigorous. However, in qualitative or socio-cultural research on sport, exercise and population health there are many circumstances where it is not feasible, required or even theoretically sensible to engage random sampling. We can divide non-probability sampling methods into two broad types: *serendipitous* or *purposive*. Most sampling methods are purposive in nature because we usually approach the sampling process with a specific plan in mind. Wherever, for example, we rely on non-randomly selected volunteers, students in a course we are teaching, or the average 'person on the street' for data collection process we are sampling through *serendipity* – taking whomever we can get! Other researchers commonly refer to this technique as *convenience sampling*. Clearly, the problem with all of these types of samples is that we have no evidence that they are representative of the populations we're interested in generalising about – and in many cases we would clearly suspect that they are not.

Purposive, non-probability sampling procedures take on a variety of forms. By definition, in purposive sampling we sample with a substantive or theoretical *purpose* in mind. We usually would have one or more specific pre-defined groups we are seeking. Purposive sampling can be very useful for situations where you need to reach a targeted sample quickly and where sampling for proportionality is not the primary concern. Another typical purposive sampling method is called *modal instance sampling*. When we do a modal instance sample, we are sampling the most frequent case, or the typical case. I might have learned that there is a 'typical' child, with very particular biographic details who is trafficked from South America to Europe. A modal sampling approach would seek to find those children in the geographic areas studied in Uruguay. Expert sampling involves the assembling of a sample of persons with known or demonstrable experience and expertise in some area. I might sample a range of former trafficked children currently living in Europe to provide their expert opinions on how the process unfolds.

In *quota sampling*, you select people non-randomly according to a fixed 'target' number of units in several categories or types of people who might have different knowledge about your subject at hand. I might, for example, create two main groups in the child trafficking study; those at risk of being trafficked and those formerly trafficked into Europe. Because I feel that each group has unique knowledge about the trafficking process, I determine that I will need to sample at least 100 children from each cluster in order to ensure I develop some empirical breadth and depth in my understanding of trafficking as a social process.

The last, and, I argue, the most common non-probability sampling method is *snowball sampling*. In snowball sampling, you begin by identifying someone who meets the criteria for inclusion in your study; say, a child who is at risk of being trafficked, or one who has been trafficked to Europe. After you administer your questionnaire or interview with them, you then ask them to recommend others who they may know who also meet the criteria. This technique is also referred to as the chain-referral method or the network sampling procedure. Although this method rarely leads to representative samples, there are times when it may be the best method available. Snowball sampling is especially useful when you are trying to reach populations that are esoteric, inaccessible or hard to find.

PROBLEMS, PITFALLS AND CONTROVERSIES

Samples are notoriously curmudgeonly, and this is especially true in the case of quantitative research. One might have the most pristine sampling frame from which to draw units and still people are reluctant to participate, they withdraw easily, or promise to participate and never show up for the study! Any of these situations may throw a sampling strategy into disarray. While it is best practice to have samples sorted before the study begins in order to random sample or ensure randomisation in an experimental process, such is rarely the case in real world research. Samples often 'evolve' as the research progresses. Studies of performance, health or illness conducted in kinesiology labs around the world operate on the basis of volunteerism. That is, people volunteer to participate in one protocol or another. No volunteers, means no study! My time, like the time of my colleagues, marches on and we occasionally must begin a study without the full complement of subjects required for completion. With respect to the eventual sample, then, we often do not know if the group will be well representative of the population of interest because we are forced to sample from potential volunteers who email, phone, or wander into a lab answering a posted call for participants placed somewhere on a university campus, sports complex or other public area. Once again, therefore, our empirical conclusions are shaped by the sample.

In qualitative research ventures, among the most consistent issues in sampling is that of selecting too many 'likes' in the study. Snowball sampling and convenience sampling have tendencies to produce incredibly homogeneous samples because of the social network effect inherent in the strategies. Once a researcher taps into a social network and samples therein, we often find more experiential similarities between people than differences. If one of the goals of non-probability sampling is to keep sampling people until we reach a point of 'data saturation' (i.e. where we are no longer learning anything new about the subject at hand), then sampling a group of people who are very much like one another is not the best strategy! If I used snowball sampling in the child trafficking study and my resulting sample was comprised of 47 children living within a three and a half block radius of one another in the city of Montevideo, I am probably doing something wrong with respect to the spirit of data saturation. Critics of qualitative research also note how the researcher's own tastes and preferences for particular people or their stories may colour the sampling process (normally discussed as an aspect of 'bias' in a study). Similar criticisms are launched against media, narrative/discourse and historical research efforts in that the clear majority of content analytic or semiotic studies contain degrees of arbitrariness in the sampling process.

See also: *Distributions; Inferential Statistics; Reliability; Validity.*

KEY READINGS

Bausell, R. and Li, Y.-F. (2006) *Power Analysis for Experimental Research: A Practical Guide for the Biological, Medical and Social Sciences.* Cambridge: Cambridge University Press.

Levy, P. and Lemeshow, S. (2009) *Sampling of Populations.* New York: Wiley.

Lohr, S.L. (2009) *Sampling: Design and Analysis.* Pacific Grove: Duxbury.

Rubin, D. (2006) *Matched Sampling for Causal Effects.* Cambridge: Cambridge University Press.

Positivism

Most of my students are positivists at heart, because from the time they were eight or nine years old, they have been exposed to the idea that science is the legitimate means of producing knowledge or for discovering the truth about the nature of the universe. Science is associated with facts, numbers, evidence and expert opinion. Scientific information is presented as the opposite of faith, irrationality, commonsense, intuition and emotional behaviour. But do we often understand the nature of positivism and its relationship to science? Are the central implications of positivism on our definition of science well known? Amazing to me is how few of my students actually know the axioms and principles comprising positivist epistemology and its relationship to science. Let's spend a bit of time examining some of the core elements of positivism.

WHAT IS THIS CONCEPT?

Positivism is the brainchild of Enlightenment philosophers including Auguste Comte and Henri de Saint Simon, and is practically synonymous with science. The two terms are often conflated. Positivism is, from one perspective, the pursuit of knowledge about the cause and effect nature of the world. *The roots of positivism are thus grounded in a belief in the nature of reality that is ultimately knowable through the application of the right methods of observation.* Embedded in this statement are a few fairly important assumptions. First, positivists believe that the world of reality, of truth, of facts is ultimately knowable; that is, human beings can perceive the rules and orders of our biological, psychological and socio-cultural universe. Another embedded assumption is that everything worth knowing is measurable. Human beings can, through the use of our senses, directly observe truth or reality. In classic scientific terms, positivism is based on the idea of empirical observation. The preferred method of observation among positivists is the very traditional conceptualisation of the 'scientific method'.

Based on Aristotle's laws of logic, the scientific method refers to a body of techniques for investigating phenomena, acquiring knowledge, or correcting and integrating previous knowledge. To be termed 'scientific', a method of inquiry must be based on gathering observable, empirical and measurable evidence, subject to specific principles of reasoning. A scientific method consists of the derivation of hypotheses about a phenomenon from theory, the collection of data through (most traditionally via experimentation) techniques designed to test the hypotheses, and the proposition of tentative conclusions about the hypotheses based on observed data. Steps in the scientific method must be repeatable or replicable, in order to test the veracity or accuracy of any one study, and to predict future results. Scientific inquiry is generally intended to be as objective as possible, to reduce biased interpretations of results. Why? Because positivists tend to believe that good knowledge is universal knowledge produced without any bias from a particular value set or ideology (Hacking, 1981).

WHY IS THIS RELEVANT TO ME?

Here is an experiment any student can undertake in their first, second or third year of study. Examine the textbooks you are currently using in your programme. If you are enrolled in a sport, kinesiology, health, or physical activity programme, you were likely required to enrol in biology/physiology, psychology, biomechanics, public health and/or human anatomy courses very early on in your programme. Examine each one of those books and search for alternative epistemologies to positivism. In psychology … maybe; population health … perhaps. But positivism will stand out as the main epistemological framework.

SHOW ME HOW IT'S USED!

Certain sports are almost by definition aggressive. Contact sports like rugby, American or British football, ice hockey, boxing and Olympic wrestling are indeed aggressive in a range of ways. What is especially fascinating about sports aggression is its impact on spectator emotions and behaviours. Pretend that I have asked you to design a study to investigate the theoretical 'catharsis' argument; that watching violent or aggressive acts in sport helps to curb via a safe release (rather than amplifying or provoking) the natural tendencies towards aggressive behaviours common amongst spectators. The theory is predicting a causal, testable relationship between two variables: player aggression and feelings of aggression among players.

A classic experiment on the subject would be very easy and probably preferable to conduct. Here, we could bring 20 people into our lab (let's not worry about the rigours of sampling at the moment) and show them an hour-long highlight reel of sports aggression, measuring their feeling states (using a tool like the Profile of Mood States inventory) before and after watching the footage. We might also measure the mood states of 20 people who have not been exposed to the footage, twice, at a time interval corresponding to the first group. We would then compare pre- and post-footage scores for the 'aggression' group and the two scores for our control group. If pre/post scores differ for the experimental group and are aggregately higher or lower than those for the control group, we may have found correlational evidence of the link between watching aggressive sport and aggressive feelings. If catharsis theory is accurate, I would expect to see statistically significant lower feelings of aggression in the group who had watched the video highlights.

A very similar study could be conducted through a long questionnaire sent out to people by directly asking them how they feel when they watch aggression in sport. Here, a survey methodology could be utilised in order to test a range of theories predicting the relationship between viewing aggression and feeling aggressive. There are fewer controls built into survey methodologies in comparison to experiments, but one could nevertheless explore a range of predictions regarding the psychological and sociological links between watching aggressive sport and emotions. Finally, even historical or archival analysis could be employed in the spirit of a positivist study of the spectating–aggression link. Historical research in sport, exercise and health often unfolds as a positivist enterprise, as history is described as the '[social] laboratory of the past'. Research within a country, region or city could be conducted to determine if sports aggression has the opposite effect as predicted by catharsis theory. How? One might examine a case selection of particularly violent or aggressive sports events in a particular area over a 50- or 60-year period. Then one could examine crime/police records, news reports or hospital records in the same area as a method of 'roughly' testing whether or not there is what social psychologists call a 'spillover effect' directly following aggressive events – violence in sports leads to violence in the street, which should be reflected in spikes in police arrests (battery, sexual assaults, disorderly conduct, vandalism, etc.) or hospitalisations due to violent altercations between people. Now, this would be the least 'scientific' of all the applications of positivism discussed here, but I am sure you can understand the logic of the approach. While historical or archival research does not have the built-in controls of experiments, or the direct questioning of surveying, quality historical research might reveal the actually lived and embodied (rather than lab-simulated or self-reported) responses to watching aggressive sports common (or not) in people.

PROBLEMS, PITFALLS AND CONTROVERSIES

Critics of positivist epistemology remind students and researchers that not all 'quality' knowledge can be framed by positivist parameters. Two major philosophical challenges to positivism have been initiated in universities and colleges in the last 100 years. The first is the rise of interpretivism as a rival epistemology. Interpretivism (as discussed in this book) asserts a somewhat 'radical' alternative to positivism, by focusing less on the inherent rules of reality and the universal nature of 'good' knowledge, and more on the socially constructed, interpreted and reflexive nature of human knowledge. The philosophical descendants of interpretivism, including variants of existentialism, postmodernism, feminism and post-structuralism, equally challenge the positivist emphasis on causality, objective order, universalism and the cross-cultural 'value freedom' of knowledge. Most members of these research camps not only assert different perspectives about the nature of reality as proposed by positivists, but also about the essence of empiricism, evidence, and even 'proper' science itself.

Second, the rise of *post-positivism* (also called *post-empiricism*) is a meta-theoretical stance that critiques and amends positivism itself. Why? Because what we might call 'pragmatic positivists' have increasingly realised that many of the more unbending axioms of positivism (universality, objectivity of knowledge, causal ordering of the world) may be untenable. Further still, rarely if ever do positivists produce verifiably 'true' causal statements about the nature of the world. As a result, post-positivists like Karl Popper and Thomas Kuhn believe that human knowledge is based not on unchallengeable, rock-solid foundations, but rather upon human *conjectures*. As human knowledge is thus unavoidably conjectural, the assertion of these conjectures is *warranted*, or, more specifically, justified by a set of *warrants*, which can be modified or withdrawn in the light of further investigation. The translation: this perspective is also a 'light' version of positivism – not nearly as relativistic as interpretivism, but more cautious around claims about the nature of knowledge and objective reality. So, post-positivism is an amendment to positivism that recognises these and other critiques of traditional positivism.

See also: Experiments; Hypotheses; Questionnaires; Research Questions.

KEY READINGS

Hacking, I. (1981) *Scientific Revolutions*. Oxford: Oxford University Press.

Krige, J. and Dominique P. (2003) *Science in the Twentieth Century*. New York: Routledge.

Mises, R. (1951) *Positivism: A Study in Human Understanding*. Cambridge, MA: Harvard University Press.

Newton-Smith, W. (1994) *The Rationality of Science*. London: Routledge.

Popper, K. (2002) *Conjectures and Refutations: The Growth of Scientific Knowledge*. London: Routledge.

Popper, K. (2002) *The Logic of Scientific Discovery*. New York: Routledge.

Rollin, B. (2006) *Science and Ethics*. Cambridge: Cambridge University Press.

positivism

Quantitative vs. Qualitative Research

From the very first days of my undergraduate training I heard stories about the vast differences between qualitative and quantitative research and how the two main 'camps' are the academic equivalent of the Capulets and the Montagues. How different the approaches to research are in theory and practice, the degree to which they create divisions between students and colleagues, and their impacts on knowledge generation processes are subject to enduring debate. An understanding of the essential, or perhaps ideal-type, bases of each approach is fundamental in assessing the role of each style of research in the contemporary academy.

WHAT IS THIS CONCEPT?

A *methodology* is an overall approach to the accumulation of knowledge based on theoretical and philosophical principles about what can be known by people and how it can be known through particular techniques of knowledge acquisition. A *method* refers to the techniques of knowledge acquisition. While the two terms are used synonymously, consider a method as a sub-component of one's overall methodology.

Quantitative methodology is based on the interconnection between the practice of deductive theory testing, a belief in objectivism, and the application of positivist methods of inquiry. Deductive theory testing means using principles derived from theories that explain events, happenings, processes, entities, phenomena in the world as the basis for our research. In the deductive approach to research, evidence is gathered in to test whether or not pre-existing theoretical ideas are accurate and predictive when applied to 'real-world' data. A general belief in objectivism refers to the philosophical idea that the world is organised by general, universal social and biological laws governing life. These laws pattern or structure the world, and exist independently of human subjective interpretation of them. Finally, quantitative researchers 'know' the world by collecting data through positivist techniques such as large-scale surveys, standardised scales and questionnaires, and, most importantly, through experimental protocols. These techniques measure concepts in the world numerically, and privilege the statistical analysis of data to test research hypotheses. The goal of quantitative methodology is to examine whether or not research hypotheses (as derived from theory) have any predictive and explanatory value in the world as evidenced by patterns in objective, numeric data. Quantitative methodology is most popular among sport and exercise physiologists, biomechanists, psychologists and nutritionists.

Qualitative methodology, by contrast, is based on the interconnection between the goals of inductively developing theoretical understandings of the world, a belief in constructionism/subjectivism, and the application of interpretivist methods of inquiry. Induction refers to the process of collecting data in order to tease out or build a theoretical understanding of the world. In the inductive approach to research, academics may commence a study with only a very loose or fragmented understanding of a subject and build a more conceptual, general theoretical description of the subject through careful observation of it over time. Constructionism or subjectivism refers to a philosophical position that the reality of social (and to a degree social psychological or psychological) experiences is a matter of subjective interpretation. There are no fixed laws governing all life or social processes, but, rather, the realities of life are constructed by people on an ongoing and everyday basis. Thus, interpretivist methods are explored in research practice. Interpretivist methods are those designed to allow researchers to understand how people construct and understand the realities of their lived experiences. Qualitative

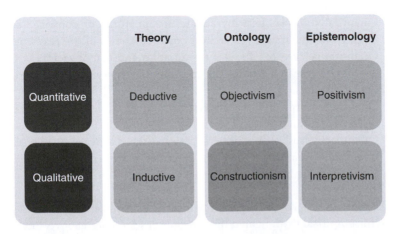

Figure 4 Quantitative and qualitative methodologies

methodologists argue that, to understand others, techniques of data collection such as observation, ethnography, interviewing and narrative analysis are required.

The nature of a research question itself indicates the researcher's methodological standpoint or preferences. Consider the following examples and identify which methodological camp gives rise to the question:

- Does the consumption of a maltodextrin-fructose drink (250ml) every 25 minutes of competition delay onset of perceived muscle fatigue for elite-level women tennis players during matches lasting two or more sets?
- What are elite-level women tennis players' definitions of femininity in the sporting world?

WHY IS THIS RELEVANT TO ME?

I could most likely spend the better part of the next year researching and reviewing all that has been written about the apparent differences between quantitative and qualitative methodologies. Quantitative methodologies tend to be privileged amongst students as 'science', while qualitative methodologists are generally understood as interesting and relevant but biased and unscientific. The key differences focused upon by students and academics alike are the following:

- Quantitative data, as numeric, are objective while qualitative data, as words, images and texts, are subjective.
- Quantitative researchers investigate in 'unnatural' or contrived settings, while qualitative researchers conduct studies in the real world.
- Quantitative research focuses on variables and causal factors while qualitative research studies the meaning of experiences within particular cultures.
- Quantitative research is always deductive while all qualitative research is inductive.
- Quantitative research is directed toward the discovery of scientific laws while qualitative research identifies patterns in how people assign meaning to life.

Like most myths, commonly held beliefs, or general assumptions, there is some empirical truth behind the dichotomies presented above. But the problem with the acceptance and reproduction of binaries lies in the ways in which students are asked, if not forced, to develop a 'this or that' mentality regarding what counts as legitimate knowledge. Rather than internalising and fully understanding the age-old methodological credo that the method(ology) should follow the question at hand, students often develop a mindset geared towards methodological tunnel vision.

SHOW ME HOW IT'S USED!

I love conducting quantitative research because of the linearity of the methodology. A well-planned quantitative study is elegant in both design and execution. If you are a person who believes in the scientific method, and who sees the world as organised (or some might say, 'determined') by factors, variables and forces, then quantitative methodology is for you. Quantitative research is conducted through a very common series of steps. First, a researcher develops a curiosity about the causal relationship between two 'things' in the world: say, between the consumption of a sports drink and fatigue during long bouts of exercise. Based on theory (bio-physical, in this case) the researcher is led to predict that a particular maltodextrin concentrated drink will delay fatigue in the body more effectively than water alone (this becomes the researcher's hypothesis). From there, the researcher determines the best way to measure the effects of drinking the concoction on fatigue, and how best to observe the process unfold in the body. Subjects are selected for the study and the researcher's hypothesis is tested in a standardised, controlled manner using the group. The relevant data are collected and transformed into numeric observations, and then analysed through a statistics computer program. From there, the researcher examines whether or not the numeric data reveal any definitive patterns regarding the original hypothesis, and concludes whether or not the theory of how maltodextrin drinks affect the body is supported by the evidence. The methodology is simple, clean, focused and efficient.

Despite the generationally reproduced reputation of qualitative research as 'soft' or as somewhat 'easier' than quantitative research, the reverse is most likely the case. Conducting qualitative research is far messier than quantitative research for at least a dozen reasons. First, qualitative research begins with a curiosity about something in the world, but does not commence with the guiding framework of theoretical axioms. Qualitative questions do not start with a predictive statement such as 'I bet this is related to this in this manner' (like quantitative

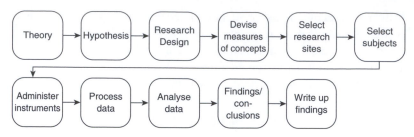

Figure 5 Steps in quantitative research

research questions), but are general and open-ended. 'How do women tennis players construct femininity?', 'What is it like to live with cancer as a competitive athlete?', or 'How do young people experience medical discourses about obesity?', are all open-ended qualitative questions. Supposedly unguided by extant socio-cultural theories, a researcher who poses a question like 'How do women tennis players construct femininity?', must then select a group of women tennis players to study. From there, decisions regarding how one actually 'measures' their constructions of femininity follow; that is, how can we observe or learn their subjective constructions of femininity (the dominant method of choice is interviewing). Data are collected through a qualitative method, and then 'openly' analysed. Using words, phrases, actions or observations made regarding how women construct femininity, a researcher is presented with the task of abstracting concepts and potentially theories about gender from the data. It is precisely the opposite technique to that employed in quantitative research, and requires creativity, analysis and re-analysis of data, reframing the main questions underpinning the study over time. Although this seems insane to students at first, the true

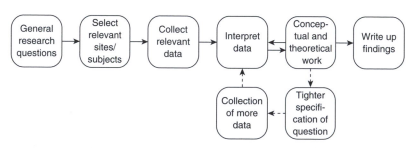

Figure 6 Steps in qualitative research

(substantive and theoretical) focus of the study may not emerge until midway through or even near the end of a project.

Qualitative research is, then, inherently frustrating for many students at first because it is not nearly as 'structured' or tightly packaged as quantitative methodology. Measurement procedures can be vague and not guided by templates or rules.

PROBLEMS, PITFALLS AND CONTROVERSIES

There is a fine line to be walked in the discussion, instruction and practice of qualitative and quantitative methodologies. While the methodologies are inevitably presented and practised sequentially in a research skills course as opposites, their respective contributions to the knowledge generation process should not be treated as anti-thetical to one another. Two stereotypes about the methodologies are also worth noting briefly. First, the commonly held notion that quantitative research cannot attest to meaning because it does not examine the contexts of life can be a warranted criticism but is not universally accurate. Survey methods in particular can measure context and examine the situated nature of how life unfolds. Additionally, survey and experimental methods can be used to examine meaning, motivation, situational reaction and subjective construction by people/groups, and how they define things in the world as real.

Second, the widespread notion that qualitative research is undertaken inductively is perhaps one of the grossest misrepresentations of actual research practice. While induction is, in fairness, the ideal-type approach to theory and conceptual development when engaging in qualitative research, qualitative research practitioners often commence studies with pre-figured theoretical and conceptual guides in mind for 'reading' their data. As qualitative researchers develop theoretical preferences for understanding the world, studies evolve as ways of applying (but not testing!) concepts and theories in new ways or in new social contexts. While this might seem to be a small criticism or technicality, the use of theory or concepts as 'sensitising' challenges the very philosophical heart of qualitative methodology. Using well-defined theories and concepts to entirely direct a qualitative study is conceptually the reverse methodological 'offence' to the practice of 'data mining' for correlations (or the practice of 'exploratory factor analysis') in quantitative research. Methodologists including Alan Bryman (2004) have noted that, given the above trends and others, perhaps the immutable differences existing between the two camps are more of a textbook reality than an empirical one.

See also: *Applied vs. Pure Research; Research Questions.*

KEY READINGS

Andrews, D. and Silk, M. (2005) *Qualitative Methods in Sports Studies.* New York: Berg Publishers.

Bryman, A. (2004) *Social Research Methods.* Oxford: Oxford University Press.

Cicciarella, C. (1997) *Research in Physical Education, Exercise Science, and Sport: An Introduction.* Scottsdale: Gorsuch Scarisbrick.

Gratton, C. and Jones, I. (2003) *Research Methods for Sports Studies.* New York: Routledge.

Williams, C. and Wagg, C. (2003) *Data Analysis and Research for Sport and Exercise Science: A Student Guide.* London: Routledge.

Questionnaires

Every once in a while my telephone rings at around 6:30pm and I cringe. I'm never expecting a call from my mother, workmate or a friend at that time. Perhaps foolishly, I pick up the phone and sheepishly say, 'hello'. On the other end of the line is normally a young woman who immediately says, 'Hi there, sir, I am from Company X, and I was wondering if you had a few minutes to answer some questions we have for you about your [household needs of some sort].' Why am I so stupid, and answer the phone every time! But then I quickly remember that she and I are not so different. We are both just researchers trying to gather empirical information about a subject at hand. I reflect and ask myself, do I make other people cringe when I ask them to participate in a survey of mine? That's a very sobering thought, so about 9 times out of 10, I say to the young researcher, 'sure, no problem at all' because I understand the role of survey research as an important data collection tool across social institutions.

WHAT IS THIS CONCEPT?

Many elite athletes use visualisation techniques in training and competition. There are many stories of athletes who've used these techniques to cultivate not only a competitive edge, but also to create renewed mental awareness, a heightened sense of well-being and confidence. All of these factors have been shown to contribute to an athlete's sports success in existing sports psychological research. Generally speaking, visualisation is the process of creating a mental image or intention of what you want to happen or feel.

But do athletes, in general, know anything about visualisation and its effectiveness? How do athletes feel about and understand the importance of visualisation in their training and performance regimens? How ubiquitous is visualisation in sports cultures? Are there key socio-demographic differences between athletes who employ visualisation and those who do not? What leads an athlete to these techniques? I could develop a whole range of predictive hypotheses to test my theoretical ideas regarding how athletes come to use visualisation and how they experience the effects. Rather than interview several hundred athletes, I could develop a survey to collect my information. Surveys are a classically positivist approach to hypothesis testing. Designed to minimise the impact of researcher bias in the question-asking process, surveys are lauded as standardised research instruments that ask respondents to 'score' or rank themselves on the variables we are measuring in a study. Because survey questions are standardised (i.e. every respondent receives the same survey questionnaire, using the identical question wording, ordering and general appearance), the survey approach to measurement lends itself well to replication, and therefore, may generate high levels of reliability and external validity.

Survey/questionnaire-based research is common in the social and psychological study of sport and exercise, and is normally undertaken for either purely descriptive or deductive/theory-testing purposes. There are literally dozens and dozens of existing questionnaires and surveys that researchers use to study everything from population level involvement in organised, leisure and physical activity, to the psychological mood states and profiles of athletes, to attitudes about sport programmes offered in an area. Not only do academics within universities employ survey methods quite widely, government and 'official statistics' agencies regularly survey groups in order to track health behaviours, physical activity pursuits, and knowledge of physical activity opportunities in a region. Surveys are used from time to time to gather information from a small group of people, but the data collection technique is ideal for collecting and statistically analysing large amounts of information on people.

Surveys are regarded as ideal tools for data collection when researchers need to gather simple descriptive information on people's behaviours and backgrounds, or when they seek to measure people's attitudes about a given subject. Surveys take on a variety of forms (see below) but normally contain three basic types of question. The questions on surveys are the empirical measurements (indicators) for variables in the hypotheses guiding our research. Even more importantly, they represent or stand in for the empirical concepts in the theory(ies) which initially inform the hypotheses themselves. Very cool. Questions on a survey are categorised as *closed, open-ended* or *scale-based*. Closed questions represent the lion's share of measures on a survey, and are structured so that how participants' answers vary is determined by the researchers' themselves before the survey is administered. A question is asked, and then respondents select from a standard, pre-determined range of responses available to them. Open-ended questions are more qualitative questions in which researchers ask subjects to briefly describe something or provide a subjective reaction to a statement provided on the survey related to the research question.

Finally, scale-based questions are a special and revered form of attitude measurement. Many socio-cultural and psychological researchers of sport believe that we can measure both conscious and subconscious attitudes people have pertaining to sport, exercise, physical activities, health and wellness. These attitudes can be measured by a series of projective and inferential techniques, or by straightforwardly asking people to self-evaluate how they feel about a particular subject, or a personal characteristic. Scale questions in general ask respondents to rank or quantify their attitudes or the frequency of their behaviours (from which we infer attitudes). Popular are Likert-type scale and visual analogue questions in which people are asked a question in a 'statement format' (such as 'Visualisation has improved my self-confidence in the past year') and then presented with a numeric scale underneath the question on which they rank how strongly they agree or disagree with the statement. These scales normally range from 1 to 5 or 1 to 7, with numbers corresponding to answers including, 1 = strongly disagree; 2 = somewhat disagree; 3 = neither agree nor disagree; 4 = somewhat agree; 5 = strongly agree).

WHY IS THIS RELEVANT TO ME?

Survey research designs have been around for a long time, and all indications suggests they will continue to thrive in academia. Surveys are tailor-made techniques for hypothesis testing in scenarios when experiments are inappropriate or unneeded, but we need standardised data on a large number of people. It's just that simple. Surveys are most relevant for psychologists, sociologists, pedagogues, policy analysts and management experts in sport and exercise because they are generally used to measure people's personal 'characteristics', attitudes, behaviours and emotions (or mood states) related to sport, exercise and health phenomena.

Sport England's 'Active People Survey' has been collected in the UK since 2005. The survey provides by far the largest sample size ever established for a sport and recreation survey and produces previously unavailable levels of detailed analysis on patterns of participation in physical activity and how they vary from place to place and between different groups in the British population. The survey measures, among other things, the proportion of the adult population who volunteer in sport on a weekly basis, club membership, involvement in organised sport/competition, receipt of tuition or coaching, and overall satisfaction with levels of sporting provision in the local community. In the first year of the survey alone, 363,724 adults in England (aged 16 plus) responded to the Active People Survey questionnaire. Since then, a minimum of 1,000 surveys have been completed in every local authority in England (354 local authorities) on a yearly basis. The questionnaire is designed to enable analysis of the findings by a broad range of demographic information, such as gender, social class, ethnicity, household structure, age and disability.

SHOW ME HOW IT'S USED!

The steps in the survey process come about as close to a tried, tested and true formula as one could find in research methodology. The real 'grunt work' in conducting survey-based research is in the initial phases of survey construction. Constructing a survey from scratch is a time-consuming and frustrating task. Without delving into too much detail, copious amounts of time are devoted to ensuring the survey questions themselves well capture the meaning of the concepts/variables they are measuring (validity issues) and are also consistent as measures (reliability issues). Indeed, months may be spent testing the reliability of our questions, especially when multiple questions are used to measure a single variable (here, we employ techniques like the split-half or test-retest method in 'large' pilot tests in order to examine reliability). A 'minor' checklist of issues to consider when designing a survey is comprised of at least the following:

- Whether we have done well in translating the theoretical meaning of concepts into variables and then measures on our survey;
- Whether or not we have achieved 'full dimensionality' (i.e. whether the measures capture the full meaning of the concepts);
- How we can maximise response rate for the survey (e.g. are there too many questions for people; is too much knowledge assumed; is the layout of the survey frustrating or confusing for people?).

We reflexively examine our surveys in order to inspect them for systematic error at this stage. But in order to really test the survey's strength, we need to conduct a pilot test using a convenience sample of respondents. A pilot test is crucial for examining whether there is any systematic measurement error in the survey and if/when/how random error emerges – threats to reliability and validity in our research can be identified quite quickly at this stage.

If everything is fine during the pilot testing, then we proceed on to the full administration of the survey. There are three general formats of surveys: *the self-report survey*, *the telephone survey* and the *face-to face survey*. Self-report surveys are 'sent' to the sample of respondents in one manner or another (normally through the mail or via an online survey site). Self-report surveys are more cost effective than other survey techniques, allow researchers to cover a wide geographic distribution of respondents, provide heightened anonymity for respondents and reduce desirability effects in the data collection process. However, they tend to produce lower response rates than other techniques, and are normally shorter than other forms of surveys. Telephone surveys are like self-report surveys (questions, format, etc.) but are administered to people directly over the telephone. They are quite cost efficient techniques with the potential to reach geographically spread-out members of the population, and tend to have higher response rates than self-report surveys (think about that … it's easier to throw away a mailed survey, or delete an emailed request to fill in an online survey than it is to say no to someone on the phone). But what about people who cannot be contacted by phone easily? Does the 'presence' of an administrator influence how people answer? How long can we keep someone on the phone, and does the length of the survey potentially affect how people answer? Finally, face-to-face surveys are exactly as they sound; a survey administered to someone directly to them in person. Face-to-face surveys produce the highest response rates and can effectively combat problems with random error (usually due to respondent confusion over one or another question), but with them comes a massive (personnel) cost and a large risk of social desirability effects entering into the process.

Wonderful, great, now how do we proceed after all of the surveys are returned? Every answer, to every question, for every respondent is transformed into a number and entered into a master file in a data processing or statistics program like SPSS, STATA, R, or Excel. All of the rules and orders for the coding process need to be established long before any shred of empirical evidence is gathered. Given the statistical results, inferences are then drawn as to what can be concluded about the hypotheses under investigation in our research.

PROBLEMS, PITFALLS AND CONTROVERSIES

Even though I fully understand the need to participate in surveys as a researcher myself, my response rate for surveys that come across my email, desk or home is probably less than 30%. Low response rates in survey methods is very, very common and kills one's confidence in the results. Why? Because when the potential pool of respondents is lowered by 50% or more, one's sense that the respondent sample will be a microcosm of the broader theoretical population is reduced – limiting the inferences allowable from the data and their overall credibility. This is why there are any number of built-in mechanisms within the method (the use of online surveys, follow-up letters, monetary incentive, phone call reminders, carefully worded introductions to the survey proclaiming how important the research is and how grateful the researchers are that one is participating) to try and bolster response rates.

Surveys obtain information by asking people questions. Those questions are designed to succinctly measure some topic of interest, and the validity and reliability of survey questions is often critiqued. Careful crafting of survey questions is essential, and even slight variations in wording can produce rather different results.

Among the best ways of ensuring the reliability of respondents' answers is to use multiple questions on a survey that measure a behaviour, or gather a large enough sample that will 'correct for' tendencies in under- and over-reporting amongst some subjects. Even when reliable and valid questions are asked, there can still be serious problems due to missing data. Missing data comes in three varieties: people who refuse to participate (the issue of response rates), questions that are left unanswered (the issue of items missing values), and (in longitudinal studies), respondents who are lost to follow-up (the issue of attrition). The problem is that missing data results in: (1) biased findings if the people for whom data is missing are systematically different; (2) inefficient statistical estimates due to the loss of information; and (3) increased analytic complexity in reading sample data. Finally, perhaps the most important limitation of cross-sectional surveys has to do with their relative lack of ability to empirically demonstrate causal relationships.

See also: Causality; Descriptive Statistics; Distributions; Hypotheses; Inferential Statistics; Populations and Samples; Reliability; Validity.

KEY READINGS

Cohen, L., Manion, L. and Morrison, K. (2000) *Research Methods in Education*. New York: Routledge.

Frazer, L. (2000) *Questionnaire Design and Administration: A Practical Guide*. New York: Wiley & Sons.

Martin, S., Kellmann, M., Lavallee, D. and Page, S. (2002) 'Development and psychometric evaluation of the Sport Psychology Attitudes – Revised Form: A multiple group investigation'. *The Sport Psychologist* 16: 272–290.

Patten, M. (1998) *Questionnaire Research: A Practical Guide*. Los Angeles: Pyrczak.

Shephard, R. (2003) 'Limits to the measurement of habitual physical activity by questionnaires'. *British Journal of Sports Medicine* 37: 197–206.

Reliability

Have you ever learned a new skill in sport or exercise? Did it feel natural at first? Probably not, unless you are one of those rare and gifted people who take to athletics naturally. For most people, learning how to paddle a canoe, for example, is a strange event. Not until dozens or perhaps hundreds of hours have passed in the canoe will you develop enough practice with paddling before the motion seems natural. Exercise physiologists suggest that it takes anywhere from 4,000 to 10,000 repetitions of a task before enough 'muscle memory' sets to make the task comfortable. When the muscles develop certain movement intelligence, the body moves consistently and quite predictably. Novice golfers are certainly envious of professional who have swung clubs so many times that the clubs are like extensions of the body itself; the swing is so consistent, so repeatable, so known, that any irregularities are shocking. In human movement then, consistency, repeatability and predictability are the same things. They are valued characteristics in performance and people spend their young lives training to achieve them. In the world of research, consistency and repeatability in the measurement process are equally valued and sought after.

WHAT IS THIS CONCEPT?

Reliability is a benchmark concept in quantitative research. A preliminary definition of reliability is the degree to which repeated measurement produces similar results over time. Kirk and Miller (1986) identify three types of reliability referred to in conventional research, which relate to: (1) the degree to which a measurement, given repeatedly, remains the same; (2) the stability of a measurement over time; and (3) the similarity of measurements within a given time period. Reliability thus generally refers to the consistency of a measure, and so a test assessing one's introversion or extroversion is considered reliable if we get the same result for individual subjects repeatedly. If a test is designed to truly measure a trait such as introversion, then each time the test is administered to a subject, the results should be approximately the same for that subject. Sounds reasonable enough, yes? If I choose to measure someone's height, their drive for perfectionism, their age, their body fat percentage, their religious beliefs, or their self-efficacy, the respective measures I select for each must be consistent if people are measured again and again (that is, as long as nothing has changed about that person during the periods between measurement!). If a measurement tool is not consistent and thus results are not repeatable, there is no reliability in my research design. Why is this important? Well, because defending the degree of reliability in our research process is an important stage in defending the knowledge claims we offer through the research itself.

The (lack of) reliability of the measurement process can be influenced rather heavily by random and systematic error. Random error in the measurement process can be produced by a million different events, factors or slip-ups normally out of the researcher's immediate control. A printer might inaccurately print a question on a survey, or a subject might come to an experiment feeling atypically angry or sad that day and thus her performance in the experiment is affected. Any number of uncontrolled variables in a study can influence the measurement process and therefore the consistency of results. Systematic error is far more worrying for researchers than random error. Imagine a weigh scale that is miscalibrated by 2kg. Every time I get on I weigh 70kg, but my weight is actually 72kg! While ostensibly reliable, the results are inaccurate (biased and therefore not valid) because of a systematic error in my measurement tool. So, while random error varies throughout the research, systematic error is constant in the measurement process.

Qualitative researchers approach the notion of reliability with trepidation. The type of reliability described above is informed by the positivist epistemology and a realist ontology. Because qualitative research is not as concerned with theory testing and measuring 'true' or consistent scores for people on variables, assessments of reliability in qualitative research are staged on alternative ground and carry different implications. Guba and Lincoln (1994) propose that inspections of the quality or integrity of qualitative measurement are better conceptualised as a process of assessing the dependability of findings. Dependability, or 'trustworthiness', is a general interpretive assessment of whether or not the researcher has reflexively accounted for how interpretive, contextual conclusions were reached within a study. Guba and Lincoln (1994) encourage 'audits' of qualitative research (basically reviews by colleagues) to assess whether or not the inductive conclusions offered in the results appear logical or 'dependable' given the described research context and protocol.

WHY IS THIS RELEVANT TO ME?

There are two main reasons as to why reliability is relevant in the research process. The first is discussed *ad nauseam* in methodology manuals, while the other very infrequently. First, if I cannot demonstrate that my measurement process has any *internal consistency* or *dependability*, then I am in a significant amount of trouble! Imagine measuring one's social background on a survey and receiving different results for that person each time! Second, there is a major assumption about measurement underwritten in the idea of reliability; true score theory (TST).

True score theory assumes that a complex concept like one's introversion or extroversion (what we could call *social character*) is a 'real thing' that can be accurately measured and quantified if we ask valid questions. I find this construction of reality to be among the most consequential ideas in science. Based on the scales researchers manufacture to measure social character, everyone will have a 'true' score representing how much of an introvert or extrovert they are in life. *Ceteris paribus*, one's social character should be stable over the life course and our method of measurement should reveal their true score.

True score theory maintains that every measurement is an additive composite of two components: *true ability* (or the true level) of the respondent on that measure; and *random error*. We observe the measurement – the score on the social character test, but we do not observe random error, unfortunately. A measure that has no random error (i.e. is all true score) is perfectly reliable; a measure that has no true score (i.e. is all random error) has zero reliability. Reliability is never perfect, however, because we can never totally account for random error in the measurement process.

SHOW ME HOW IT'S USED!

There is no way to perfectly assess or determine the reliability of a given measure. What a frustrating situation! But quantitative researchers examine four kinds of reliability in assessing the quality of any given study. Tests of reliability may be undertaken before a study commences, but typically occur after at least a portion of data has been gathered. The four reliability 'tests' are:

1. *Inter-rater or inter-observer reliability*: Used to assess the degree to which different raters/observers give consistent estimates of the same phenomenon. When multiple people are giving assessments of some kind or are the subjects of some test, then similar people should lead to the same resulting scores. It can be used to calibrate people, for example those being used as observers in an experiment. Inter-rater reliability thus evaluates reliability *across different people*. Two major ways in which inter-rater reliability is used are: (a) testing how similarly people *categorise* items; and (b) how similarly people *score* items. This is the best way of assessing reliability when you are using observation, as observer bias very easily creeps in. It does, however, assume you have multiple observers, which is not always the case. Inter-rater reliability is also known as *inter-observer reliability* or

inter-coder reliability. Observers being used in assessing hospital patients' stress are asked to assess several 'dummy' people who are briefed to respond in a programmed and consistent way. The variation in results from a standard gives a measure of their reliability.

2. *Test-retest reliability*: Used to assess the consistency of a measure from one time to another. An assessment or test of a person should give the same results whenever you apply the test. Test-retest reliability evaluates reliability across *time*. Reliability can vary with the many factors that affect how a person responds to the test, including their mood, interruptions, time of day, etc. A good test will largely cope with such factors and give relatively little variation. An unreliable test is highly sensitive to such factors and will give widely varying results, even if the person re-takes the same test half an hour later. Generally speaking, the longer the delay between tests, the greater the likely variation. Better tests will give less retest variation with longer delays. Of course the problems with test-retest are that people may have become accustomed to it and that the second test is likely to give different results. This method is particularly used in experiments that use a no-treatment control group that is measured pre-test and post-test. Various questions for a social character test are tried out with a class of students over several years. This helps the researcher determine those questions and combinations that have better reliability.

3. *Parallel-forms reliability*: Used to assess the consistency of the results of two tests constructed in the same way from the same content domain. One problem with questions or assessments is knowing what questions are the best ones to ask. A way of discovering this is to do two tests in parallel, using different questions. Parallel-forms reliability evaluates different questions and question sets that seek to assess the same construct. Parallel-forms evaluation may be done in combination with other methods, such as *split-half*, which divides items that measure the same construct into two tests and applies them to the same group of people. For instance, an experimenter develops a large set of questions measuring social character. They split these into two and administer them each to a randomly selected half of a target sample.

4. *Internal consistency reliability*: Used to assess the consistency of results across items within a test. Imagine I have created 17 questions to measure your social character on a survey. Different questions that test the same construct should give consistent results. If all of

the questions are measured on a scale from 1 to 9 (1 indicating introvert and 9 indicating extrovert) then extroverts should answer 9 or very close to it on all 17 questions. Internal consistency reliability evaluates individual questions in comparison with one another for their ability to give consistently appropriate results. This is a kind of reliability assessed through statistical techniques such as *average inter-item correlation, average item total correlation, split-half correlation* and *Cronbach's alpha*.

PROBLEMS, PITFALLS AND CONTROVERSIES

Reliability does not ensure valid, and therefore meaningful, results. Remember the example of the scale I provided earlier in this entry. Reliability is evaluated and managed in pilot studies of a research protocol and seemingly verified by post hoc statistical analysis of results. But consistent and therefore repeatable results do not reaffirm that the conceptualisation and operationalisation procedures leading to measurement were sound. Poor conceptualisation and operationalisation may in fact be masked by consistent results. Maybe my questions about social character actually measure self-efficacy! The results would be internally consistent and probably repeatable, but unless we perform a series of checks on the validity of our measurement process, notions of reliability in our survey only present half the diagnostic story.

Controversy arises regarding the appropriateness of the concept of reliability in qualitative research. The ways in which reliability is assessed in qualitative studies (if at all – I cannot remember any reviewer of any qualitative article I have published raising questions of reliability in a review of my work) tends to be as interpretive and reflexive as the data analysis process itself. How sound is the theoretical interpretation? Does the question fit with the methods employed, and are the results reasonable given the context of research? Would another researcher armed with this qualitative data reach similar interpretive conclusions? Is there any plausibly transferable or trans-contextual evidence produced in this study? These sorts of questions and others are utilised to assess the reliability of qualitative research from time to time. But be aware, the answers to the questions are not reached in an objective manner. So, how reliable are these assessments of reliability! Richardson (1999), among others, advocates the abandonment of positivistic criteria for assessing research entirely, and proposes that the 'reliability' of qualitative research be judged by its illumination of the human condition,

reliability

its communication of believable knowledge about lived experience, its emotional impact on audiences, and even its aesthetic value.

See also: Quantitative vs. Qualitative Research; Validity.

KEY READINGS

Guba, E. and Lincoln, Y. (1994) 'Competing paradigms in qualitative research', in N. Denzin and Y. Lincoln (eds), *Handbook of Qualitative Research*. Thousand Oaks, CA: Sage. pp. 105–117.

Hopkins, W. (2000) 'Measures of reliability in sports medicine and science'. *Sports Medicine* 30: 1–15.

Kirk, J. and Miller, M. (1986) *Reliability and Validity in Qualitative Research*. Beverley Hills, CA: Sage.

Richardson, L. (1999) 'Feathers in our CAP'. *Journal of Contemporary Ethnography*, 28: 660–668.

Traub, R. (1994) *Reliability for the Social Sciences*. London: Sage.

Viswanathan, M. (2005) *Measurement Error and Research Design*. New York: Sage.

Walker, I. (2010) *Reliability in Scientific Research: Improving the Dependability of Measurements, Calculations, Equipment, & Software*. Cambridge: Cambridge University Press.

Representation

Almost every evening when I come through the door on my return from work, my eldest son Eoghan greets me to ask me about my day, 'What did you do today, dad?' Given the day, I might have spent anywhere from two or three to ten hours out of my house. What do I tell him? His mind would numb at some of the finer particulars of my workday. His eyes might roll from an account of the tedium of meetings, or writing and reading endless emails. So I selectively edit, providing him a portrait of my day he will find interesting. I don't lie to him – fashioning a narrative of me saving people from burning buildings or fending off criminals in a corner shop – but I simply string together bits and pieces he might find amusing or at least worthy of his attention. In essence, I've selected to represent what constitutes a 'day' in my life in a four- or five-minute narrative. The representation is selective, deliberate, audience sensitive and dialogical with his question. As simple as recounting a day is to one's five-year-old son, representing years of fieldwork among dozens of participants, hundreds of hours in a lab with 80 subjects, or data on 200 survey questions from several thousand respondents is not so easy to represent. In what follows the process and politics of academic 'representation' will be discussed.

WHAT IS THIS CONCEPT?

Representation is the process of assembling, sifting through, reducing and ultimately summarising data in a research project. In its most simplistic form, representation is the process of telling and showing people your research results in a written or graphic form. In a much more complicated form, representational processes cut across the entire research act. Among the most difficult set of interrelated tasks in the research process is deciding upon a way of collecting data which 'represent' a theoretical concept under scrutiny, reducing the mass of data one might acquire into a manageable form and then presenting one's conclusions to audiences such that one's narrowly defined research question is answered. Here's an example to help clarify. I recently initiated a study of Developmental Coordination Disorder (DCD) among a group of youth in Canada. DCD is an intriguing condition; it manifests as a fine motor skill disorder, and those afflicted with it struggle considerably with simple tasks such as tying their shoelaces, writing, balancing in non-routine ways, and even running. Children with DCD tend to fear and eventually withdraw from physical education entirely; as such, they tend to have higher rates of obesity, lower self-efficacy and aversions towards sport in comparison to their peers (Cairney et al., 2007). DCD's aetiology in the body is relatively unknown, as sufferers do not present physical trauma, brain lesions or other markers typically associated with neurological/motor skill problems. I am studying how youth (a sample of 210 children, aged 6–10) effectively manage DCD in playground and physical education settings, how they construct their physical disabilities, and what might be done to work with children with DCD in order to facilitate a greater range of sport and physical activities for them in school and elsewhere. This is a qualitative and quantitative study, employing observation, survey scales, interviews and photo-elicitation techniques.

By the end of the study, I will have interviewed 135 children, surveyed 205, used photo-elicitation techniques with 75 and conducted classroom observation in six settings over the course of 80 hours or more. In other words, I will have data capturing or 'representing' the lived realities of DCD shared by the kids. Interview data will provided

representation

descriptive accounts of everyday life with DCD (including the social, emotional and cultural aspects of it), the quantitative data will represent the psychological profiles of the children, and the observational data will shed light on how DCD is performed socially in physical activity groups and pedagogical contexts. But imagine the amount of written and recorded data I will have at the end of the study. Consider how, for example, a 45- or 60-minute interview with one child might produce 75 or so pages of typed transcripts. We simply cannot report everything we have collected over the course of a study; this is would be impossible. A major task, then, in the act of research is developing a system of representation in order to 'concisely' answer the research questions fuelling our studies, and to summarise the data in an aggregate manner. Other chapters in this book outlining techniques of data analysis provide information on how the process of reduction is accomplished given specific methodologies. Of far greater concern in the remainder of this entry are the contested philosophies of representation implicit in the research process and the consequences of particular styles of representation on academic knowledge creation and dissemination.

WHY IS THIS RELEVANT TO ME?

In order to represent DCD in a written report, I have to boil down vast amounts of data into categories, concepts, themes, patterns and typologies. Findings I perceive as interesting, common, contradictory and especially illuminating might be included, and the banal, rare, or undeveloped bits of data jettisoned. The great majority of the messy details of participants' lives, identities, mindsets and social relationships are excluded. This occurs as a necessary stage in the research process. Consider any laboratory study of the effects of smoking on the body. Researchers will not, in any given study, examine every body system, but instead might focus on the lungs, or the throat, or even the tongue alone. Even then, the examination might be contoured as a cancer study alone. Examinations of the world are selective and reductive by design. But just as we reduce in practice, we then reassemble. All of the fragments of data – strewn across endless document files on my computer, including word processing files and spreadsheets – will stare up at me like paint cans brimming with fresh colours. Through prescribed data analytic techniques, I will search for patterns, themes and commonalities in the data. In their discovery I am assembling 'realist' knowledge; here is the truth of DCD emerging to me. Extracting and collating data to represent the reality of DCD are the acts of scientific narrative; as a system of knowledge production through storytelling. We collect and examine many 'texts' (e.g. field notes, interview transcripts, pictures, coded answers from questionnaires, and so on) and transform them into an academic text.

SHOW ME HOW IT'S USED!

The act of representation through report writing is a process of making an argument and offering a related set of conclusions regarding one's original research question. How one argues with data (the essence of the research process) is closely related to one's method(ology), among other things.

Quantitative researchers argue with numbers. They represent bodies, minds, groups and societies through tables packed with coefficients, estimate values and probabilities. Numeric data contained in a table is a text like any other text; it is a stand-in, an avatar for complex physiological, mental, emotional, social or cultural phenomena. Vast amounts of data on these complex systems are then reduced to several numeric figures upon which decisions about hypotheses and their supporting theories are to be based. Qualitative researchers generally favour written, verbose texts. Instead of carefully arranged tabular data, qualitative researchers offer 'evidence' of social construction via excerpts from interviews, field notes from observational work or typologies created in the data analysis process. More recently, qualitative research in sport and exercise fields are turning to photographic evidence as a way of capturing (that is, getting closer to in another sensory way) the 'real' in their practices of representation. Documentary analysis and representation along with the use of multimedia data are being included in online journal publishing activities – where short video clips may be embedded in a published article. Trends towards methodological reform or innovation strive to place readers 'closer' to lived experience than 'disembodied' books, chapters and articles. To this end, an even more radical form of data representation is at the academic doorstep. For more than a decade, qualitative researchers have called for the use of art, poetry and even embodied performance art as academic texts intended to represent lived experience. These researchers argue that in order for academic representations of reality to become more 'real' for people and move them to think, feel, act and consider, they must be aesthetically opened and crafted as non-traditional texts. Thrift (2007) pushes boundaries even further, suggesting that the next stage in the evolution of academic research might very well be non-representational; meaning, that representational practices which portray embodied realities must themselves emerge from written texts and evolve into fully embodied and visceral performance pieces.

PROBLEMS, PITFALLS AND CONTROVERSIES

Anthony Giddens's (1984) compelling discussion of the 'double-hermeneutic' establishes yet another issue in representation for contemplation. Giddens discusses how researchers, particularly qualitative, strive to interpret other people's interpretations of the world. Confusing, yes, but very true. Sociologists of sport, for example, routinely employ theory to make sense of how people make sense of the world! Any experience under empirical scrutiny and eventually represented in a textual document (such as the experience of DCD among children) is multi-layered by a range of subjective interpretations – giving even more credibility to the ontological assumption that no experience can be perfectly (realistically) represented. All representations are thus narrated approximations of 'some' truth. Giddens's (1984) observation applies to all of science, as what we choose to use as empirical data and how we come to interpret those data is a process of hermeneutic 'reading'. So even large and dense statistical tables brimming with coefficients, probability estimates and effect sizes are selective readings of an object under study.

Finally, if representation is an imperfect process, then the generalisability and therefore utility of academic findings, discussions and conclusions is always in question. While quantitative researchers rally behind statistical significance values and sample sizes to buttress claims of generalisability – and qualitatively oriented colleagues champion generic social concepts in their research in the same pursuit – the inevitably subjective aspects of representational processes raise doubts about any perfectly generalisable conclusions. Rojek (1986), in drawing on the work of Norbert Elias, encourages an ideology of methodological pragmatism here by suggesting we should strive to produce the most 'reality congruent' theories and analyses possible without fetishising the need for universal truths.

See also: Critical Theory; Translation; Triangulation; Visual Methods.

KEY READINGS

Brachman, R. and Levesque, H. (2004) Knowledge Representation and Reasoning. Los Angeles: Morgan Kaufmann.

Cairney, J., Hay, J., Mandigno, J., Wade, T., Faught, B. and Flouris, A. (2007) 'Developmental coordination disorder and reported enjoyment of physical education in children'. *European Physical Education Review* 13: 81–98.

Giddens, A. (1984) *The Constitution of Society: Outline of the Theory of Structuration*. Cambridge: Cambridge University Press.

Rojek, C. (1986) 'Problems of involvement and detachment in the writings of Norbert Elias'. *British Journal of Sociology* 37: 584–596.

Thrift, N. (2007) *Non-Representational Theory*. London: Routledge.

Research Ethics

Whenever a researcher conceives of a potential project, among the first considerations is whether or not the study can be conducted safely. This is especially relevant when we conduct research involving human subjects; when we bring people into a lab and run physical tests on them, administer psychological tests on them, or observe them and interact with them culturally in the field of everyday life. As academic researchers we simply cannot allow our own ambitions for knowledge discovery, curiosities about the world, or goals for career/personal advancement to get in the way of a fundamental belief we must uphold as researchers; that of protecting subjects from undue harm in the inquiry process. Codified and institutionally enforced principles of research ethics help to guide us in making decisions about what is appropriate or inappropriate in research practice. In what follows we will review and unpack some of the core principles and debates about research ethics, and ethics review boards, within universities and colleges.

WHAT IS THIS CONCEPT?

Research that involves human subjects or participants raises unique and complex ethical, legal, social and political issues. Research ethics is specifically interested in the analysis of ethical issues that are raised when people are involved as participants in research. There are three objectives in research ethics. The first and broadest objective is to protect human participants from being harmed in the research process. The second objective is to ensure that research is conducted in a way that actually serves the interests of individuals, groups and/or society as a whole. Finally, the third objective is to examine specific research activities and projects for their ethical soundness, looking at issues such as the management of risk, protection of participant confidentiality and the process of informed consent.

For the most part, research ethics has traditionally focused on issues in biomedical research. The application of research ethics to examine and evaluate biomedical research has been well developed over the last century and has influenced many of the existing statutes and guidelines for the ethical conduct of research. However in humanities and social science research, different kinds of ethical issues arise. New and emerging methods of conducting research, such as auto-ethnography and participatory action research raise important but markedly different ethical issues and obligations for researchers. Research involving vulnerable persons, which may include children, persons with developmental or cognitive disabilities, persons who are institutionalised, the homeless or those without legal status, also raises issues in any research context.

Given all of the above, every study undertaken in a university by a student or professor must pass an ethics review by at least one (but normally two or three) ethics review committee(s). This rule includes all work performed in courses, and research undertaken for thesis work. Researchers submit full proposals to the ethics committee or 'board' in their university or college, and an interdisciplinary panel of experts reviews its contents to ensure the research protocol fulfils institutional ethical standards. Depending on the time of year, the review process may take a week or several months to complete. Until researchers receive a 'green light' from an internal review board, no data can be collected for a proposed research project. If there is an ethical dilemma posed by the potential research, those undertaking the project are requested to revise their protocol or, in some cases, instructed to abandon their project outright.

WHY IS THIS RELEVANT TO ME?

An important issue arising in the ethical review of scientific research involving human participants is risk of harm. Notions of risk and harm in human participant research have evolved from a biomedical tradition born out of atrocities such as medical experimentation carried out by Nazi physicians in the Second World War and the Tuskegee Syphilis

Study, alongside tragic events such as the Sonoma State Radiation experiments and the experimental use of thalidomide in the 1950s and 1960s in North America. However, there have also been ethically questionable research endeavours in the social sciences and humanities, such as sociologist Laud Humphrey's ethnographic study (*Tearoom Trade*), psychologist Philip Zimbardo's Stanford Prison experiment and social psychologist Stanley Milgram's experiments on obedience to authority.

Clearly, there is risk of harm involved for those who take part in many kinds of sport or physical activity related research, not just biomedical or health research. Harms resulting from participating in research may be physical, social, psychological, emotional, financial or legal. Physical harms might include side effects from being given an ergogenic drug about which little information is known, or being given a well-known drug for a new use. Most physical harms arise in biomedical research but there may be some experimentation in social sciences that involves risk of physical harm. Social harms may include having something about a participant publicised without prior consent and the participant, as a result, being embarrassed or marginalised by the exposure of these views, opinions or attributes. Psychological or emotional harms may result from being deceived in research or from being asked to recall or recount traumatic or difficult experiences without adequate preparation or counsel. Financial harms may come from having participants' employment security placed in jeopardy because of participation in a research study. Legal harms may result from the exposure of participants to involvement in illegal practices.

Many research projects in sport, exercise and health are what we would classify as involving 'minimal risk' of harm – usually meaning that by participating in the study, participants face no greater personal risks that those they encounter in their everyday lives. That does not mean, however, that we should then not attend to the risk of potential harms that do exist. As always, risk of harm should be considered in a contextual manner. Moreover, risk of harm must be considered against the potential for benefit to individuals and society in all types of research. Finally, noting that risk of harm will always be present and to some degree uncertain, the burden rests with the researcher, alongside research ethics boards in universities and colleges, to put strategies in place to mitigate potential harms and minimise risks.

Many professional associations, government agencies, and universities have adopted specific codes, rules and policies relating to research ethics. These codes provide the guidelines for how we may, or may not, sample,

research ethics

measure variables, collect field data, report findings, and even interact with research subjects. Many government agencies, such as the National Institutes of Health (NIH), the National Science Foundation (NSF), the Food and Drug Administration (FDA), the Environmental Protection Agency (EPA) and the US Department of Agriculture (USDA) have ethics rules for funded researchers. In Canada, research ethics in universities are generally outlined by the 'Tri-Council Policy Statement: Ethical Conduct on Research Involving Humans', developed by the Canadian Institutes of Health Research (CIHR), the Natural Sciences and Engineering Research Council (NSERC), and the Social Sciences and Humanities Research Council (SSHRC). Other influential research ethics policies include the Code of Ethics (American Society for Clinical Laboratory Science), Statement on Professional Ethics (American Association of University Professors), the Nuremberg Code and the Declaration of Helsinki (World Medical Association).

SHOW ME HOW IT'S USED!

Codes of research ethics exist to protect, fundamentally, the rights of subjects and to ensure they are not exploited for the sake of scientific inquiry or the pursuit of academic knowledge. These codes contain core ideas, or principles, that guide how researchers treat people in the research process. All of these principles must be considered when designing a study. The principle of voluntary participation requires that people not be coerced into participating in research. Closely related to the notion of voluntary participation is the requirement of informed consent. Essentially, this means that prospective research participants must be fully informed about the procedures and risks involved in research and must give their consent to participate. Ethical standards also require that researchers not put participants in a situation where they might be at risk of harm as a result of their participation. There are two standards applied in order to help protect the privacy of research participants. Almost all research guarantees the participants' *confidentiality* – they are assured that identifying information will not be made available to anyone who is not directly involved in the study. The stricter standard is the principle of *anonymity*, which essentially means that the participant will remain anonymous throughout the study – even to the researchers themselves (whenever this is possible, but the principle is most easily achieved in experimental research). Increasingly, researchers have had to deal with the ethical issue of a person's right to service. Good research practice often requires the use of a no-treatment control group – a group of participants who do not get the treatment or programme that is being studied. But when that treatment or programme may have beneficial effects, persons assigned to the no-treatment control may feel their rights to equal access to services are being curtailed.

Other ethical principles promoted within particular policy documents in governmental and non-governmental agencies include: honesty (in reporting data, results, methods and procedures); objectivity (striving to avoid bias in research design, data analysis, data interpretation, peer review, personnel decisions, grant writing, expert testimony, and other aspects of research where objectivity is expected or required); disclosure of stakeholder relationships (disclosing personal or financial interests that may affect research); integrity and carefulness (avoiding careless errors and negligence; carefully and critically examining your own work and the work of your peers); openness (sharing data, results, ideas, tools, resources); respect for intellectual property (honouring patents, copyrights and other forms of intellectual property, not using unpublished data, methods, or results without permission); responsible mentoring (helping to educate, mentor and advise students through research studies); social responsibility (striving to promote social good and prevent or mitigate social harms through research, public education, and advocacy); and animal care (showing respect and care for animals when using them in research).

PROBLEMS, PITFALLS AND CONTROVERSIES

Many of my methods students wonder why they are required to receive training in research ethics. You may believe that you are highly ethical and know the difference between right and wrong. You would never fabricate or falsify data or plagiarise. Indeed, you may also believe that most of your colleagues are highly ethical and that there is no ethics problem in research. Indeed, the best evidence we have shows that misconduct is a very rare occurrence in research, although there is considerable variation among various estimates. The rate of misconduct has been estimated to be as low as 0.01% of researchers per year (based on confirmed cases of misconduct in federally funded research) to as high as 1% of researchers per year (based on self-reports of misconduct in anonymous surveys). According to the 'stressful' or 'imperfect' environment theory, misconduct occurs because various institutional pressures, incentives and constraints encourage people to commit misconduct, such as pressures to publish or obtain grants or contracts, career ambitions, the pursuit of profit or fame, poor supervision of students and trainees, and poor oversight of researchers. Erroneous or fraudulent research often enters the public record without being detected for years. To the extent that the research environment is an important factor in misconduct, a section on research ethics in a course is likely to help students get a better understanding of these stresses, sensitise them to ethical concerns, and improve future ethical judgement.

Still, research ethics boards are routinely criticised for being 'out of touch' with the real world, or creating a 'cotton wool' climate in universities. Ethics boards and codes of ethics tend now to err on the side of caution when it comes to research. Here's an example: in the mid-1990s I conducted an ethnographic project on ticket scalpers in Canada. I lived with a couple of them, hung out with them on a daily basis and went to sports contests to watch them in action. Over the course of time I witnessed quite a bit of criminal behaviour, some violence, and found myself in more than a couple of 'rough' situations in the field. Today, I would be hard pressed to have the study pass an ethics review because of the inherently 'dangerous' nature of the group.

Finally, one of the most challenging issues to be confronted in the study of ethics is that they can rarely be learned out of a textbook. While certain codes and principles are easily understood, one of the benchmark ideas – minimal risk – is a very tough concept to operationalise and standardise. My students have asked for my opinion on a full range of ethics issues, including: accepting money from private organisations to 'find' particular data in a study; the development of 'personal' relationships with research participants; the use of profane comments from interview subjects; the use of Internet data and website contents; performing muscle biopsies on children under the age of 16; and even the appropriateness of giving out one's personal email or phone number to a subject. Some of the above dilemmas are more easily answered with a 'right' or 'wrong' than the others. Codes of ethics provide a framework for managing these problems, but in some instances proper judgement, keen interpersonal skills and gut instincts all come to the fore.

See also: Research Proposals; Research Questions; Unobtrusive Methods.

KEY READINGS

Case, S. (2000) *Textbook of Research Ethics: Theory and Practice.* New York: Springer.
Elliott, D. and Stern, J. (1997) *Research Ethics.* Hanover: University Press of New England.

Haggerty, K. (2004) 'Ethics creep: Governing social science research in the name of ethics'. *Qualitative Sociology* 27: 391–414.

Hoonaard, W. (2003) *Walking the Tightrope: Ethical Issues for Qualitative Researchers*. Toronto: University of Toronto Press.

King, N. and Henderson, G. (1999) *Beyond Regulations – Ethics in Human Subjects Research*. Chapel Hill: University of North Carolina Press.

Research Proposals

Methods textbooks provide straightforward definitions of research proposals. A research proposal is a technical document outlining a research problem, how the problem will be studied, and the proposed benefits of the research. But a research proposal is also a position paper in many respects; it argues and begins to frame academic knowledge about a subject in a specific manner. Even less spoken about within the walls of a methods classroom is how the research proposal acts as an intentional 'hurdle' in the research process that both students and faculty must leap at times. In what follows, we will review certain technical aspects of a research proposal, but focus squarely on the more subtle procedural dimensions pertaining to the document's place in the research process.

WHAT IS THIS CONCEPT?

While there is no universal, trans-disciplinary roadmap guiding the preparation of a research proposal, we can tease out a simple definition of its form and content. A research proposal is a written document describing, in quite some detail, an idea for empirical (or theoretical) research that an individual or group has developed. This definition is in part misleading, however, because 'new' research ideas that are embedded in proposals often follow previous research efforts and knowledge developed from others' published work. And, indeed, quite a bit of reading (research via literature reviews) is involved in crafting a research proposal. But suffice it to say, a research proposal is a 'mapping' document, outlining the plan of attack a person has developed for answering an academic question they have stitched together. Proposals are vital documents to prepare as they help to organise a researcher's thoughts on his or her subject of interest, and provide focus and a concrete direction for the study. In essence, they are the architectural blueprints of research. Before we dig into the ground in order to build knowledge upon it, we must have an idea of what the house 'should' look like at the end of the process!

Here is a generic example of the contents of a research proposal for sport, exercise and health students. Again, proposals vary by sub-discipline and substantive area, but each of the following will typically be addressed in a proposal:

(i) *Problem justification*: Good practice is to establish the scientific and or social relevance of the phenomenon you wish to investigate. The convention is to convince readers of the relevance of the problem you are investigating and the need for research in the area. Although it might sound a touch controversial, a mentor of mine once told me: 'Not all questions we think of need to be answered, and sometimes gaps in the literature are there for a reason.' Imagine I propose to study career trajectories of ex-Olympic athletes. We know very little about what ex-Olympians do after retirement from elite sport. Interesting, but I have to convince readers on social scientific grounds that this is a worthwhile project of study.

(ii) *Question/problem*: Following a brief discussion of the topic's relevance, a researcher will state the specific question or hypothesis propelling the research act. In the case of qualitative research the question might be very open-ended and exploratory. 'How do ex-Olympians define their sense of self following retirement?' Quantitative research commences in a far more directed manner. Instead of an open-ended question here we would have a definitive hypothesis such as, 'Ex-Olympians who participated in team sports became employed in more white-collar managerial jobs than athletes who competed in individual sports.'

(iii) *Existing literature*: After a discussion of the significance of the research and the main problem/question to be 'solved' during the collection and analysis of evidence, a literature review is sure to follow in most cases. The aims of the literature are manifold, including: to review others' main findings on the same (or conceptually similar) subject; to establish whether or not the researcher seeks to replicate previous findings or fill a gap in the literature; to critically examine mainstay or innovative ways to theorise the subject;

to review the methods used to study the subject to date; to further illustrate why the main research question is being posed; and to demonstrate the researcher's substantive competency (or, simply, 'homework' completed) with the subject. Common practice is to re-state the research question at the end of the literature review to emphasise the goal of the proposed study.

(iv) *Methods*: Methods, methodology or 'procedure' sections of a research proposal vary considerably depending on one's research question and topic of interest. Quantitative (experimental or survey-based) research proposals are incredibly specific with respect to each and every aspect of data collection and analysis, while qualitative (ethnographic, historical, interview-based, media analytic, and others) proposals are far less rigidly procedural. Across both quantitative and qualitative proposals, though, the methodological sub-topics typically reviewed are: sampling procedures; the development of research instruments and lab/field protocols; the measurement process; the administrative steps in the research process (who is in charge of what); techniques for data analysis; storage and handling of data; and how the data will be summarised and disseminated. Appendices of any documents the participants will need to sign, reviews of protocols or written instruments presented to them will be attached as well.

(v) *Ethics*: From time to time, the discussion of research ethics and potential threats to participants posed by the research protocol may be contained within the broader discussion of methodology. However, institutional (ethics) review boards in departments or faculties are increasingly requesting ethics details to be presented in a separate section. Here, a researcher (conducting a study involving human participants) needs to outline each step taken in the protocol to ensure the research effort conforms with the accepted ethics principles codified in their particular institution, workplace, professional association or other relevant governing body.

(vi) *Budget and resources required*: Finally, a rather small section will appear at the tail end of the proposal highlighting any infrastructural, technical, financial, time and personnel resources needed to complete the project. The envisioned operating costs and timeline are often the most crucial aspects of this section.

While a research proposal is a technical document and its explicit significance is easily understood as a part of the preparatory work in the research process, its implicit role and how the proposal is employed is not nearly as obvious.

WHY IS THIS RELEVANT TO ME?

When a student finds cause to lament about a research proposal exercise, I am quick to remind them that I spend copious amounts of time yearly writing proposals. Faculty members do not escape the tedium of the research proposal process. I really do not need to write a formal, 20- or 30-page research proposal to organise my research; but other stakeholders in university research need to review my proposed investigations. Faculty members find cause to prepare proposal documents (again, with the organisational role of the proposal aside) for two main purposes. First, we write proposals so that an internal ethics review board in our university or college may review the protocols and raise flags about, or ask for further clarification on, a potentially 'sticky' aspect of the research procedure. The research ethics review process can be quite arduous, depending on one's subject of inquiry and intended procedure of study, so professors now spend great amounts of time crafting 'airtight' proposals in order to ensure (and illustrate) that participants will be treated with respect, dignity and due care. Second, proposals are often expanded as part of applications to funding agencies (both public and private) in the effort of seeking money for research. A research proposal undertakes a rather long inter-institutional walk in this regard. I prepare a proposal and will most likely hound one of my colleagues to review its contents and provide pragmatic and conceptual feedback. Then, a proposal heads its way to my research ethics board for review – first within my faculty, and then at the larger university ethics review panel. Once it has been cleared by the ethics committees, I begin to send the proposal to funding agencies like the Social Sciences and Humanities Research Council of Canada, or the Canadian Institutes of Health Research for funding consideration.

SHOW ME HOW IT'S USED!

I instruct my students to think about a research proposal as something akin to the opening statements a lawyer offers to a jury in a criminal trial. It is an outline, and as such an argument about the study and its relevance to the knowledge production process in universities and colleges. It is a person's first opportunity at framing the subject in the way that he or she envisions it in a theoretical and real-world sense. Here is an example. One might initially scoff at my idea of studying the career trajectories of ex-Olympians. This is not a statistically huge group and many might assume they are well cared for following their sports careers. In other words, the jury has potentially already reached its verdict! A proposal has the ability to alter perceptions of the problem and the need to understand it better through investigation. I could draw on institutional and anecdotal evidence to highlight the number of athletes actually involved, their dispersion across the country, their relative lack of higher education or certification in anything other than sport, and discuss existing studies from professional sport which testify to the relative lack of quality career opportunities outside of sport that athletes face. I could then draw on existing theories of the self and identity to paint a portrait of the significance of work (or lack thereof) to one's master status, cite theories from the sociology of education and occupations outlining the relationship between academic credentialism, social mobility and career prospects, and review social psychological theories which unpack enduring associations between occupational alienation, unemployment and self-efficacy. All of a sudden the topic, because of how we might frame it using existing theories of human behaviour, becomes far more relevant (at least we hope).

Now that the jury is listening with a bit more of an open mind, we need to demonstrate our first-hand knowledge of the subject. The ability to converse with ease and insight about the academic 'state of play' in one's area of investigation is absolutely imperative. Imagine if my literature review section in a proposed study of ex-Olympic athletes contained only a few spotted references and hints that I had just recently begun to understand this area of inquiry. By contrast, a rounded discussion of the related literatures, theories and main reasons how/why people have studied 'life after sport' would go a long way in convincing people that the study is worthwhile.

Yet the entire research plot can be lost in the methods section of a proposal. The demonstration of methodological expertise is paramount in a quality proposal. In truth, I might read a proposal submitted to an ethics board or a grants review panel on which I sit in an area of research this is not my own. The theories and topics might be entirely foreign to me, but methods are universal. Poorly designed methods stick out like a sore thumb in a proposal, and cannot be concealed by erudite literature reviews and compelling arguments regarding the significance of the subject. In many cases, a researcher has failed to provide enough detail about how, in technical terms and explicit stages, the research protocol will unfold. The root of the problem is often that the researcher has preferred to devote more space in the proposal to literature reviews and problem justification than methodology. A general rule of thumb is to place enough step-by-step information in the methods section so that if another researcher wanted to replicate the research, they would be able to do so with ease – just from one's proposal alone. There is no surer way to receive a returned proposal that has been rejected by one committee or another than through the neglect of one's methodological procedures. Finally, exemplary proposals contain a critical section towards the end of the document, that others may have ignored: a clear, reasonable and well-articulated plan for the use of data emerging from the study and the potential implementation of findings in institutional practice or policy.

PROBLEMS, PITFALLS AND CONTROVERSIES

The process of writing a research proposal is associated with strikingly few controversial issues or highly contested ideas. The lion's share of problems and pitfalls accompanying the process has to do with how a researcher envisions this step in the inquiry process, or how seriously the document is treated. If a researcher has little concern or respect for the process, that attitude will be immediately apparent in the document's brevity. I am equally suspicious of proposals in which an author appears to have already made empirical conclusions about the question under investigation, or pre-determined the theoretical conclusions to be drawn from the research.

Lastly, the tell-tale sign of a poorly conceived (or at least a far too ambitious) research proposal stems from its empirical or ethical unfeasibility. My students regularly conceive of wonderful projects that, in practice, simply cannot be conducted. I, for one, would love to better understand the subcultures of doping in elite sports through an ethnographic analysis of steroid use among Olympians, but this project will never happen. On more practical grounds, research requiring technical abilities (lab skills, fieldwork expertise, survey scale construction) that neophytes may not possess creates barriers in the research process. Students (or faculty, for that matter) may not have the time, money, size of research team, or access to a sample needed to carry out a research idea, despite assurances offered in a proposal. Participants' rights to be safeguarded from undue harm may not be guaranteed sufficiently in the proposal. Promises in research proposals regarding the use of four or five or six methods of data triangulation rarely develop into a research reality, and neither do claims regarding how the findings will be published in 10 or more journal articles and as the backbone of two academic textbooks. The bottom line is that best practice in writing proposals is to be thorough, pragmatic, convincing and forever realistic.

See also: *Applied vs. Pure Research; Literature Reviews; Research Ethics; Research Questions.*

KEY READINGS

Gratton, C. and Jones, I. (2003) *Research Methods for Sports Studies*. New York: Routledge.

Krathwohl, D. (1988) *How to Prepare a Research Proposal: Guidelines for Funding and Dissertations in the Social and Behavioral Sciences*. Syracuse: Syracuse University Press.

Thomas, J. and Nelson, J. (2001) *Research Methods in Physical Activity*. Champaign: Human Kinetics.

Research Questions

Translating an idea or curiosity one has into a researchable question is a tough task. I am very interested, for example, in non-traditional forms of structural-skeletal-muscular rehabilitation. I read a lot about the Alexander Technique and Structural Integration (Rolfing) methods, and wonder why these techniques, by comparison to chiropractic or Active Release therapy, are not recognised by most health insurance providers as scientifically legitimate (or at least worthy of financial coverage). But how could I transform a general insight or curiosity about this discrepancy into a research question? Ideas for research fly through the heads of faculty members and students on a daily basis. Carefully thinking through an idea and crafting it into a research question, however, takes quite a bit of work. There is both an art and science of research question formation, and generating a researchable question is an essential skill to master early on as an investigator.

WHAT IS THIS CONCEPT?

One's research question is the driving force of an investigation. It provides the purpose, mandate, orientation and legitimacy of all the fact finding and data analysis in the research. Another way of thinking about the research question is to conceive of it as a statement of the very specific puzzle you aim to solve through the process of data collection and analysis. Depending on one's area of research interest and the paradigm from which one operates, we generally ask four main types of research questions. None of the question types is inherently better or more scientific than the others.

(i) *Descriptive*: These questions focus on identifying and outlining common patterns, events, characteristics or trends in bodies, minds and societies. Examples include, 'How many people living in Surrey (UK) from working-class backgrounds have a form of cancer?'; 'What is the growth rate of Active Release therapy certifications in the United States?'; 'How many girls play organised tennis in Canada in comparison to boys?'; or 'What is the risk rate of ankle injury in minor league football in the United States for children aged 13–14?' Descriptive questions and the studies they lead to provide us with important information about the distributional or categorical nature of our phenomenon of interest. Descriptive studies in sport, exercise and physical activity research are almost always quantitative, using numbers, charts and other forms of numerically summative ways to answer a research question.

(ii) *Explanatory*: These questions are the hallmark of scientific inquiry. An explanatory question is derived from a theory, whereby the axioms and principles of a theory are used to predict an outcome in the 'real world'. Explanatory questions are part and parcel of deductive research processes. A theory explains how and why something in the world will behave in a particular manner. For instance, if I swing a particular alloy golf club at a particular angle and velocity, at a ball lying in the sand trap buried to a particular depth, on a day with wind coming at me from a particular angle and speed, then theoretical physics and biomechanics theories will predict where my ball will fly. If these theories have any 'empirical legs', then they will be able to predict, with great accuracy, where my ball will go or not go. Explanatory questions do not, then, commence by proposing we will eventually explain the nature of a phenomenon under study; explanatory questions propose/predict that we already know how and why things work, and we need to test whether or not our understandings are accurate. A straightforward explanatory question might be, 'Is there an optimum golf club loft angle (between 50 and 65 degrees) to maximise accuracy when striking from the sand?' Here, we would be testing the theoretical idea that certain loft angles produce more accuracy out of sand trap scenarios. Or, we could rephrase as, 'Titanium golf clubs with a loft angle of 60 degrees produce greater accuracy in striking scenarios when the ball is buried 2cm or more in sand by comparison to titanium clubs with a loft angle of 50 degrees.' Notice that such explanatory 'questions' are often not phrased as questions *per se*. Explanatory questions are quite regularly phrased as definitive *statements of relationship*; when they adopt such a form, we call them *hypotheses*.

(iii) *Exploratory*: This category of question can be easily identified at times, while at other times they are confused with descriptive questions. Exploratory questions form the basis of inductive inquiry, and initiate a programme of investigation intended to 'flesh out' a tentative or working understanding (not explanation) of a phenomenon. Here, we might only have a general theoretical or substantive clue about what is going on with respect to a phenomenon (no past theories or studies accurately account for it or provide us with direction), and therefore we embark on a very loosely structured programme of data collection and analysis to arrive at a tentative understanding. Exploratory research questions are devised at times as the basis of pilot studies in experimental research protocols or survey-based inquiries, but are more typically associated with qualitative or 'grounded' empirical investigations. Examples of exploratory questions include, 'Is there a relationship between gender and violence in sport?'; 'What are the nutritional strategies of elite rowers?'; or 'How do people construct and understand barriers to physical activity participation?'

(iv) *Evaluative*: These questions can be descriptive, explanatory or exploratory in nature. These questions address whether or not a programme, policy or product developed to produce a result in the world is actually operating as intended. Evaluation-based questions are frequently posed at the request of a public or private group or institution seeking the systematic assessment of one of their initiatives. Quite bluntly, a group may wish to know, 'Does our programme work?' For instance, does the creation of a staff exercise facility promote physical activity participation at the worksite? A city council might seek to examine the effects of hosting a major games like the Olympics or Commonwealth Games on healthy, active living in the city. A chocolate manufacturer might seek information on whether or not dark or white chocolate plays a role in muscle recovery following long bouts of intense exercise. When we are commissioned or charged with evaluating others' programmes and products, we may be required to provide descriptive information, informed theoretical explanations of the results, or answers from exploratory frameworks and perspectives.

WHY IS THIS RELEVANT TO ME?

If we believe that a research question is a statement that identifies the parameters of the phenomenon to be studied, we must be our own harshest critics and ask whether or not our questions are relevant, neatly defined and timely. I encourage students to create a checklist of questions to ask themselves with regard to their own research questions. Here are only some of the items for inclusion on those lists:

- *A strong research idea should pass the 'so what' test.* Think about the potential impact of the research you are proposing. What is the benefit from answering your research question? Who will it help (and how)? If you cannot make a definitive statement about the merits of your research question, you should most likely reconsider why you are asking it beyond your own academic curiosity. Let's remember that people may have not asked this question in the past because it is not worth asking!
- *A research question should be narrow and not broad-based.* For example, 'What can be done to prevent substance abuse?' is too large a question to answer in any specific study. It would be better to begin with a more focused question such as, 'What is the relationship between the experience of physical abuse before the age of 10 and substance-abusing behaviours during adolescence?'
- *The answer to the question is not immediately obvious.* This is not a question that commonsense, or reams of pre-existing research, could already answer with much confidence.
- *The question is clear enough for other people to understand.* Is the question stated clearly enough that someone in your academic field would know exactly what you set out to research?

- *Is the question challenging; does it point to inadequacies in our current understanding, or question taken-for-granted ways of knowing?* Good research questions tend to probe for new insight into a phenomenon, or apply commonly accepted academic knowledge in new ways.
- *Is it actually researchable?* That is, could we find the information required to actually provide an answer to our question? Further, can the information be collected in a reasonable amount of time?
- *Do I have the background and expertise to conduct this research?* Most importantly, what disciplinary knowledge is needed to find answers to the question, analyse the data and summarise the results?

From a methodological perspective, all of these questions should be answered sufficiently and affirmatively before research commences. Courses and textbooks in research method can provide guidelines for evaluating the soundness of a research question, but students also need to develop an intuitive feel about the relative worth and potential impact of their questions.

SHOW ME HOW IT'S USED!

There are no definitive, step-by-step guidelines for writing a research question, but there are generic processes researchers pass through on the way to creating a research question. Most of us start with a general idea or observation like, 'Hey, why is it that Rolfers get ignored or receive a "bad rap" from insurance companies?' The idea may sit with me for days, or weeks or months before I become committed to pursuing a line of investigation on the subject. From there, I would hit the library (or virtual library) and examine what has been written about Rolfers, their credentials, insurance company practices, ideas about professionalism and prestige in the health care industry, and so forth – anything, basically, that would provide insight on what we know about the phenomenon, theories that have been utilised to explain health care credentialism, major findings or conclusions and insight on the relevance of the subject. From an extensive and time-consuming literature review will emerge a much more specific focus of research than when I started to poke and prod around in the area. I might refine my interests in this case to examine the role of professional associations in influencing university curricula as a means of 'legitimising' the professions. I might find that the more established and sanctioned health care professions seem to have a strong 'curriculum foothold' in mainstream universities and colleges, and therefore can influence ideologies about what professions are legitimate. But, seemingly, no one has addressed the link in a targeted and focused research effort. And further still, the extant research indicates a need to empirically examine if the use of the term 'alternative' therapy by university researchers and in course readings/teachings in health sciences in reference to techniques like Rolfing are ostensibly correlated with insurance company scepticism about the latter's legitimacy. I started with a general interest in Rolfing and insurance coverage, but have teased out a very specific subject to research by reviewing what we know, and potentially don't know about the subject: 'Is there a relationship between use of the term "alternative" in university/ college constructions of a rehabilitation technique and health insurance subsidisation of related therapy for people?'

If I sought to test a particular theory predicting the use of the term alternative with health insurance provider scepticism, then the question would be explanatory. If I sought to examine if there is a connection, describe its nature and offer tentative answers to the meaning of the connection, then the study would be classically exploratory in thrust. Again, neither approach is more 'ideal' than the other. The defining line is whether or not I would use theory to pre-explain the nature of the correlation and then test if the theory is accurate or not.

PROBLEMS, PITFALLS AND CONTROVERSIES

There is much confusion over how to write a researchable question. Students have difficulties in narrowing down their interests into manage-ably narrow questions, and express frustration over the difference between hypotheses and research questions. With regard to the latter, incredible ambiguity and inconsistency exists in methodology textbooks. An hypothesis (a predictive statement of relationship between two variables) is but one type of research question and its structure should never be confused with the ideal-type research question. Even more confusion results when students learn about statistical hypotheses (i.e. null and alternative hypotheses) and their role in the quantitative research process. Best practice is to remember that hypotheses (while wonderful teaching aids in the classroom because they are the most narrowly defined of all research questions) are not the model structure for all questions. By contrast, my qualitatively oriented students occa-sionally fight tooth and nail to retain a level of openness, ambiguity and lack of definitive direction in their questioning in order to remain 'true' to some idealised notion of inductive research. But overly broad and undirected questions immediately lead to a lack of focus, even in the most traditional of grounded theoretical approaches to inductive inquiry.

There is also a major difference between a general 'problem' one sets out to investigate and the more circumscribed question within the problem area one chooses to investigate. I may set out to examine the problem of credentialism for Rolfers/Structural Integration therapists as my main area of investigation. But my research question is a narrow focus of interest within this problem area, such as the role of the term 'alternative' in university and college discussions of the practice in creating credentialism dilemmas for therapists with health care/insurance providers. A question leads to the examination of one small piece of the overall problem; remember, I could never fully solve or understand how the problem of credentialism manifests for Rolfers with one study, but I can develop a rich empirical grasp of one component. I disambiguate the idea of a 'research problem' in the classroom as a means of illustrating the ways in which many researchers ask related questions about/within a similar problem area, and how knowledge from seemingly dissonant studies should be collated in the process of building better academic understandings of the world.

See also: *Grounded Theory; Hypotheses; Literature Reviews.*

KEY READINGS

Gratton, C. and Jones, I. (2003) *Research Methods for Sports Studies*. New York: Routledge.
Krathwohl, D. (1988) *How to Prepare a Research Proposal: Guidelines for Funding and Dissertations in the Social and Behavioral Sciences*. Syracuse: Syracuse University Press.
Thomas, J. and Nelson, J. (2001) *Research Methods in Physical Activity*. Champaign: Human Kinetics.

Theory

Theory is a frustrating concept to teach, and certainly daunting for students to learn at first. Theory is dense, conceptual, and far too 'textbooky' for many undergraduate and graduate students. But if research is the vehicle of knowledge discovery, theory is most certainly the engine. Colleagues of mine may disagree with me, but I teach students that theory is the life-blood of any academic discipline. Our theories help explain, describe, predict, interpret and draw comparisons between bodies, actions, movements, thoughts, ideologies, emotions, environments, space, and all other aspects of the human condition. Theory and methods should be taught together as one scarcely exists, with any practical value, without the other. Unfortunately, methods textbooks are notoriously poor in providing clear, rich and nuanced descriptions of the relationship between the two. When students develop a 'healthy' appreciation of the methods–theory connection, an ability to conduct sound research almost always accelerates.

WHAT IS THIS CONCEPT?

Theories, then, are nothing more than a series of paradigm-related statements about the ways in which the biophysical, socio-cultural or behavioural world operates. Theories explain how and why people do and experience things: such as, why our bodies are able to move in particular ways, why we become ill, how social inequality affects people and where it comes from in our societies, how confidence operates in one's mind, and so on. Theories generally attest either to why something happens and what causes it to happen (these theories come from a positivist orientation), or to how people come to understand, organise and experience life in particular socio-cultural environments (these theories come from an interpretivist orientation).

With respect to the generic characteristics of a theory, we could focus on three main features. First, a theory must be *testable*. People must be able to observe whether or not theoretical ideas seem to work (or not) in the world. Statements or ideas we must simply accept or reject on faith alone are not theories as much as they are ideologies or dogma. Second, and related to the principle of testability, theories must be *falsifiable*. Theories that are not falsifiable are called *tautologies* – by their own definition, they are true and universal. Finally, theories should strive to be *parsimonious*. Parsimony is the idea that the simplest and most logistically straightforward explanation is the best. As a theory becomes more complex (interweaving more and more central concepts and axioms), it becomes less parsimonious.

Concepts are the building blocks of theory. Concepts are fuzzy ideas, and I often begin by telling my undergraduate students that concepts are not 'natural' things in the world but rather ideas we have made up. The stated relationship between concepts (i.e. the way they are connected within a theory) is what makes a theory unique. For example, alienation is a concept – a tough one to define – but let's just accept for now it's an idea or a label we apply to the way people feel. Socio-economic class is also a conceptual idea. Alienation and socio-economic class are not theories. But, if I start to connect them and make statements about their relationship (people who are in the most marginalised social classes feel alienated in a society preoccupied with material wealth and the accumulation of capital), then I have a theoretical idea working here! Theories are simply very short or very long-winded statements of explanation (and in many cases prediction) about the relationships between concepts. Theories are all about concepts. What amazes me is how sociocultural students of sport and health tend to grasp this idea right away, but their colleagues with physiological, biomechanical or motor-behavioural leanings do not (at first) see how even the body, a bone, energy, the nervous system, force, carbohydrates, or disease are indeed concepts linked together by complex theoretical systems of knowledge embedded within a specific academic paradigm.

Finally, the eventual *research question* one asks in a study is a product of everything above. Hypothesis-driven research is positivist in its orientation, and tends to privilege ways of knowing the world 'objectively' through the application of the scientific method in pursuit of causal relationships. An hypothesis is ultimately a prediction of a causal relationship between two observable concepts (derived from a theory, and its explication of why and how the two concepts are causally related). Or, research questions take on more general forms than causal hypotheses, and reflect the paradigmatic orientation of interpretivism, e.g., 'What do physical literacy skills mean to a young adult?' These types of research question, while still directed by one's interest in the conceptual relationships between things, underline the exploratory thrust of much interpretivist work. Here, the goal is not (typically) to test theories but rather to explore and expand upon existing theoretical ideas or to generate new theories.

WHY IS THIS RELEVANT TO ME?

A solid grasp of the main, competing and innovative theories in your field is critical for becoming an expert in your research subject of choice. Becoming an expert in an area of historical interest for academics is not an easy task at times. To engage in a study of racial differences in sport participation, one would sift through hundreds of journal articles pertaining to racialised differences in sport, and the dominant theories used to study the ways in which racial/ethnic stratification is linked to athletic

theory

participation. Here is a perfect example of what we have been talking about so far in this entry. To potentially explain ethnic differences observed in swimming involvement, one might first become an expert in theories of ethnic/racial stratification (and there are many!) in society. Theories on this topic will explain what stratification is, how it occurs, how it is reproduced, and how it manifests in cultural practices like swimming. Students often begin the other way around, clamouring to find everything written about swimming (from one's disciplinary perspective) and then teasing out existing explanations offered for observed racial differences in swimming rates. If no theories are found to be satisfactory in the search, one then looks for different theoretical ideas in race/ethnicity theory or embarks on a so-called grounded theoretical study. The second approach, while methodologically fine, too often encourages students and young researchers to think about the subject first before theory, and to lose sight of the theoretical mandate of the study. In this example, your goal might be to emerge as an expert on a particular theory of racial stratification in society, and to use swimming as a case study for testing if the theory has any explanatory power. Here, I am reminded of a sage, old methods saying, 'Whatever it is you think you are studying, remember that it ain't.'

SHOW ME HOW IT'S USED!

There are a million and one ways in which theory creeps into a research effort, and limited space within this entry cannot detail each and every instance of use. Theories are predominantly deployed in three main ways in sport, exercise and health research.

1. *At the beginning of a study*: A theory can be the main driver of a study at its inception in two main ways. First, a theory can be used as the basis for deriving hypotheses to be tested in a study. Such is the classic deductive method of inquiry, wherein statements about general conditions outlined by a theory (e.g. the way in which ethnic stratification works in a society) are drawn upon to test specific empirical conditions (e.g. differences in sports participation between ethnic groups). In this instance, theory is used to develop causal hypotheses, and empirical results relating to the hypotheses are then used to assess the explanatory and predictive power of the original theory. Second, researchers can take conceptual fragments from a theory to lead to a more qualitative and exploratory study.
2. *As the study emerges*: In a traditional quest for the discovery of grounded theory, conceptual ideas are built inductively through

empirical observation in one or many settings of interest. The use of theory is therefore delayed in this type of investigation because researchers believe the best theoretical explanations of the world are formed by observing and then conceptualising. Tradition holds that exploratory, 'ground-up' research should conclude with the discovery or development of testable theoretical propositions about a subject matter under investigation.

3. *As a form of social/political commentary*: Scores of 'critical theorists' hotly debate the role of theory and its connection to the empirical research process. Critical theorists frequently contend that traditional scientific modes of knowing/theorising are privileged over others. To them, researchers overly fetishise empirically oriented research and common ways of gathering and interpreting data, and tend to neglect their roles in proposing socially challenging theory. Critical theorists stress the need to explore many ways of knowing and representing reality, but fundamentally press for the use of theory as a means of commenting on extant socio-political conditions in or across societies. As result, critical theorists increasingly position themselves less as social scientists bound by a particular research canon, and more as progressive, and ofttimes radicalist, cultural commentators.

PROBLEMS, PITFALLS AND CONTROVERSIES

Any researcher can develop a modicum of theoretical blindness. I have acquired a penchant for several theories over the past few years, and I must admit to being tempted to see the entire world through their respective lenses. I know I probably shouldn't engage all of my qualitative work with pre-configured theoretical ideas in mind, but it is terribly difficult to divorce what one feels to be conceptually compelling from one's empirical inquiry. Theoretical blindness is a definite roadblock in the knowledge production process. What would our disciplines be like if researchers still held firm to theoretical ideas from 20, 50, or 100 years ago? Knowledge production, dissemination and use occur by engaging theoretical ideas in active research and constantly probing their empirical validity against one form of data or another. When we dogmatically adhere to the principles of theory without critically inspecting its reality-congruence, it becomes little more than a collectively habituated ideology or philosophy. To be sure, the most zealous and unreflexive followers of a theory never let empirical facts stand in the way of its principles.

More complicated dilemmas arise in our research when we seek to integrate and synthesise various conceptual ideas and theoretical chains

theory

into a study in an attempt to test many theoretical ideas, or to fashion a new hybrid theory. This scenario arises quite regularly in the contemporary university or with colleagues, as a result of trends in multi-disciplinary team building and research. Integrating theories and concepts derived from disparate disciplines and across paradigms can be a tricky task, and unless one is well versed in theoretical integration it is probably best to err on the side of theoretical and conceptual parsimony. I often tell my undergraduate students that if a reader walks away with a clear understanding of the main theoretical point one is arguing in a book or article, the encounter has been a success. Studies attempting to test or wield many theoretical and conceptual ideas tend to read as academic patchwork, often without a main theoretical point of the study emerging. Meta-reviews of how theories or particular concepts have been applied by many researchers on a given topic are probably the best exception to this rule.

See also: *Critical Theory; Epistemology; Grounded Theory; Hypotheses; Meta-Analysis; Ontology; Variables.*

KEY READINGS

Guba, E. and Lincoln, Y. (1994) 'Competing paradigms in qualitative research', in N. Denzin and Y. Lincoln (eds), *Handbook of Qualitative Research*. Thousand Oaks, CA: Sage. pp. 105–117.
Kuhn, T. (1962) *The Structure of Scientific Revolutions*. Chicago: University of Chicago Press.
Mohr, J. (2008) 'Revelations and implications of the failure of pragmatism: The hijacking of knowledge creation by the ivory tower'. New York: Ballantine Books.
Schick, T. (2000) *Readings in the Philosophy of Science*. Mountain View: Mayfield Publishing Company.

Translation

There are hundreds, if not several thousand researchers of sport, physical activity and health in their respective labs, field settings or media rooms at this moment immersed in the study of life. They will no doubt produce reams of findings and innovative suggestions pertaining to the problems they study. They will receive various types of institutional and peer kudos, accolades and even awards for their research. But how much of this research will be utilised by people outside of the university? If it is used, how long will it take for their conclusions to trickle down through institutional pathways into policy and practice? Will audiences beyond university and college boundaries understand their complex theories, methods, systems of analysis and recommendations? Over the past two decades, health researchers in Canada and the United States have lobbied for increased knowledge transfer or translation as a critical component of contemporary research practice – the process of shortening the period between 'lab results and bedside practice'. Knowledge transfer, literally the 'transferring and application of state-of-the-art knowledge generated by academic research', is an echoed mantra within sport and health sciences, and can no longer be regarded as the territory of the 'applied' researcher alone.

WHAT IS THIS CONCEPT?

Academic research for the sake of academic research is rapidly becoming a thing of the past. Knowledge transfer/exchange/translation is a system of collaborative problem-solving between researchers and decision makers within or across institutional settings predicated upon the assumption that good knowledge is worth sharing – and worth sharing quickly. In plain terms, knowledge transfer refers to the process of first translating esoteric knowledge generated by a researcher or held within a sub-discipline and then sharing it with relevant others (individuals, institutions or groups who could benefit from such knowledge). Too often cutting-edge research produced within universities remains within universities or buried in academic journals. I run with a group of marathoners every Tuesday and Thursday evening. They eat rather horribly. From conversations with colleagues who study sports nutrition, and my own reading in sport science nutrition journals, my attitudes about eating and my dietary practices have shifted considerably. But what about my friends who 'pick up' slivers of nutritional knowledge here and there? They learn to eat through trial and error. They fat load, carbohydrate load, calorically restrict, gobble ergogenics and shovel in high-sugar energy drinks in ways largely discounted in the extant literature! Finding ways to translate, transfer and exchange knowledge gained through sports nutrition research with the athletes on the front lines would help tens of thousands of runners around the world perform and feel better in their sport of choice.

The Canadian Institutes of Health Research (CIHR) in 2004 referred to knowledge transfer/translation as 'a dynamic and iterative process that includes synthesis, dissemination, exchange and ethically sound application of knowledge to improve the health of Canadians, provide more effective health services and products and strengthen the health care system' . The CIHR has been a global leader in the promotion of knowledge exchange and translation between university researchers and stakeholders across institutions. The very fact that this term has gained visibility in health research represents a major shift in research priorities.

WHY IS THIS RELEVANT TO ME?

A dual emphasis on the production of high-quality, evidenced-based (normally meaning empirical) research and on finding means and avenues to communicate findings to a spectrum of others alters the nature of what academics do in practice. The next time you are sitting in a lecture theatre or in a seminar room listening to your professor, ask yourself, 'How could someone use this research?' Do people use the evidence in any way? Could it be used? Over three or four years of study in an undergraduate programme, students have learned hundreds of conceptual ideas and been exposed to innumerable findings from innumerable studies. How much of this corpus of knowledge is transferred and translated into social practice anywhere?

The term *knowledge transfer or translation* is increasing in importance and use in the fields of public health, medicine and rehabilitation research. Knowledge transfer is a relatively new term that is used to describe a relatively old problem; the under-utilisation of evidence-based research. Under-utilisation of evidence-based research is often described as a gap between what is known (by knowledge producers) and what is currently done in practice settings. Think of a field of your interest, any field at all. What about the use of imagery as a relaxation technique, for example? I would bet, and would be willing to wager my PhD on the outcome, that no more than 5–8% of Canada's or Great Britain's population know of 'imagery' or visualisation techniques (even fewer could accurately explain them!). But if current research is accurate at all, imagery can be employed in a full spate of therapeutic ways to treat any number of anxiety disorders. Still, odds are that contemporary practice in the clinical treatment of anxiety is about 10 to 15 years behind what we know right now about the effectiveness of imagery.

SHOW ME HOW IT'S USED!

Once again, the term knowledge transfer or translation most readily appears in medical and health care literature, and primarily pertains to the assessment, review and utilisation of empirical research. Sport scientists are only now calibrating their research efforts around the concept and the practice, and are searching for helpful advice or templates of instruction. Regrettably, there is not one set manner for performing knowledge transfer (KT). KT can be conducted in a range of ways, depending on the type of research/knowledge produced, the subjects at hand, and the audiences potentially affected by the research efforts. The primary purpose of KT is to address the gap between the large volume of research data and its systematic review and implementation by key stakeholders; how this occurs can be flexible. But are there no commonly accepted 'elements' of doing KT? Yes, there are, in fact. The practice of KT involves the *translation* of complex and esoteric knowledge into accessible and incorporable ideas; the identification of *key stakeholders* or beneficiaries of our ideas; and the multi-method communication of results to the stakeholders (with emphasis placed on the practical usability of ideas generated via research).

While the term KT may appear similar to the rudimentary concepts of dissemination or diffusion of findings, it can also be differentiated by its emphasis on the 'quality' of research prior to dissemination and implementation of research evidence within a system. KT advocates do not suggest researchers rush to translate or transfer all academic knowledge, but rather research based on sound principles and techniques that has been rigorously reviewed. Further, unlike simple dissemination activities designed to make complex findings accessible to beneficiaries (e.g. distributing user friendly information written in plain language, developing research briefs and summaries, etc.), KT requires coordination and process improvement within a complex system to influence behaviour change and outcomes. In an effort to advance KT as a generically and universally accepted stage in the research process, several academic programmes and international organisations have established centres that conduct KT-related research, development, and dissemination activities, including the following:

- Agency for Healthcare Research and Quality (AHRQ): Translating Research Into Practice (TRIP) Program – An initiative focusing on implementation techniques and factors associated with successfully translating research findings into diverse applied settings (http://www.ahrq.gov/research/trip2fac.htm);

- Campbell Collaboration (C2) – An international organisation that conducts systematic reviews of education, social welfare and social science research (http://www.campbellcollaboration.org);
- Canadian Institutes of Health Research (CIHR) – The major federal agency responsible for funding health research in Canada, it has established charges for KT research, development, and dissemination (http://www.cihr-irsc.gc.ca/e/29529.html);
- Cochrane Collaboration – An international organisation that conducts systematic reviews of health and medical research (http://www.cochrane.org);
- Knowledge Translation Program (KTP) at the University of Toronto, Canada – A multidisciplinary academic programme developed to address the gap between research evidence and clinical practice and the need to focus on the processes through which knowledge is effectively translated into changed practices (http://www.stmichaelshospital.com/research/kt.php);
- Knowledge Utilisation Studies Program at the University of Alberta, Canada – A health research programme focusing on nursing, the social sciences and research utilisation in the nursing profession (httpkusp.ualberta.ca /);
- National Health Service (NHS) Centre for Reviews and Dissemination at the University of York (UK) – An organisation that conducts systematic reviews of research and disseminates research-based information about the effects of interventions used in health and social care in the United Kingdom (http://www.york.ac.uk/inst/crd/welcome.htm);
- What Works Clearinghouse (WWC) – A clearinghouse established by the United States Department of Education's Institute of Education Sciences to provide educators, policy-makers, and the public with a central, independent and trusted source of scientific evidence of what works in education (http://ies.ed.gov/ncee/wwc/).

As I have become intrigued by the potential 'transferability' of my own research, I have come across a number of design plans for incorporating the practice of translation into the research process, such as the Ottawa Model of Research Use (Logan and Graham, 1998) or the Lavis framework (Lavis et al., 2003). In addition, authors in the medical and health care literature agree that KT is a complex and lengthy process, and one that requires innovative and dedicated action on the part of knowledgeable strategic planners and change agents.

PROBLEMS, PITFALLS AND CONTROVERSIES

Knowledge transfer is a lofty, wonderful idea but can be plagued by two inherent problems. First, not all academic research projects are meant to be translated for broader audiences. Think of highly theoretical or basic research in the university. There continues to be a niche for research pushing the boundaries of theoretical conceptualisations of the world. These books, articles and essays are like private conversations shared among small groups of researchers. But these in-group conversations may germinate into fruitful lines of empirical inquiry in the future when they are played around with by other researchers. Second, not all research is easily transferable into immediate 'use contexts'. Small-group, case-study research often carries low external validity or reliability and is not necessarily appropriate for translation or transfer. The lack of transferability of knowledge gleaned from such projects does not render them socially irrelevant, but does limit their use-value in translational terms.

Finally, the spirit of KT is multidirectional but in practice operates in a predominantly uni-linear fashion; that is, researchers 'teach' others about how to solve problems as opposed to a situation where a range of participants are asked to pool and exchange knowledge in the problem-solving process. Research on athletes with anorexia is a prime example here. For more than four decades psychologists of sport have been called upon to translate what they know about the personality characteristics of the average anorexic in sport to parents, coaches and other team officials (in the process of identifying young athletes at risk of developing an eating disorder). An approach reflective of the spirit of KT would see a problem-solving scenario that involves an examination of how parents, athletes, clinical psychologists, peers, friends, coaches, trainers and nutritionists understand the aetiology of disordered eating. By pooling/exchanging knowledge between those experienced with different dimensions of the phenomenon, a more rounded understanding of the process might emerge and better solutions for combating the disorder might develop. The majority of contemporary translational efforts in the area are built, almost entirely, upon researchers' disciplinary understandings of the disorders.

translation

215

See also: Applied vs. Pure Research; Evidence-Based Research and Practice; Interdisciplinary Research; Triangulation.

KEY READINGS

Canadian Institutes of Health Research (2004) *Knowledge Translation Strategy 2004–2009: Innovation in Action.* Ottawa: Canadian Institutes of Health Research. Available at http://cihr-irsc.gc.ca/e/39033.html.

Jacobson, N., Butterill, D. and Goering, P. (2003) 'Development of a framework for knowledge translation: Understanding user context'. *Journal of Health Services Research & Policy* 8: 94–99.

Lavis, J.N., Ross, S., Hurley, J., Hohenadel, J., Stoddart, G. and Woodward, C. (2002) 'Examining the role of health services research in public policymaking'. *Milbank Quarterly* 80: 125–154.

Lavis, J., Robertson, D., Woodside, J.M., McLeod, C. and Abelson, J. (2003) 'How can research organisations more effectively transfer research knowledge to decision makers?' *Milbank Quarterly* 81: 221–248.

Logan, J. and Graham, I. (1998) 'Toward a comprehensive interdisciplinary model of health care research use'. *Science Communication* 20: 227–246.

Pope, C. (2007) *Synthesizing Qualitative and Quantitative Health Research.* New York: Open University Press.

Stratus, S., Tetroe, J. and Graham, I. (2009) *Knowledge Translation in Health Care.* Oxford: Wiley-Blackwell.

.... Triangulation ....

For the better part of the last 10 years, a staple research exercise in my undergraduate classes requires students to use observational methods, interviewing, surveys and media analysis to answer a research question of their choice. I love this exercise for at least a hundred reasons. Chief among the reasons is that it forces students to think in different ways about a subject of their choice and to inspect it from a variety of angles. These types of assignments are more appropriate for 'social-cultural' questions regarding sport, health and exercise, but not exclusive to them. An exercise like mine is predicated on the belief in and practice of *triangulation*. Since the early 1970s, the idea of using mixed or multiple methods within a study has grown in popularity as a strategy for adding depth and scope to a single research method.

WHAT IS THIS CONCEPT?

Triangulation can be defined as the mixing and matching of different research methods and data in a single study in order to pursue different forms of knowledge about a question at hand. The culling of different types of data by various methods (e.g. interviews, surveys, content analysis) is believed to enhance the internal and external validity about a subject under scrutiny. Why? Well, because when a researcher studies a subject from a series of vantage points, then a more rounded and potentially informative set of conclusions results. Johnson and Onwuegbuzie (2004: 18) describe the fundamental principle of mixed methods or triangulated research as the task of 'combing the methods in a way that achieves complementary strengths and non-overlapping weaknesses'.

What do Johnson and Onwuegbuzie mean by strengths and weaknesses of a particular method? Here's a research example. An amateur sport like soccer in Canada operates through the co-operation of thousands of people including paid and volunteer referees. Among the most pressing problems in sports like football is that of coach retention. A new set of stories about growing referee attrition in the sport crop up on a yearly basis. Common explanations revolve around burnout, competing time and social commitments, and systematic abuse from coaches, players and spectators. A quantitative, survey-based study of 2,000 amateur referees in the sport could be designed and administered in order to test prevailing theories of burnout and attrition. These data would be very helpful in understanding attrition patterns and potential causes. But quantitative data are not particularly insightful for addressing the meaning of refereeing to people, how it is experienced, the contexts in which it occurs, and how the 'exiting' process unfolds over time. By contrast, qualitative studies are not designed for analysing large-scale patterns of exiting across big groups of people. The deficiencies of one method are, then, hopefully addressed by strengths of the other.

The applications of triangulation do not end with the above example. Norman Denzin (1970) extended the idea of triangulation beyond its conventional association with mixing research methods alone. He distinguished four forms of triangulation:

triangulation

1. *Data triangulation*: entails gathering data through several sampling strategies, so that slices of data at different times and social situations, as well as on a variety of people, are gathered;
2. *Investigator triangulation*: the use of more than one researcher in the field to gather and interpret data.
3. *Theoretical triangulation*: the use of more than one theoretical position in interpreting data;
4. *Methodological triangulation*: the use of more than one method for gathering data.

While number (4) in the list above is perhaps the preferred method of triangulation the others listed are certainly worthy of extended exploration.

WHY IS THIS RELEVANT TO ME?

The philosophy of pursuing a triangulated design is based on methodological pragmatism. Generally speaking, the idea of triangulating methods, data, theory or even investigators as part of a study design is a bold move forward towards the end of 'turf wars' among academics. Pragmatism cares little about how you, me or someone else prefers to see and study the world as a matter of disciplinary perspective. A methodological pragmatist favours a mentality of 'let's use whatever helps us best answer a question' when it comes to research design. To this end, questions and the task of acquiring answers to questions are placed at the forefront of the research process – not paradigms, not theories, not any one particular method itself. The specific combination of methods or techniques to be used in a study follows from the question itself. If a question could be 'better' answered by the use of several techniques of data collection and analysis, then so be it! Side-stepped in this process are messy ontological and epistemological questions and ignored are stereotypical and dated ways of seeing quantitative or qualitative research traditions as two solitudes of inquiry.

SHOW ME HOW IT'S USED!

A friend of mine is a parent of a 13-year-old football player. Over lunch one day he remarks that he cannot help but notice the high turnover rate of referees in his son's league over the past two seasons. I decide at this very moment that the subject is worthy of some investigating. I start with a problem: what is going on with referee attrition in this league?

At this point I need to make a very important decision. Will my empirical venture into this area focus on testing a theory of group behaviour, shall it focus on the need for statistical data, or will I become preoccupied by studying the practice of refereeing *in situ* in order to understand the joys and hazards of being a referee in such leagues? I have a few 'alternative' options at my disposal.

First, I might conduct what we have been discussing as *a triangulated study design*. Triangulated studies are generally described as 'one-shot' or 'one-phase' designs in which two different kinds of data are gathered on the same subject. I might send out, for example, a 45-item question-naire to 500 former referees in southern Ontario, Canada, to examine whether or not a series of variables effectively predict and explain their decisions to leave the role. At the same time, I might identify and inter-view 25 or so referees between the ages of 13 and 25 to speak with them about the exiting process, and what it meant to them as people. Just for good 'measure', I might spend hours hanging around youth football fields in the region watching people referee in practice in order to achieve a better understanding of the referee environment.

Second, I could engage in what methodologists call a *concatenated study design*. This type of study is what I normally have students conduct as a research exercise in my methods undergraduate classes. Here, I might approach the problem of referee attrition by first collecting exploratory, qualitative data (interviews and observation) and then using empirical evidence and conceptual understandings of the process gleaned in this stage in order to develop a survey questionnaire for dis-tribution among a greater number of referees. Concatenated (strung or hinged together) studies operate in several phases, where one phase of data collection and analysis informs the focus and content in subsequent phases. The goal in the initial stage(s) is to gain a better understanding of the phenomenon from the 'ground level', and in the later stages to test emerging understandings of the phenomenon on a wider scale.

Third, I could pursue what is often called an *embedded study design*. Embedded studies are ones in which there is a main methodological 'player' at work in the research and a second method is utilised in a sup-porting role. I first send out a survey to 5,437 referees in the southern Ontario region and test several theoretically derived hypotheses about burnout and attrition. To supplement these data, I have, from the outset, intended to interview a sample of 15–20 of these referees in order to explore their responses with them, and to ask them for further information on the exiting process. I might ask them to provide more detail about their frustrations, time commitments, degree of burnout, and so on, but also ask them if I missed anything important concerning the attrition/exiting process in my original survey. Embedded designs are structured to provide a chance for follow-up data that helps to flesh out empirical observations and patterns noted in the first phases of data collection and analysis. Additionally, interviews or even observational methods like ethnography can be tapped in embedded designs to help explain surprising data from the original questionnaires that greatly challenge the researcher's assumptions going into the study. If, for example, I discovered in my surveys that young referees cite the *lack of* a competitive culture in and around the playing field as the number one reason why they left the role, I would certainly seek out interviews with referees to learn more!

PROBLEMS, PITFALLS AND CONTROVERSIES

Triangulation can be a time-consuming, onerous and unwieldy task. Critics of triangulation are quick to mention that simply employing a series of techniques in order to study a subject is not, in and of itself, a magic bullet for combating limited or otherwise poor research. A far more damning criticism is that despite pragmatist emphases on question answering, there are still important philosophical disagreements and potentially overwhelming ontological and epistemological differences between qualitative and quantitative approaches to the study of life. Researchers are well aware of these differences, and thus come to favour one main technique of data collection in a study, merely tacking on others to appear as if a study is progressively sensitive to the need for studying a subject in the round. Questions are to be raised, then, regarding whether or not quantitative data in a largely qualitative study are providing anything more than descriptive statistical icing on the research cake, or whether qualitative data in a primarily quantitative study are there to add a 'human face' to numeric data.

Silverman's (1993) well-cited criticism of triangulation attacks the very thrust of the approach, claiming that the idea privileges the positivist assumption of objective truth. To Silverman, using mixed or triangulated methods is undertaken to make sure researchers find the truth about a subject by studying it from all angles. Rarely are new or innovative theories of human behaviour gleaned from triangulated research processes, and more often than not, notes Silverman, 'additional' sources of (qualitative) data are gathered to illustrate the validity of theories tested in quantitative research. Here, the qualitative cases are provided as in-depth analyses of how and why the patterns identified in the quantitative phases of research operate as they do in the world. Qualitative researchers may equally abuse the task of triangulation, by using numeric 'evidence' gathered from a survey as a means of highlighting the commonality of contextual processes and situational events observed in small-scale interaction.

See also: *Evidence-Based Research and Practice; Interdisciplinary Research.*

KEY READINGS

Denzin, N. (1970) *The Research Act*. Chicago: Aldine.
Johnson, R. and Onwuegbuzie, A. (2004) 'Mixed methods research: A research paradigm whose time has come'. *Educational Researcher* 33: 14–26.
Nirantranon, S. and Nirantranon, W. (2009) 'Theory to practice: Prospective sport science curriculum of institute of physical education', *The Social Sciences* 4: 654–656.
Plano, C. and Creswell, J. (2008) *The Mixed Methods Reader*. Thousand Oaks, CA: Sage.
Silverman, J. (1993) *Interpreting Qualitative Data: Methods for Analysing Talk, Text and Interaction*. Thousand Oaks, CA: Sage.
Thurmond, V. (2001) 'The point of triangulation'. *Journal of Nursing Scholarship* 33: 253–258.

Unobtrusive Methods

Every once in a while I read a returned survey questionnaire, examine self-report data or review notes I have transcribed from an interview and question whether or not the respondent has provided the 'full truth'. The highly personal and oftentimes sensitive nature of our research questions can certainly encourage non-disclosure or even deception among participants. Wiggling our way into people's lives with requests that they speak, move or think along lines that we ask them to, can be rather disruptive and may alter the course of their everyday lives. So when people are incorporated into the research process we must always question whether or not we are encountering the 'real person'. For these reasons alone, an entire strand of research techniques called unobtrusive methods are explored by academics as a way of studying people without bothering them. Unobtrusive methods receive an unwarranted 'bad rap' in academic circles and are not employed nearly as frequently as they might be in the study of human life.

WHAT IS THIS CONCEPT?

Unobtrusive methods (also called *non-reactive methods*) are techniques of data collection in which a researcher does not come into contact with respondents first-hand in any type of interactive scenario. They are most appropriate when a research question focuses on social behaviour in a particular context or milieu. The popular topics selected for unobtrusive observation by undergraduate students of mine include drinking and party behaviours among fans at sports contests. Unobtrusive methods may place researchers and subjects in close proximity with one another, but they do not engage in any sort of interpersonal interchange or communication. Students curious about unobtrusive methods typically start researching them by reading Webb, Campbell, Schwartz and Sechrest's (1966) classic text, *Unobtrusive Measures: Non-Reactive Research in the Social Sciences*. The most simple and straightforward unobtrusive method Webb et al. discuss is *simple observation*: an anthropological method of studying culture used for well over a hundred years prior to their book. Simple observation is precisely what the name implies. A study based on simple observation involves a researcher going out to a setting in order to observe, record and later analyse patterns of behaviour found there. I am quite fascinated with how people eat when outside of their homes. It is relatively easy to eat 'well' in the home, but not so easy given many of the quick and easy choices available in malls, restaurants, vending machines, and elsewhere. What fascinates me even more is how people will mainly report healthy eating behaviours in surveys and interviews, but frequenting a range of restaurants and public venues which sell food might teach us something very different about people's food choices. A simple observation study could be constructed around the idea that in order to understand how the food environment shapes eating behaviours, we need to go out and unobtrusively observe how people eat outside of the home without them knowing they are being watched – just imagine if you knew a researcher was observing you and observing the contents of your grocery cart!

Other researchers are a touch more 'aggressive' with their perspective on unobtrusive methods. They favour what the Australian social psychologist Stephen Bochner (1979) called 'manipulative experiments'. Bochner advocates the use of social experiments in order to test human behaviour in a variety of typical public scenarios. For instance, Bochner staged fake collapses on trains to assess people's willingness to help others, shoplifting incidents to assess public morality (i.e. whether other customers would report him), and other events. The advantages of unobtrusive research have been well summarised by Rathje (1979). First, unobtrusive measures tend to assess *actual* behaviour as opposed to *self-reported* behaviour. Second, unobtrusive measures are usually safe, both for researchers and other people. Observations, if made discreetly, are harmless and non-disturbing to others. Third, unobtrusive methods, because they do not disrupt others, are easily repeatable. This enables re-checking of findings and allows questions of reliability to be re-examined by others. Because of the non-disruptive nature of these methods, the fourth advantage is that people do not react to the researcher. Fifth, access is not usually a problem. Because researchers rarely need the co-operation of others, research access is much easier. The sixth advantage is that unobtrusive research is usually inexpensive. Observations, archives and physical trace work are simple, and the major expense is time and a record book, compared with typing, printing and copying expenses for surveys or statistical data analysis, and time and skill in processing survey results. Finally, because unobtrusive methods are so non-disruptive, inexpensive, accessible and safe, they are ideal for longitudinal study designs – those that follow activities over a period of time.

WHY IS THIS RELEVANT TO ME?

There are any number of places to go and observe social life happen and to learn by watching. Sports grounds, fitness centres, public parks, city streets, malls, parades and festivals, schools and workplaces are only a few prime spots for observing health and physical activity behaviours. In the second place, the sheer volume of recorded information about health and physical activity practices available for people to observe is staggering. Fitness magazines, sports media, websites, sports organisation records, historical archives housed in university libraries, policy documents and a huge range of other recorded materials about sport, health and exercise are waiting to be observed by people. Even the most unsystematic studies of sport's popularity among Internet sites teach us something about its cultural relevance. A study of public blogs about weight loss narratives could be crafted quite easily. An analysis of media sharing sites such as

YouTube for posted videos on alternative sport could be useful for documenting how this phenomenon has mushroomed worldwide. Policy documents and publicly released information about the money spent by a local government for improving fitness opportunities for the disabled could be employed in a study of enduring barriers to sport access.

SHOW ME HOW IT'S USED!

For the sake of conceptual clarity and distinction, let's bracket unobtrusive methods into two main streams: *simple observation* and *content analysis*.

Simple observation methods, as previously outlined in this entry, are the most straightforward and probably the most interesting for students. There is a certain sneaky thrill associated with studying people who are unaware they are being watched. When conducting a simple observation study, researchers have to consider if they can in fact gain public access to behaviour or events of interest (e.g. while the study of locker room culture might be fascinating, I'm not likely to find a sports team who wouldn't notice me hanging around their club room during halftime!), and whether or not my covert observation of their actions poses any ethical dilemmas (e.g. the observation of criminal behaviour, sexual activity or financial interactions). Simple observation is best suited to common, everyday, or socially unproblematic public behaviour. It is an appropriate method for studying the natural rhythms and flows of a culture. Let's stay with my example of eating patterns and food choices. A grocery store is a great place to watch people make food choices, to observe the content of their choices and to infer something about the culture of eating in our societies. The research might be able to teach us a great deal about how people eat as a cultural phenomenon. Food choices and the accumulation of one's dietary resources are directly observable. Also observable is how the context of a supermarket is assembled for people: how it looks, smells, sounds, is decorated, where food is placed, its advertising, where it is located geographically, and how the people there work and interact with customers, are all aspects of the food environment that is the grocery store in your neighbourhood.

But there are also many, many instances of human action, attitudes and patterned behaviour that exist in 'trace' form. Physical artefacts that are built up in a space over time, and those that disappear in a space can signal something potentially important to us as researchers. *Measures of accretion* are artefacts of culture that have proliferated or been built up in a space. In my local grocery store, the 'organic' food section existed as only a small corner of one remote shelf at the back of the store a decade ago. Today, the organic section has an entire aisle to itself, with organic products scattered throughout the store in other places as well. The expansion of the organic food section potentially signifies shifting consumer tastes and preferences for healthy food, the success of the organic food lobby to affect cultural eating patterns, or even a supermarket chain's motivation to at least appear to offer healthy options for consumers. *Measures of erosion* are precisely the opposite of measures of accretion. Here is a neat way measures of erosion could be employed in the supermarket study. I enter my local grocery store two minutes after it opens in the morning. I notice that the evening shift workers have restocked all of the shelves and the products are nicely arranged in tight and orderly lines for the day's consumers. To test popular food choices and whether or not people make 'healthy' food choices, I count how many apples and heads of broccoli are in the produce section, and how many bags of potato chips and bottles of pop are in the 'party' aisle. At the end of the day (and I have been careful to note in previous visits to this store that they do not restock apples, broccoli, chips or pop during the day), I return to the store and count how many of each item remains on the shelves. Of course, what I am interested in here is how many are actually gone; or the rate of erosion for each. Measures of erosion tend to indicate the relative importance of an object within a space (i.e. its use frequency), or in special cases can symbolise the decaying significance of a cultural product (consider the disappearance of particular food products in the store and their lack of replacement because of lack of consumer interest).

Although I am not completely convinced content analysis falls under the category of unobtrusive methods, it is regularly discussed in the array of techniques deemed 'non-reactive'. The use of historical archives and records has long been exploited by researchers in the pursuit of 'accrued' measures of events and social processes, but of booming popularity is the use of television commercials, films, television shows, music, movies, Internet sites, weblogs, and social media spaces like Facebook as sources of data for unobtrusive observation. There is considerable anonymity in the observation of most of these data forms, and they are (much of the time) readily available for observation. Consider a study of fantasy sports pools and leagues, fan-produced websites devoted to particular athletes or professional sports teams and the ways in which sports and activity symbols are inscribed into people's profiles on sites like Facebook or MySpace. My bone of contention with the inclusion of (mainly media based) research in the category of unobtrusive methods relates back to the issue of social desirability. Mediated or mass communicated messages are given to be read to wide audiences in many cases and are as such often fabricated with social desirability in mind. There is an amplified performative aspect of mass mediations, and questions about whether or not they are measures fitting into the original spirit of unobtrusive methodology – that of analysing people and their behaviours when they believe they are somewhat 'off camera'.

Students often conflate unobtrusive methods with unobtrusive measures. An unobtrusive method is the non-reactive technique of data collection; usually in the form of simple observation of 'live' people, or the collection of content from archives, media or web space. Unobtrusive measures are the bits and pieces of data we observe. The conflation is produced and compounded by scores of existing research manuals and texts using the terms interchangeably.

PROBLEMS, PITFALLS AND CONTROVERSIES

Unobtrusive methods are not the easiest to defend in front of hardnosed scientists in our faculties and departments. The highly interpretive and subjective aspects of 'reading' human behaviour, or its traces, are quite the hermeneutic endeavour. Here are merely a few criticisms of unobtrusive methods/measures I encounter on a regular basis.

First, the methods are inherently detached from the cultural contexts of study. Stated in a different way, by studying a context as a foreigner and not interacting with people therein, one is observing behaviour or its traces without a deep cultural understanding of what the behaviour, events or expressions studied actually mean to the people there. Motivations and attitudes are notoriously impossible to infer beyond a shadow of a doubt via unobtrusive methods. Second, unobtrusive methods are criticised for being highly selective with respect to what is actually recorded and reported as data. Imagine you were asked to sit at a food court in a shopping mall for four hours a day, for a week's duration. No doubt you would witness hundreds of meals being eating and a wide range of social behaviours. Simple observation studies, like research efforts relying on measures of accretion and erosion, are notoriously reductionist with a strong tendency among practitioners to focus on the more 'sexy' rather than the mundane findings emerging from the observations. Third, if one is truly committed to an unobtrusive protocol, the size of one's methodological tool kit in the study is severely reduced. Reliance on a single method is justifiable in many research scenarios, but unobtrusive methods pose a unique problem as the methodological driver of the study. Of all research techniques, questions of internal validity are paramount and potentially devastating to unobtrusive-based projects.

See also: Archival Analysis; Discourse Analysis; Media Analysis.

KEY READINGS

Bochner, S. (1979) *Unobtrusive Measurement Today: New Directions for Methodology of Behavioral Science*. San Francisco: Jossey-Bass.

Bouchard, T. (1976) 'Unobtrusive measures'. *Sociological Methods Research* 4: 267–300.

Lee, R. (2000) *Unobtrusive Methods in Social Research*. New York: Open University Press.

Rathje, W. (1979) 'Modern material culture studies', in M. Schiffer (ed.), *Advances in Archaeological Method and Theory*. New York: Academic Press. pp. 1–37.

Webb, W., Campbell, D., Schwartz, E. and Sechrest, L. (1966) *Unobtrusive Measures: Non-Reactive Research in the Social Sciences*. Thousand Oaks, CA: Sage.

Validity

Methods instructors often hurry through the discussion of validity in undergraduate modules. There is a tendency to think about the concept as a highly specialist idea, consequential only to the most geeky of all researchers or those in the final stages of data analysis. These assumptions could not be further from the truth. The assessment of a research project's 'validity' commences in its earliest phases and is relevant across its duration. There are, in fact, many aspects of validity to be mindful of in the research process, and how one judges the relative validity of a project varies for given methodologies.

WHAT IS THIS CONCEPT?

There is no single, universally agreed upon definition of 'validity' amongst academic researchers. The first way research methodologists view validity is a rather simple but profound one. Here, we ask ourselves, am I truly measuring what I think I am measuring? This is, by and large, the most common understanding of validity in sport, exercise and health sciences. There is a massive leap sometimes between the theories and concepts underwriting our research and the ways in which we choose to measure those concepts. Take a concept like self-efficacy. Self-efficacy is not a real 'thing' in the world, right? We have defined it as something like 'belief in one's own ability to perform a task', or 'the feeling of self worth, optimism and competence to intrinsically motivate an individual'. What is frustrating about conceptual definitions is that they contain even more concepts!

There is no inherent thought or action that is objectively a self-efficacy. It is an abstract idea, a concept, or a label that we apply to observed behaviour indicating or representing that concept. There are any number of surveys available that have been designed to measure the concept of self-efficacy. Questions on the survey such as, 'Do you agree or disagree with the following statement: Whenever I play a game with my team, I feel like a valued member of the group?' are intended to stand in as measurable indicators of the concept. Whether or not that question or others like it actually measures self-efficacy with respect to how we define it, is our question of validity. Am I really measuring someone's belief in their ability to perform a task or their feelings of self-worth as a person through that question? If not, we say the question is not a valid (truthful) measure of the concept. From time to time, students will see this generic concern with validity referred to as *internal validity*.

The second way of viewing validity is more or less a question of research design beyond the level of conceptualisation and the selection of appropriate indicators. Here, we worry about and scrutinise whether or not the design of the study itself or the ways in which the research process unfolded produced a level of bias that skews results or limits their applicability to the 'real world'. Experimental researchers are quite preoccupied with this type of validity (often also referred to as internal validity), and it is often called *test* or *experimental validity*. Questions regarding whether biases in the sampling process, defects in the technical aspects of the measurement process (i.e. problems with data recording instruments), and whether or not the appropriate techniques of data analysis have been employed and interpreted correctly in the study are at the forefront here. Researchers will further examine and critique whether or not the study's findings appear to be externally valid, meaning whether or not we would expect to find similar patterns and tendencies in the data if we studied another group of people (*external validity, or generalisability*). Here, methodologists also question whether or not empirical patterns observed in the laboratory would indeed be likely to appear in the real world (we call this a special kind of validity known as *ecological validity*).

WHY IS THIS RELEVANT TO ME?

Validity is everywhere and anywhere in the research process, from the formation of the research question, to the literature review, to the collection, analysis and reporting of data. To ensure research is valid, among the most important characteristics of the mindset of a careful researcher are attention to detail and intense self-scrutiny. Why? Well, colleagues will inevitably disagree with me, but a fundamental aim in the research process should be the production of accurate, or reality-congruent, research. If we conceive of research papers, journal articles, books, technical reports, or research abstracts as arguments about the nature of the world based on some form of observation, then the quality of one's argument is fundamentally predicated upon the validity of the research process. Steps in each phase of the research process must unfold with validity in mind. If one's findings have no accuracy due to poor conceptualisation, operationalisation and measurement, or if improper techniques of data analysis are employed, knowledge claims offered in a study are utterly untrustworthy. Also, with little to no rigour in the process of collecting data, worthless results emerge. Imagine a lab researcher who never thought to calibrate heart rate monitors, or a survey researcher who failed to test their survey instrument in a pilot test or against a known, valid questionnaire. Without undertaking the appropriate steps to ensure we are measuring what we have sought to measure, and have measured it in a technically 'tight' manner, we have wasted a great deal of time and money.

SHOW ME HOW IT'S USED!

I used the example of self-efficacy earlier in this entry to illustrate the idea of internal validity. Let's return to the concept of self-efficacy to illustrate the sub-dimensions of internal validity and then experimental (test) validity.

Examinations of the internal validity of research efforts focus on the ways in which concepts are defined and linked to empirical measures. There are two main branches of internal validity: content validity and criterion validity. Let's begin with content validity. Say I developed a new survey to measure self-efficacy in people, and say I used 15 questions as empirical measures of self-efficacy. I first need to assess whether or not the questions have any *face validity*. Face validity is like a methodological laugh test; if our internal conceptualisations and indicators do not appear, on their face, to be even closely linked, reasonable or logical, then we have an issue here. If, for example, I chose to measure self-efficacy by asking people if they owned a pet, the question would have no face validity. If our conceptual definitions and measures pass this internal test, we normally assess whether or not they have a certain degree of *content validity*. A fuzzy concept like self-efficacy has many dimensions or aspects to it, as we have defined it above. Particular measures I would choose as questions on my survey might tap into many of those dimensions; if they do, we say they have very good content validity.

Let's turn our attention now to criterion validity. In constructing empirical measures for our concepts, best practice teaches us to test or compare what we have chosen as measures against existing ways of measuring the concepts (e.g. as indicated in the literature). We are assessing the validity of our measures against accepted measures in the literature or those believed to be valid among research experts; we use accepted measures as a benchmark or as criteria. The four main types of criterion validity are: *predictive validity, concurrent validity, convergent validity* and *discriminant validity*. We do not have enough space to delve into each of these sub-types on internal (and then criterion) validity, but a few more words might help us understand their role in the research process. In content validity, the criteria for assessing whether our measures fit well with our concepts are based on our internal definitions of what the concepts mean. In criterion-related validity, we usually make a prediction about how the measures will *perform (theoretically)*, based on how others have conceptualised and measured in comparable extant research.

PROBLEMS, PITFALLS AND CONTROVERSIES

While there are real-world limitations placed upon studies in which validity is called into question, we must remember that validity is predominantly a matter of conceptualisation, definition, statistical estimation and argument. Quantitative researchers devote significant amounts of time at the front end of a study to conceptualising and operationalising their measures. Because there is no perfect fit between concepts and indicators (the fancy term in the methods literature is the 'epistemic correlation'), how one chooses to define and then measure something is always an act of social construction (yes, even for the so-called 'hard' sciences!), and so assessments of validity are also social constructions. In qualitative research (especially when conceptualisation unfolds inductively) it can be difficult to externally assess the relative validity of a project, as no one, save for the principal researcher(s), has been privy to the mass amounts of empirical indicators/measures leading researchers to conceptual conclusions. A few interview or field note excerpts presented as indicators in a paper are not nearly enough to judge the internal validity of someone's work. So, while researchers collectively agree upon the importance of validity, it is oftentimes slippery and elusive to critique in practice.

Critics of qualitative studies find occasion to deride such techniques because of the lack of external validity apparent in these methods. True enough. I would venture to guess that probably 75 out of 100 published articles employing qualitative research techniques are not generalisable, at least statistically, to a larger population. But qualitative researchers focus less on generating statistically generalisable substantive findings, and more on the trans-contextual relevancy of concepts and ideas generated through the research process. Qualitative researchers often fight back by criticising the 'scientific' connection between concepts and measures in one's office or lab and the fetishisation of statistical (external) validity. With respect to the first criticism, a great deal of theorising about what concepts mean and how they should be appropriately measured is undertaken before 'empirical life' is observed. With respect to the second criticism, statistical generalisability (which has much to do with sample size and sampling error in a study) does not ensure ecological validity. An over-emphasis on whether or not numeric results are likely to apply to a bigger population may obfuscate whether or not an experiment is replicating 'real life' in the lab or elsewhere.

See also: Quantitative vs. Qualitative Research; Reliability; Research Questions.

KEY READINGS

Brustad, R. (2009) 'Validity in context – qualitative research issues in sport and exercise studies'. *Qualitative Research in Sport and Exercise* 1: 112–115.

Gadamer, H. (1995) *Truth and Method.* New York: Crossroad.

Whittemore, R., Chase, S. and Mandle, C. (2001) 'Validity in qualitative research'. *Qualitative Health Research* 11: 522–537.

Zeller, R. and Carmines, G. (1980) *Measurement in the Social Sciences: The Link Between Theory and Data.* Cambridge: Cambridge University Press.

validity

Variables

The language of science is discourse about the numeric relation between variables in the world. A discussion of variables usually features in the first or second week of an undergraduate methods course. When people have a foundational understanding of the idea of variables, science becomes a whole lot easier and exciting. Apart from the concept of a distribution – a statistical way of seeing variability – there is no other concept as important as variables for learning the quantitative research ropes.

WHAT IS THIS CONCEPT?

You won't be able to accomplish very much with quantitative research unless you know how to talk about variables. A *variable is any entity in the physical, cultural or social sphere that can take on different value for people*. Okay, so what does that actually mean? Anything that researchers can measure and people can score on differently is a variable. For instance, *age* is a variable because it takes on different values for different people. There is naturally occurring variability of age in a population of people. There are hundreds of variables in the world we can measure and score people on with 'naturally occurring numbers', like age, income, height, VO_2 max, red blood cell count, intelligence, and so forth. We love these kinds of variables because statistical tests were built for them! But variables are not always naturally numerical. *Country of residence* can be considered a variable because a person's country of residence varies around the world. But there is no naturally numeric way to count country of residence. Your personal country of residence score can be assigned a value, however, if we simply assign numbers to countries. The variable 'gender' typically consists of two assigned values: male and female. We can assign quantitative values in place of these two 'named' values.

In all cases mentioned so far, what makes a variable a variable is its different attributes. A variable's *attributes* are a set of response categories or scores assigned to it which researchers must decide upon before collecting data. Stated differently, we establish how a variable's attributes are to be defined, and, in doing so, the different scores people will be able to receive for the variable. We then actually determine how the variable will vary! For instance, the variable *gender* regularly has two attributes: *male* and *female*. If you are male, you might get a score of (1) on that variable, and if you are female, you are assigned a (2). In all cases of quantitative research, we transform a person's scores on a variable into a numeric code. But in a different study we might assign three attributes to the variable: male (1), female (2) and transgendered (3). The variable *sports you play* might be defined as having five attributes: tennis, soccer, hockey, rowing or baseball. Anyone who has even heard of sport knows this list is not exhaustive.

Another important preliminary distinction having to do with the term 'variable' is the difference between an *independent* and *dependent* variable. This distinction is particularly relevant when you are investigating cause and effect relationships in the world through experiments or longitudinal surveys. It took me the longest time to learn this distinction as an undergraduate student – much like the difference between objectivity and subjectivity. I originally thought that an independent variable was one that would be free to vary or respond to some programme or treatment, and that a dependent variable must be one that *depends* on my efforts (i.e. it's the treatment). But this is entirely backwards! In fact the *independent variable is what you (or nature) manipulates* – a treatment, or programme or cause. The *dependent variable is what is affected by the independent variable* – your effects or outcomes. For example, if you are studying the effects of a new sports coaching intervention on team cohesion, the new coaching programme is the independent variable and team cohesion is the dependent variable. There are also special variables called *control variables*,

WHY IS THIS RELEVANT TO ME?

Given the centrality of (the relationship between) variables in the scientific process, how researchers decide to set the parameters of a variable's attributes is extremely significant in any quantitative study. Deciding how to determine a variable's attributes (thus deciding how we will allow it to vary in our study) is a messy task. Epidemiologists, for example, will present very convincing arguments about the overt relationship between variability in social class and premature mortality. Members of the working class on average do seem to die earlier than members of the middle or upper class, and contract a wider range of illness more frequently. But how do we actually measure class? Is it as neatly defined as lower, middle and upper? The determinants of what defines each of the three attributes are widely contested by socio-cultural and demographic researchers. Generally speaking, class is determined in theory by one's employment status (i.e. socially ranked status), level of educational attainment, and occupational income. The more you have of each, the higher your class position. Simple, right? No, and here is where the equation is a bit confusing. A tradesperson does not normally possess university degrees, has low occupational prestige, but can make more in income than many, many middle-class workers. Where do we place that person in our class scheme? One of your professors, especially junior professors, might have high occupational status and levels of education, but less income than many blue-collar workers. A kinesiology student might graduate with a PhD, become a personal fitness instructor, make a boatload of money, but still have low occupational prestige. Other scholars have argued that class is not determined by the 'holy trinity' of education, income and occupational prestige at all, but by one's access to social, cultural, physical and economic forms of capital. Urggggh! All of the above illustrates that what counts as variability is subject to human construction, definition and interpretation in many cases. For your own benefit, try to determine how something like health or illness varies in a group of people. How would you measure those variables?

SHOW ME HOW IT'S USED?

Variables are used to test theories, measure concepts, build hypotheses, observe relationships and draw empirical conclusions in our research projects. They are the centrepiece in scientific research, and determine what kinds of statistical analysis we may perform to examine our data. In order to understand the mechanics of variable analysis, we need to first understand the different levels of measurement of our variables. We can distinguish between two classes of variables according to the level of measurement:

- Continuous variables;
- Discrete variables.

A continuous variable (income, age, red blood cell count, etc.) is one in which the attributes are naturally occurring numbers. A discrete variable is one in which the attributes are not naturally occurring numbers, but rather 'names' or 'terms' or 'categories' (marital status, gender, nationality, level of sport played, etc.). Let's examine each in a bit more detail, because how you decide to measure your variables 'counts' (I know, bad pun) a lot in the research process.

I. Continuous (or naturally quantitative) variables

Continuous variables can be classified into three sub-categories:

Interval-scale

Interval-scale data has order and equal intervals. Interval-scale variables are measured on a linear scale, and can take on positive or negative values. It is assumed that the intervals keep the same importance throughout the scale. They allow us not only to rank order the items that are measured but also to quantify and compare the magnitudes of differences between them. We can say that body temperature of 38°C is higher than 36°C, and an increase from 36°C to 40°C is twice as much as the increase from 36°C to 38°C. Body Mass Index score is another example of an interval-scale variable.

Continuous ordinal

These occur when the measurements are continuous, but one is not certain whether they are on a linear scale, the only trustworthy information being the rank order of the observations. For example, if a scale is transformed by an exponential, logarithmic or any other nonlinear monotonic transformation, it loses its interval-scale property. Here, it would be expedient to replace the observations by their ranks.

Ratio-scale variables

These are continuous positive measurements on a nonlinear scale. A typical example is the growth of a bacterial population in the body. In this model, equal time intervals multiply the population by the same ratio. Ratio data are also interval data, but they are not measured on a linear scale.

II. Qualitative or discrete variables

Discrete variables are also called 'categorical variables'. A discrete variable, X, can take on a finite number of numerical values, categories or codes. Discrete variables can be classified into different types, with the most common being:

- Nominal variables;
- Ordinal variables;
- Multiple response variables.

variables

Nominal variables

Nominal variables allow for only qualitative classification. Their attributes are words rather than naturally occurring numbers, with no rank order among them. That is, they can be measured only in terms of whether the individual items belong to certain distinct categories, but we cannot quantify or even rank order the categories. Nominal data has no order, and the assignment of numbers to categories is purely arbitrary. Because of lack of order or equal intervals, one cannot perform arithmetic (+, −, /, *) or logical operations (>, <, =) on the nominal data. Typical examples of such variables are: gender, religion, birthplace and favourite sport.

Ordinal variables

An ordinal variable is like a nominal variable, but its different states are ranked in a meaningful sequence. Ordinal data has order (sounds logical enough by definition!), but the intervals between scale points may be uneven. Because of lack of equal distances, arithmetic operations are impossible, but logical operations can be performed on the ordinal data. A typical example of an ordinal variable is the socio-economic status of families. We know upper middle class is higher than middle class in theory but we cannot say how much higher. Ordinal variables are also quite useful for subjective assessment of people's opinions, values or preferences. Ordinal scale data are very frequently used in social and behavioural research to measure these mental states. Almost all opinion surveys today request answers on three-, five-, or seven-point scales (a Likert-scale format). Such data are not appropriate for analysis by classical, linear statistical techniques, because the numbers are comparable only in terms of relative magnitude, not actual magnitude. Consider, for example, a questionnaire item on the perceived relevance of family support in long-term athlete development. Respondents (elite athletes) are asked to indicate their perceived level of family support during their first stages of sport involvement:

1 = Nil; 2 = Low; 3 = Medium; 4 = Great; 5 = Very great

Here, the variable 'Family Support' is an ordinal variable with five attributes. Ordinal variables often cause confusion in data analysis. Some statisticians treat them as nominal variables, while other statisticians treat them as interval scale variables, assuming that the underlying scale is continuous.

Multiple response variables

Multiple response variables are those on which an individual can receive a score on several of the variable's attributes. A typical example is a survey questionnaire about the types of physical activity in which one has participated over the last month. The respondents would be asked to check or circle all that applied:

Organised sport
Recreational or 'pick up' sport
Fitness class (aerobics, step, Pilates, yoga)
Weightlifting
Trail hiking or rock climbing
Walking
Gardening

In this instance, I would circle 1, 2, 3 and 5 (I should have scored 7 as well but became complacent) and would therefore have four scores for the variable.

PROBLEMS, PITFALLS AND CONTROVERSIES

Researchers take a massive empirical leap between concepts and variables. Consider a concept like health or performance in sport. If we spoke about health or performance in sport during a conversation, my guess is that we would roughly understand what the concepts mean without ever having to explicitly define them. Well, that's not nearly adequate enough for researchers. Science is frustrating initially to students because of the precision required in our language and the degree to which we all need to be on the same analytic page when it comes to our concepts and the indicators selected to represent those concepts (i.e. as variables in a study). Why? Because a concept like health has a quicksilver quality to it, for example. Researchers involved in a variety of studies on the subject may define the concept differently. To some, it may refer to organ functioning, tissue or cell regeneration, body mass composition, or the ability to ward off and then fight viruses. To others, health is a state of mind, or a degree of existential wellness. For others still, health refers to balance in life, a complex blend of social ties, bonds, friendships, biological health and personal contentment. In all cases, we need to select indicators/variables as the defined measures of our concepts. There has to be a degree of 'epistemic correlation' between how we define concepts and how we measure them, and this is never a perfect or infallible process. Any leap from concepts to measures is one of *reductionism*, and, as such, opens a door for criticism. When we quantify the world, our bodies, social networks, behaviours, minds, personalities, and so forth into tidy variables, we lose a lot of information about them. The loss of information in the process of quantitative measurement and variable analysis is among the principal criticisms of positivist science offered by qualitative researchers. Can our overall health be grasped, known, understood or measured by simply our BMI score?

There is a noted tendency among quantitative researchers to fetishise variable analysis over solid theoretical development. In these cases, researchers are more concerned with distributional relationships between variables and how to model them statistically, than with theory testing and development. Methodologists might refer to such a process as the proverbial 'tail wagging the dog'. Other manifestations of 'illness' in this area are revealed in shotgun or kitchen sink approaches to variable analysis. Here, researchers include variables from a range of competing theories, or those suggested as main correlates by other studies, with the goal of concluding which ones reign supreme in gathered data. When scientists become atheoretically concerned with examining if and how variables are related, and then determine the best way to demonstrate such a relationship statistically, the goal of science as a knowledge production process has been abandoned. There is an innate and intricate link between theory, research and knowledge, and, without this, one must question the purpose or merit of the exercise.

See also: Analytic Epidemiology; Causality; Descriptive Statistics; Distributions; Experiments; Hypotheses; Inferential Statistics.

KEY READINGS

Biddle, S., Markland, D., Gilbourne, D., Chatzisarantis, N. and Sparkes, A. (2001) 'Research methods in sport and exercise psychology: Quantitative and qualitative issues'. *Journal of Sport Sciences* 19: 777–809.

Fallowfield, J. (2005) *Statistics in Sport and Exercise Science*. Chichester: Lotus Publishing.

Field, A. (2009) *Discovering Statistics Using SPSS*. London: Sage.

Gratton, C. and Jones, I. (2003) *Research Methods for Sports Studies*. New York: Routledge.

Newell, J., Aitchison, T. and Grant, S. (2010) *Statistics for Sports and Exercise Science: A Practical Approach*. Toronto: Pearson Education.

Thomas, J. and Nelson, J. (2001) *Research Methods in Physical Activity*. Champaign: Human Kinetics.

Williams, C. and Wagg, C. (2003) *Data Analysis and Research for Sport and Exercise Science: A Student Guide*. London: Routledge.

Visual Methods

Researchers spend dozens, hundreds, and in some cases thousands of hours studying a topic of interest. We then wade through reams of empirical data, scores of personal accounts, a dizzying number of recorded events, and try to make some sort of academic sense of what we have observed. At the end of the process, we magically reduce so much evidence from the world into a few representative statistics, or extract and showcase several typical excerpts from interview transcripts into written reports. We are highly skilled experts in transforming the physical, social and the ideological into neatly written texts. But for many researchers, 'seeing' is believing. A growing number of researchers in sport, exercise and health fields actively use visual aids, visual data or visual data collection techniques as means of producing knowledge about the world.

WHAT IS THIS CONCEPT?

Whenever researchers incorporate photographs, drawings, visual aids, videos or other printed/graphic materials into the process of data collection or analysis, visual methods have been tapped. In brief, 'visual methods' is a catchphrase referring to the use of (mainly) still or moving pictures in the research process. We must think about visual methodologies as alternative ways of knowing – an important epistemological point to remember. I could tell you about the many times I have been to Old Trafford in Manchester to watch United play. I could regale you with stories about how the pitch looks from close up, what it feels like to sit in the middle of the Stretford End, or describe the collective energy produced by a stoppage time goal. All of these things make the experience meaningful to me and to thousands of others who attend the matches. Without grasping the relevance of these visual and auditory stimuli, it is difficult for me to communicate the feeling of being a spectator there. So much of culture and its experience is seen and felt. Or, I could tell you about the first time I went to a beach in California and sat for hours watching the surfers play in the waves. Or, I can ask 15-year-old boys about their thoughts on an ideal body image and they can tell me. But imagine if you saw a video of United fans passionately chanting, could see pictures of bronzed surfers peppering the beach, or if boys showed us pictures of the ideal body. Would it change our understanding of each subject? The visual presents a means of communicating the essence or meaning of a culture, an act, a scene or a thought in ways often untapped by the spoken or written word. The proliferation of visual methods in contemporary research may indeed represent a turning point in sport science epistemology.

For sport and exercise scientists who study the biomechanics and physiology of the moving body, computer simulated, generated and captured images of the three-dimensional body have paved the way for considerable discovery. The use of video, 3-D motion cameras and film in the lab, for example, has led to developments in the study of running gait and economy. A modern sports performance devoid of an array of video and motion-capture equipment would most certainly be unusual. Psychologists of sport also employ still and moving pictures of athletes in the research process in a range of ways. The use of video in psychological and pedagogical studies of the on-field interaction between coaches and athletes has produced considerable insight into the impact of particular coaching styles on athletic performance. Even a quick review of current research practices in sport, physical activity and health showcases how visual data and visual representations of data are quickly becoming indispensable tools and techniques.

WHY IS THIS RELEVANT TO ME?

There are at least five research situations in which visual methods are warranted. First and perhaps most obviously, when the subject matter itself pertains to visual culture and its reception by audiences, visual techniques are appropriate. When the research at hand centres on how people react to and make use of media texts, we may ask people to view selected images, documents or films and describe their constructions of them. Millington and Wilson (2010) describe, for example, how the socio-cultural analysis of sports films, sports websites and advertisements often involves a method whereby subjects are asked to view and then discuss, either individually or collectively, their interpretive 'readings' of the texts as classed, raced, gendered or sexed subjects themselves.

Second, visual methods are incorporated into the research process as a tool for opening up the knowledge production process. A specific visual technique called 'photo elicitation' is especially noteworthy. Photo elicitation involves the use of photographs during an interview as a means of

Figure 7 Pre-game at Old Trafford in Manchester

facilitating the exchange between the researcher and the participant. Why and how? Well, a 'good' interview (i.e. where there is free-flowing information, mutual trust, and positive energy/affect between participants) normally occurs when a certain level of *intersubjectivity* (think of this as a shared or mutual understanding of where each other is 'coming from') has been achieved.

I took this picture (Figure 7) in 2009, while sitting in the 7th row of the Stretford End. Every single aspect of the image has a meaning for me now, as it did then.

Photo elicitation is designed to stimulate conversation. Here, a researcher will show a subject a series of pictures and ask them what they 'see' in the pictures, what the images mean to them, or to provide an account of what is happening in the picture. A researcher might, for example in attempting to grasp what the Stretford End means to United fans, show me a picture of the terraces there and simply say, 'describe being here'. Just seeing the terraces stirs many thoughts, emotions and wonderful memories, each of which I could articulate, I think, to someone else. If the same researcher simply asked me (without showing me the picture and having it trigger my thoughts and emotions) to describe the End, I am not sure if the same answer would be produced.

Third, visual methods are strongly warranted when researchers want subjects to tell their own stories, from their own vantage points, as a means of knowing. 'Photovoice' is a very specialist method by which researchers encourage or ask participants in a project to take pictures of, video record or draw, people, places, events or images which mean something to them. I have conducted research with chronically ill athletes – people living with cancer, liver disease, HIV, and other conditions. At one stage of the research process I asked several participants to take one of my video cameras and film their own mini-documentaries of a week in their lives. The participants did so with much enthusiasm and produced amazing short features of their lives as wounded athletes. By having the subjects highlight what they understand to be the relevant day-to-day structures and meanings of their lives I gained a deeper understanding of how illness and sport identities must be negotiated daily. The method is very clever because the subjects themselves pick and choose the events to film; therefore, the edited videos reveal how they wish others to understand their experiences.

Fourth, visual methods are increasingly utilised as a means of representing qualitative data and breaking down barriers between researchers and potential audiences. Sarah Pink (2007) has produced intellectually and emotionally engaging visual/written accounts of what it is like to walk. Through her use of video recorders and cameras, Pink gives visual life to the joys of walking in space and place through the use of images taken while walking with others (a form of *mobile methodology*). I tried to push the visual envelope even further in a study of fell running in the UK through the use of 'infographics' (Atkinson, 2010). I borrowed the notion of infographics from street/city sign making, where a simple symbol on a posted sign provides information for a pedestrian or driver. In an account of the existential thrill of fell running, I tacked a dozen pictures of the practice into an article, with excerpts from my field notes framing each of them. The goal in such a method is to invite readers to see and potentially feel what I have studied, without being influenced by my academic interpretations of the topic. The use of visual (particularly video) data in reports or accounts of research is accelerated by the recent movement to online journals in which 'megaspace' can be devoted to the uploading and storing of mpeg and video files in research articles.

Fifth, and finally, visual methods are essential for those contemporary sport and exercise sciences requiring visual images of the performing and functioning body as their source of data. Visually tracking the angles of the limbs during a long-jump lift off, the head position during an uneven bars dismount, or the degree of 'wobble' in a muscle mass during athletic effort has become critical for developing effective interventions and innovations in sports performance technique. In short, to see the body moving is the primary means of knowing how the body moves. Additionally, the computer simulation and visual representation of 'possible' athletic movements has ushered in a new era of sports performance training. Professor Fred Yeadon at Loughborough University is a pioneer in this field. His computer models of twisting somersaults in gymnastics have been used to teach athletes how to see themselves doing – before they can even perform them – theoretically possible leaps and dismounts.

SHOW ME HOW IT'S USED!

Visual methods are indeed relevant in a trans-disciplinary context, as evidenced in the above discussion. Sociologists and media researchers of health, sport and physical activity use visual methods for collating and analysing the experience and meaning of athletics among people. Epidemiologists (people who study the factors affecting the health and wellness of a population – sometimes referred to as public health researchers) often utilise photo methods as a means of showing and therefore understanding the risk contexts leading to illness. For example, as part of the Health of Philadelphia Photo Documentation Project, Cannuscio et al. (2009) conducted a study of three separate neighbourhoods and the local urban environmental contexts of risk that might lead to differing rates of disease therein. To do this, the researchers used residents' photographs of the places and spaces in their neighbourhoods which they felt produced either illness or wellness. From the study, they developed a better understanding of the 'street aetiology' of disease and illness. Epidemiologists have also mapped contexts and zones of illness risk in urban areas as a means of understanding and representing the link between environment and disease. Chen et al. (2006), for example, mapped premature mortality rates in Boston between 1999 and 2001 according to spatially demarcated neighbourhoods. These sorts of maps are critical for alerting public health officials and policy-makers to patterned, high rates of illness in particular communities.

Psychologists of sport regularly experiment with visual methods in a range of manners. Among the most commonly employed visual methodology is, in actuality, 'visualisation'. The use of visualisation and imagery is common within applied sports psychology as a means of improving elite athlete performance. As part of a complex psychological training regimen, athletes are routinely coached to use their minds to see themselves winning, to imagine what performance will feel like, to self-scan their own bodies and to imagine that their motor skills are 'perfect'. Sports pedagogists like Laura Azzarito often use visual methodologies in educational contexts to shed light on how dominant physical education regimes and ideologies are received by students. In a research project titled, 'Moving in My World', Azzarito studied secondary school students in inner-city school physical education classes in the British midlands. She adopted visual participatory methodologies (such as photovoice) to document young people's subjective experiences of their bodies in health and gym classes, and the ways in which such embodiments are expressed in the development of their young physicalities (Azzarito and Sterling, 2010).

PROBLEMS, PITFALLS AND CONTROVERSIES

Like any other set of methods in our research toolkit, visual methods are subject to scrutiny and scepticism. A major source of concern for critics is the degree of openness and subjectivity in the visual data collection, analysis and representation process. Visual images are what semiologists call 'polysemic'; simply they are open for a million different interpretations and decodings. If the meaning of any image or moving picture is not fixed (objective), then how can researchers make any preliminary, let alone definitive, interpretation of what they mean to people; or, how can we know anything through the use of visual data? One can only imagine. This criticism applies less to the 'hard science' use of pictures and images, of course.

Related to the above, questions about validity and reliability in visual projects reign supreme. The idea that a picture or short film could consistently capture and represent complex socio-cultural or psychological processes is difficult for certain researchers to accept. The reduction of context or environmental risk factors to a map is equally a stretch. Visual methods, like all of our techniques of data acquisition and representation, are reductionist in their essence. The amount of reductionism added to the high level of subjectivity in the process of using and interpreting visual methods may be unappealing to those impressed by traditionally scientific ways of knowing. Finally, critics ask what the role of the researcher is in visual methods projects. There is a certain de-centring of the researcher's analytic role in particular incarnations of visual methods (think of photovoice here). Cynics decry the privileging of subjects' analytic role in the research process and the process of letting raw data speak for itself.

See also: Media Analysis; Representation of Data.

KEY READINGS

Atkinson, M. (2010) 'Fell running in post-sport territories'. *Qualitative Research in Sport and Exercise* 2: 109–132.

Azzarito, L. and Sterling J. (2010) '"What it was in my eye": Picturing youths' embodiment in "real" spaces'. *Qualitative Research in Sport and Exercise* 2: 209–228.

Banks, M. (2007) *Using Visual Data in Qualitative Research.* London: Sage.

Cannuscio, C., Weiss, E., Fruchtman, H., Schroeder, J., Weiner, J. and Asch, D. (2009) 'Visual epidemiology: Photographs as tools for probing street-level etiologies'. *Social Science and Medicine* 69: 553–564.

Chen, J., Rehkoph, D., Waterman, P., Subramanian, V., Coull, B., Cohen, B., Ostrem, M. and Krieger, N. (2006) 'Mapping and measuring social disparities in premature mortality: The impact of census tract poverty within and across Boston neighborhoods'. *Journal of Urban Health* 83: 1063–1084.

Harrison, B. (2002) 'Seeing health and illness worlds – using visual methodologies in a sociology of health and illness: A methodological review'. *Sociology of Health and Illness,* 24: 856–872.

Knowles, C. and Sweetman, P. (2004) *Picturing the Social Landscape: Visual Methods and the Sociological Imagination.* London: Routledge.

Millington, B. and Wilson, B. (2010) 'Media consumption and the contexts of physical culture: Methodological reflections on a third generation study of media audiences'. *Sociology of Sport Journal* 27: 30–53.

Pink, S. (2007) *Doing Visual Ethnography.* London: Sage.

Rose, G. (2007) *Visual Methodologies: An introduction to the Interpretation of Visual Materials.* London: Sage.

van Leeuwen, T. and Jewitt, C. (2001) *Handbook of Visual Analysis.* London: Sage.

visual methods